AI-Driven Sustainability

AI-Driven Sustainability: The Future of Human Resources Management is an interdisciplinary publication that demonstrates the artificial intelligence phenomenon or AI in the sustainable shaping of human resources management.

The role of AI as a support to the existing HR processes and a comprehensive changer of organizational, ethical, social, and environmental values is reviewed by authors. By providing readers with a wide scale of explanatory case studies among global business corporations and with a thorough review of law-ethical and technological issues in 10 chapters, the book suggests a "green model" of AI implementation in HR dimensions.

A must-read publication for researchers, practitioners, and leaders who want to make their business part of the conscious future in labor in the environment of digitalization.

AI-Driven Sustainability

The Future of Human Resources Management

Joanna Rosak-Szyrocka and Radosław Wolniak

CRC Press
Taylor & Francis Group
Boca Raton London New York

CRC Press is an imprint of the
Taylor & Francis Group, an **informa** business

Designed cover image: Shutterstock

First edition published 2026
by CRC Press
2385 NW Executive Center Drive, Suite 320, Boca Raton FL 33431

and by CRC Press
4 Park Square, Milton Park, Abingdon, Oxon, OX14 4RN

CRC Press is an imprint of Taylor & Francis Group, LLC

ISBN: 9781041131434 (hbk)
ISBN: 9781041131038 (pbk)
ISBN: 9781003668282 (ebk)

DOI: 10.1201/9781003668282

Typeset in Minion
by Newgen Publishing UK

Contents

Author Biographies

Joanna Rosak-Szyrocka is an assistant professor and Erasmus+ programme coordinator at the Faculty of Management, Czestochowa University of Technology. Her areas of expertise include sustainable development, digitalization, Industry 4.0, Quality 4.0, education, artificial intelligence (AI), and quality management.

She has participated in numerous teaching mobilities under the Erasmus+ programme in countries such as Italy, the United Kingdom, Slovenia, Hungary, the Czech Republic, Slovakia, and France. She actively collaborates with many academic institutions both in Poland and abroad. At the Faculty of Management, she is involved in various research teams, including interdisciplinary groups. She is also a member of the faculty's committees for dean's office research and course progression in the field of occupational health and safety, as well as the technical evaluation committee.

Her achievements have been recognized on several occasions: in 2012, she received a certificate of recognition from the Dean of the Faculty of Management for her publishing activity; in 2017, she was awarded the Dean's Medal for long-standing cooperation with the faculty; and in 2023, she was honored with the Medal for Long Service by the President of the Republic of Poland.

Radosław Wolniak is a full professor at the Department of Economics and Informatics at the Silesian University of Technology (Poland). For over 20 years, he has been dealing with issues of management, including Industry 4.0, Smart City, digitalization, artificial intelligence, and sustainability. His achievements include over 600 publications issued by national and international publishers, as well as many undertakings and projects implemented in cooperation with the business environment. He's on the Stanford List of Top 2% Scientists most cited across the globe for 2023.

Scientific interests: management, AI in management, sustainability, Industry 4.0, Smart City, digitalization, innovativeness, smart factory.

Introduction

As the McKinsey Global Institute has pointed out, between 2019 and 2022 alone, 8.6 million career changes have occurred, and by 2030, approximately another 12 million are expected; that is, the scale of professional transformation will be 25% higher than predicted. This unusual rate of change is no longer a vision of the future—it is already occurring now. Artificial intelligence is not just a propellant for this transformation; it is also the only way to comprehend, plan, and manage it sustainably. At a time when people's skills are becoming outdated at an unprecedented rate and the climate and social imperatives are becoming central to business strategies, AI is redefining the realm of human resource management, as long as it is used responsibly, morally, and humanely.

In this context, it is appropriate to quote Yoshua Bengio, an AI specialist and Turing Award winner: *AI Isn't About Just Being More Efficient – It's About Opening Up New Possibilities, Freeing Human Ingenuity, And Addressing Several Of Our Nation's Difficulties.* It is this mixture of potential transformations and extensive human values that serves as the foundation for the present book.

As Microsoft CEO Satya Nadella puts it, *AI Is Not Going To Replace People; Rather, People Who Use AI Will Replace People Who Don't Use It.* Thus, it is not enough to comprehend the technology; it is also essential to cultivate novice attitudes that enable us to utilize AI sensibly in the corporate world.

This book, *AI-Driven Sustainability: The Future of Human Resources Management*, delivers the reader with 10 chapters, each of which tackles the pertinent issues of AI's use in sustainable human resource management. In Chapter 1, the authors talk about AI's impact on the traditional work system, which is mostly seen in supporting various HR processes, such as recruitment and talent development. The authors also focus on the ethical concerns around algorithmic decision-making and the importance of adopting transparent HR policies. Chapter 2 describes the theoretical fundamentals of sustainable HRM driven by AI and includes such core values as fairness, transparency, explainability, and human agency. The chapter also describes the risks of biased data and provides an ethical model of AI implementation in HR. Chapter 3 is devoted to the implementation of AI in recruitment. Here, the authors provide case studies of Amazon, Google, PepsiCo, and others to show the potential and challenges of biased reduction, as well as methods of ensuring data quality and developing hybrid decision-making systems. In Chapter 4, the authors discuss the use of AI in fostering the employee experience, which includes well-being, work-life balance, skills development, and engagement. The authors describe the concepts of mental health chatbots, sentiment analysis, and offers of personalized learning paths. Chapter 5 covers AI utilization in human capital management in a sustainable manner. The authors show how AI-based analytics assist with forecasting turnover, optimize training, and are utilized for socially, environmentally, and ethically responsible workforce management. Chapter 6 is focused on the ethical problems and technology governance when it comes to HR. For example, the authors discuss real-world cases of AI misuse in HR, such as discrimination by algorithms, and argue in favor of control measures, like audits, impact assessments, ethics committees, and stakeholder involvement. Chapter 7 examines how AI can help achieve organizations' CSR and ESG objectives. It highlights the potential of AI in promoting fair, transparent, and inclusive HR activities and discusses the new role of HR in promoting ethical innovation. Chapter 8 provides case studies of organizations that have integrated AI in HRM through the lens of sustainable development. It discusses possible examples of sustainable AI in diversity, well-being, Green HRM, as well as strategic planning with the cases of Microsoft, Deloitte, and LinkedIn. In Chapter 9, the authors examine the current legal provisions and regulatory regimes associated with AI implementation in HR at the international level. The definitions of hard law and soft law, including GDPR, the AI Act, OECD, and UNESCO standards, and the identification of difficulties associated with the analysis of regulatory provisions are also included. Chapter 10 outlines a visionary, strategic perspective; it argues that the future-ready HR is not entirely dependent on AI law and ethics. Instead, future-ready HR promotes a culture of learning and digital savviness and prepares its workforce for a value-centered approach.

We hope that our publication will not only provide its reader with knowledge but also the inspiration for further thought and action. There is nothing more urgent in the era of fast change of technology and social life than obtaining insight that strikes you as significant and relevant to the conscious, ethical, farsighted creation of the future of work.

Joanna Rosak-Szyrocka
Radosław Wolniak

I

Foundations of AI-Driven Sustainable HRM

CHAPTER 1

Introduction to AI in HRM and Sustainability

> ***"The ultimate resource in economic development is people. It is people, not capital or raw materials, that develop an economy."***
>
> ***Peter F. Drucker***

1.1 EVOLUTION OF HUMAN RESOURCE MANAGEMENT

The growing dominance of digital technology has led to profound cultural, sociological, and economic changes around the globe (Rosak-Szyrocka & Wolniak, 2025). All things considered, because of these developments, the contemporary era is now known as the "digital age" (Rosak-Szyrocka, 2024). According to these developments, digital technologies are becoming more and more integrated into employee life and HRM, the latter of which seems to be impacted in a variety of ways. The development of HRM mirrors the change in the nature of work itself, where technology and human wellness are now defining the practices that control the modern workforce (Kaufman & Association, 2004; Becker, Huselid, & Ulrich, 1992; Bondarouk & Brewster, 2016).

Human resource management (HRM) is a systematic and cohesive approach to managing a company's most valuable assets, which are its employees, who both individually and collectively help the firm accomplish its goals (Thite, Kavanagh, & Johnson , 2012; Armstrong 2006). According to this definition, HRM is a role in businesses that aims to enhance employee performance in support of the strategic goals of their employer (Ulrich et al., 2010).

Table 1.1 shows the evolution of HRM in the age of technology.

DOI: 10.1201/9781003668282-2

TABLE 1.1 Evolution of HRM in the Age of Technology

Era/Timeframe	Key Features & Concepts	Description
Pre-Industrial HRM Before the 18th Century	Family- or guild-based informal systems of labor organization.	Work was best managed locally or by the family and attention was on apprenticeships and the development of skills. Many similarly skilled workers learned their trades through apprenticeships. HR departments did not exist and jobs were arranged through normative and blood relations. Labor management was decentralized, and jobs were more often than not informal and personal rather than being organized structures.
Industrial Revolution & Personnel Management 18th–19th Century	Rise of factories, increasing demands for organized labor management, concentration on recruiting and, primarily, welfare.	With the coming of industrialization, firms formalized their management of labor. The first personnel departments took shape, gathering into themselves hiring, wages, safety, and worker welfare. The management of staff emphasized the fundamentals of labor law and work organization more.
Human Relations Movement & Welfare Early 20th Century	Evolution of HR functions into areas concerning employee well-being, employee attitude, and the behavior of individuals in the organization.	This period witnessed the emergence of new approaches to managing workers that stressed the health, motivation, and group processes of workers. The Hawthorne Studies were important studies of their time, because they were the first to concentrate on how workplace factors affected workers' attitudes and performance. These studies found that employees' morale, their relations, and their perceptions of the work environment were essential for productivity. Accordingly, HR management transformed from a focus on simple task efficiency to a culture that was supportive and communicative. It was during this time that people in business began understanding the need for the well-being, trust, and motivation of employees. HR was never solely about managing tasks, but it became more and more about creating an environment in which employees could flourish. It is these changes that would set the stage for the follow-on HR strategies that would balance worker well-being and organizational success, and lead to the integration of technology in HRM.
Strategic HRM & Technology Integration 1980–2000	Human resources as a strategic partner in the organization, connecting HRM to business objectives.	HRM evolved into a more strategic role that corresponded to the business strategy. HR's function was no longer limited to managing staff and welfare; in fact, it was now directly contributing to the strategic objectives of the business. The emergence of new technology including Human Resource Information Systems (HRIS) transformed the way HR operated during this time. These applications streamlined numerous administrative functions, like payroll and benefits, enabling HR workers to concentrate on more strategic efforts. HR was challenged to make a real contribution to organizational performance by focusing on the alignment of talent management (TM) with wider business objectives. This period saw the beginning of the use of a quantitative approach to HR, where factors like staff performance, turnover, and effectiveness of recruitment were used to influence business decisions.

TABLE 1.1 (Continued)

Era/Timeframe	Key Features & Concepts	Description
Digital Transformation of HRM 2000–2010	Introduction of HR systems such as Human Resource Information System (HRIS), e-recruitment, & the start of HR analytics.	The penetration of HR software and systems, such as HRIS and e-recruitment platforms, was rampant in this era. These instruments enabled HR departments to better organize employee information, monitor performance, and automate certain key functions around hiring and onboarding. The emergence of HR analytics enabled HR professionals to base their decisions on data and to predict future staffing needs. Companies were able to more comprehensively assess workforce trends, enhance their hiring techniques, and even predict turnover or spot potential leaders. Digitizing HR processes also yielded enormous efficiency gains, streamlining HR teams' workload and freeing them up to concentrate on more strategic workforce planning.
AI and Predictive Analytics in HR 2010–2020	The infusion of artificial intelligence (AI), machine learning (ML), and predictive analytics (PA) in HR	New technologies such as AI and ML came along to accelerate and optimize countless HR activities. Recruitment specifically had access to AI-enabled tools that could scan resumes, do initial tests for candidates, and even predict which candidates would be the best fit for a company's culture and needs. Predictive analytics became a key resource for HR professionals, helping them predict future trends like employee turnover or a demand for specific skills. This utilization of data enabled even more precise, anticipatory decision-making. Smart AI and chatbots also started dealing with many mundane employee questions and administration, which let HR focus on more strategic concerns. Such technologies were also able to eliminate hiring biases and enhance the precision of employee performance evaluations.
Sustainable Development and CSR in HRM 2019–Present	Incorporation of Corporate Social Responsibility (CSR) and sustainable development into HRM practices focusing on diversity, work ethic, and employee well-being.	Amid increasing societal attention on environmental, social, and governance (ESG) matters, HR is being held to account to ensure that organizations behave ethically and are good corporate citizens. Diversity, equity, and inclusion (DEI) are increasingly at the forefront of HR strategies centered on providing workplaces that are socially responsible and supportive of all employees in addition to being efficient. Corporations will have to remain attentive to employee wellness, work-life balance, and mental health, to make sure that workers feel not only productive, but happy in their working environment. This emphasizes the increasing role of HR in shaping environmentally, socially, and ethically responsible and sustainable work that benefits the organization as well as society at large.

(*Continued*)

TABLE 1.1 (Continued)

Era/Timeframe	Key Features & Concepts	Description
AI-Powered Strategic HRM 2020–Present	AI workforce tools for talent management, employee engagement, and workforce planning. AI and Automation in HRM—Predictive Hiring.	This is the time where AI is coming to every aspect of HR. More and more, AI solutions are being integrated into the HR lifecycle—affecting everything from hiring and onboarding to employee development and performance management. Predictive hiring has become more sophisticated, using algorithms not just to evaluate candidates, but also to predict the level of staffing that will be required in future, based on trends and market conditions. AI now also allows HR professionals to monitor employee engagement and satisfaction and even predict the likelihood of burnout or disengagement before it becomes an issue. Automating these processes has also reduced the administrative burden for HR practitioners, who can now spend more time on strategic tasks like workforce planning and creating employee engagement programs. AI is also critical in overseeing remote teams and global workforces so that organizations can ensure productivity, communication, and engagement across various geographies.

Source: Own study.

1.2 DEFINING SUSTAINABLE HRM AND ITS IMPORTANCE

Today's organizations exist in a context characterized by numerous social, environmental, and economic problems, which affect the management of human resources. Sustainable Human Resource Management (SuHRM) is increasingly developing into not only a response but also a prerequisite of organizational resilience and long-term accountability to stakeholders. In order to meet the needs of present generations without endangering the ability of future generations to meet their own, organizations must engage in sustainable development, which takes into consideration the social and environmental effects of human and organizational activities (Imperatives, 1987).

Recent studies suggest that over 73% of companies currently combine sustainability with their main HR and business strategies, connecting it with employer branding, employee engagement, and long-term talent retention (Lee, Lee, & Kim, 2025; Labelle et al., 2025). Sustainable development goals (SDGs) are accomplished by integrating creative sustainable methods and using the organization's human resources to embrace new ecological practices (Chams & García-Blandón, 2019). Long-term factors including urbanization, biodiversity, climate change, and workforce demographics are all taken into consideration by SuHRM (Aust, Matthews, & Muller-Camen, 2020; Kramar, 2014). According to Dubois and Dubois (DuBois & Dubois, 2012), HRM holds a central role in organizational environmental sustainability. The goal of SuHRM is to achieve corporate goals while balancing the protection of natural resources with commercial expansion (Farndale & Paauwe, 2018; Bagga & Srivastava, 2014). Table 1.2 presents selected definitions of SuHRM.

TABLE 1.2 Selected definitions of SuHRM

Author	Definition of SuHRM
(Aust, 2009)	SuHRM is an idea of harmonizing the interests of employees and the organization and taking into account scarce resources and coming generations.
(Zaugg et al., 2001)	SuHRM is the ongoing and long-term approach to developing human capital, incorporating motivation, well-being, and organizational responsibility into HR practices.
(Ehnert et al., 2016)	SuHRM is implementing HRM techniques and methods that facilitate the attainment of monetary, social, and environmental objectives, impacting both internal and external stakeholders and spanning an extended period of time while accounting for unforeseen consequences and unfavorable feedback.
(Kramar, 2014)	SuHRM is value-based HR, which integrates sustainable and ethical aspects in an efficient manner.
(Figueira et al., 2024)	SuHRM is an inclusive HRM approach linked to ESG and the UN Sustainable Development Goals (SDGs).
(Faugoo, 2024)	SuHRM posits that human capital is an asset of strategy responsibility for performance and social responsibility impact.
(Sołtysik et al., 2024)	SuHRM is a new approach that connects leadership and organizational innovation with sustainability.
(Mariappanadar, 2019)	SuHRM aims to balance the economic/financial, human/social, and cultural aspects of social sustainability by investigating and comprehending the institutional-level work practices (work arrangements) that shape the characteristics and role of work that have both sustainable and unsustainable impacts on citizens' quality of life.
(Cohen, Taylor, & Muller-Camen, 2010)	SuHRM is creating a workforce with the trust, values, abilities, and drive to produce a successful triple bottom line via the use of HR tools.
(Thom & Zaugg, 2004)	SuHRM is built on a sustainable approach of recruitment, development, and release of employees and managers, making the solution responsible toward both society and the economy and combining social and performance indicators.
(Podgorodnichenko et al., 2022)	SuHRM embodies a shift of focus, from a strategic point of view, in human resources toward workforce development for environmental and societal resilience.

Source: Own study.

The growing regulatory pressure at both national and international levels is one of the main triggers for the adoption of SuHRM practices. ESG (Environmental, Social, Governance) reporting, gender pay transparency, diversity disclosures, data protection (like GDPR), etc. are all requirements that force companies toward more transparent and responsible practices in HR policies and reporting (Farndale & Paauwe, 2018; Woods et al., 2020).

One other significant driver is the rising demands of employees, customers, and investors, who are increasingly electing to do business with companies that act ethically, inclusively, and environmentally responsibly. The younger generations (Millennials and Generation Z) not only want good working conditions; they want to know their potential employer can make a positive social and environmental difference. It is in this situation that corporate values and organizational culture play an important role in an employer's branding and attraction of talent (Butler, 2025; Surugiu et al., 2025).

There are also demographic changes and aging societies; investments need to be made in employee well-being, flexible work models, and lifelong learning. The post-pandemic world has also hastened the requirement for digitalized, inclusive, and health-oriented HR practices. Through these collective factors, SuHRM is a strategic necessity for organizations in developing long-term resilience, maintaining stakeholder trust, and contributing to the world in which it operates, notably in alignment with global sustainability arrangements, including the UN Sustainable Development Goals (SDGs) (Deller et al., 2025).

SuHRM is the establishment of an HRM system that supports the company's sustainable performance and the use of HR technologies to assist in integrating a sustainability plan within the business. With policies that reflect equity, development, and well-being and support environmentally friendly practices, sustainable human resource management (HRM) simultaneously ensures the long-term health and sustainability of the organization's internal and external stakeholders while building the skills, motivation, values, and trust necessary to achieve a triple bottom line (Cohen, Taylor, & Muller-Camen, 2010). Table 1.3 presents the differences between HRM and SuHRM.

Employees' roles as recipients and consumers of HR practices are actively discussed in SuHRM. Training and development policies aim to ensure equal access to developmental initiatives and facilitate the long-term development and career progression of employees within the organization, as well as their overall employability (Berber et al., 2014; Gomes, Coelho, & Ribeiro, 2025). For instance, sustainable recruitment, selection, and staffing practices are designed to achieve social inclusion and equality (Berber et al., 2014; Shahid et al., 2025). Furthermore, according to SuHRM, performance management may help workers grow and participate in their career planning, which empowers them to have an impact on organizational procedures. The following five SuHRM tenets may significantly impact companies.

1. First and foremost, SuHRM involves long-term planning. The goal is to build occupations that benefit people, promote job stability, and do away with the outdated "hire and fire" strategy, rather than concentrating only on making fast money and satisfying exigencies. Employees who get SuHRM are seen as assets rather than merely temporary workers.
2. The significance of including workers in choices that impact them is acknowledged by sustainable human resource management. Having meaningful two-way conversations is more important than just giving instructions. In addition to fostering an environment where workers feel valued and empowered, this helps the business to obtain insights, resolve issues, and form alliances with staff members who will ultimately contribute to the long-term prosperity of the business by planning and carrying out projects that have a higher chance of success.

TABLE 1.3 Differences between HRM and SuHRM

Area	HRM	SuHRM
Strategic Objective	Strives on efficient operations, cost reduction, and satisfaction of goals. HR is a business-enabling support organization which is aligned with business Key Performance Indicators.	Seeks to integrate the bottom line with employee welfare and ethical operations and do its part to effect positive change to society and the environment. HR is regarded as a strategic partner.
Time	Concentrates on near-term measures such as turnover in a month, hiring lifecycles, or absentee rates.	Covers the long-term workforce sustainability, seeing to matters such as upskilling, career pathing, and psychological safety.
View of the Employee	Viewing employees as labor inputs or costs; emphasis on productivity and compliance.	Values employees as co-producers of organizational value; focus on respect, motivation, and autonomy.
Environmental focus	Environmental concerns are seldom cited in HR roles.	Takes an active stance on green initiatives through HR processes.
Corporate Social Responsibility (CSR) and Environmental, Social, Governance (ESG) integration	CSR is typically handled by marketing or compliance, rather than HR.	CSR and ESG strategies around workforce practices are fundamentally driven by HR.
Diversity & Inclusion	Center around standards compliance or public relations-type projects.	Drives equity, belonging, and structural inclusion through all HR systems.
Success Metrics	Success is based on output-focused metrics—things like turnover, time to fill, and employee output.	Utilizes inclusive measurement that consists of engagement, psychological safety, and the learning climate as well as social and environmental contribution.
Technologies	Utilizes simple HRIS (Human Resource Information Systems) to conduct administrative work and track payroll and reporting information.	Combines AI, predictive analytics, and digital tools to measure ethical workforce planning, transparency, and sustainability tracking.

Source: Own study.

3. Third, learning and the improvement of employee skills are the main goals of SuHRM. In addition to developing abilities for the present position, this entails planning for the future needs of the company and its personnel. The workforce's development and potential are being invested in.
4. Fourth, an essential component of SuHRM is employee care. Promoting a good work-life balance, maintaining a safe workplace, and taking care of employees' physical and emotional health are all important aspects of ensuring their well-being. When occupations are unpredictable and in unstable conditions, this care becomes even more important.
5. In conclusion, it is critical that organizational structures and processes mirror and uphold SuHRM practices. Employing sustainability criteria in job descriptions and interview questions is one practical way that businesses may implement SuHRM

concepts. Training sessions on sustainability may be required as part of onboarding. Performance reviews have to include particular sustainability objectives, and staff members should get incentives and promotions in recognition of their efforts. There should be put in place company rules that require waste reduction and energy saving. Sustainability activities should be evaluated on a regular basis and staff should be actively engaged in these projects to guarantee continuous progress (Griep et al., 2024).

The working conditions of employers and their suppliers have become a de facto norm for many businesses, as noted by Boudreau and Ramstad (Boudreau & Ramstad, 2005), because sweatshop scandals have harmed some well-known brands. Ignoring the social component of sustainable development, especially sustainable human resource management, is ineffective in this regard. The argument that SuHRM is the most important component of sustainable development would be logical, therefore.

Sustainability may be helpful for the economy in the long term in addition to being morally right (Boudreau & Ramstad, 2005). In order to attain sustainability, society must be seen holistically, with a moral and ethical viewpoint that takes into account the diversity of subgroups and looks at people as fellow humans. By doing this, the three sustainability imperatives—economic, social, and environmental—or, more accurately, equality, needs, and limits—are taken into consideration. Because people are at the core of sustainability, SuHRM is an essential component (Duvnjak & Kohont, 2021).

1.3 THE RISE OF AI IN WORKFORCE MANAGEMENT

Incorporating AI into HRM is revolutionizing how businesses recruit, develop, and retain personnel. In the present competitive business environment, using AI in HR operations is evolving from a mere technological improvement to a strategic need (Singh et al., 2025). AI makes it easier to automate repetitive and administrative tasks like payroll management, employee onboarding, and resume evaluation.

This frees up HR professionals to focus on more strategic tasks like employee engagement and talent development (Basu et al., 2023; Budhwar et al., 2022). Additionally, HR departments may estimate staff attrition, evaluate worker productivity, and enhance learning and development programs by using insights from large datasets that are retrieved by AI-powered analytics systems (Tripathi & Rosak-Szyrocka, 2024; Rosak-Szyrocka et al., 2023).

AI-powered solutions are now being integrated into HR tasks such as workforce analytics, performance management, employee engagement, and talent acquisition (Singh et al., 2025; Rosak-Szyrocka & Wolniak, 2025). AI-driven systems have the potential to reduce recruiting time and improve the caliber of hires by analyzing job descriptions, matching them with applicant profiles, and conducting initial interviews using chatbots and natural language processing (Alnamrouti, Rjoub, & Ozgit, 2022; Bujold et al., 2024).

The World Economic Forum's Future of Jobs Report 2023 indicates that about 65% of the world's companies expect to use AI in their talent management by 2027. This encompasses uses in hiring, workforce planning, and performance management among others, driving the emphasis away from administrative support and toward strategic decision-making processes (World Economic Forum, 2025). The report cites AI as one of the most influential technologies supporting this transformation in how companies find, develop, and keep talent. With the labor market transforming due to automation, demographics, and new work practices, AI is at the heart of organizational agility and competitiveness. Customized recruiting programs, artificial intelligence used in employee engagement, predictive analytics, and so on make HR capable of directly reacting to the wishes of the workforce much sooner and in a more precise manner.

The number jumps to more than 60% of large companies that have already deployed AI-based HRM systems, such as Oracle HCM Cloud, by 2024 (Khair et al., 2025). These products allow users to make autonomous decisions, such as using predictive analytics to predict employee turnover and schedule the workforce. The merger of AI with a cloud platform gives businesses more flexibility and responsiveness to change.

Authors Ali and Rafi have shown that organizations that adopted AI technology to match candidates and analyze interviews decreased the amount of time taken to personally engage with the candidates by 25%, and better matching of the candidates with the roles resulted in better hires (Ali & Rafi, 2024).

Unfortunately, while artificial intelligence helps automate and forecast HR functions, the results of the decisions being made are now falling under the handle of "algorithmic decision-making" (ADM). ADM refers to the use of structured, algorithmic systems to assist or replace human decision-making in fields such as hiring, performance reviews, and workforce planning (Suen, Chen, & Lu, 2019; Köchling & Wehner, 2020; McColl & Michelotti, 2019). Applications of AI might thus lead to respectable employment and long-term organizational growth (Böhmer & Schinnenburg, 2023). For instance, LinkedIn, Glassdoor, and Indeed users may seamlessly apply for roles leveraging their verbal profiles as resumes (Tian et al., 2023).

Numerous sources, both inside and outside the workplace, can be used to collect information about employees. These include the quantity of keyboard clicks, social media posts, phone calls, websites visited, physical presence, GPS (Global Positioning System) tracking of locations outside the workplace, emails, office movements, tone of voice, and even body language in sociometrics (Moore, 2017). In order to foster a more adaptable and inclusive workplace culture, AI approaches are being used to evaluate employee involvement and attitude in real time. These innovations ensure data-driven decision-making, less human bias, and increased efficiency (Singh et al., 2025). Table 1.4 presents the applications and benefits of AI in HRM.

1.4 THE NEED FOR AN ETHICAL AND SUSTAINABLE APPROACH

79% of 200 AI experts from German businesses surveyed said that AI is essential for gaining a competitive edge (Köchling & Wehner, 2020). Algorithmic platforms and systems are now available from a number of for-profit companies, including Google, IBM, SAP, and Microsoft, and they support modern HR procedures, including recruiting and performance evaluations (Walker, 2012). Algorithmic decision-making (ADM) is

TABLE 1.4 Applications and benefits of AI in HRM

HRM area	AI application	Description	Benefits
Talent Acquisition	CV sifting, candidate-ranking chatbots, predictive job matching—uses AI and data analysis to analyze variables (skills and qualifications, past work experience, behavioral and cognitive characteristics, personal preferences, historical hiring success trends, and even, simply, style of communication or cultural fit) and automatically predict how well a potential job candidate matches with the requirements of any particular role	AI algorithms evaluate and score CVs through keyword matching, role fit, and earlier performance metrics. Conversational bots answer candidate questions immediately and predictive analytics evaluate historical data and behavioral markers to determine the probability of success. AI makes all stages of the early-stage funnel automated. Sophisticated parsing algorithms can rapidly parse thousands of applications and extract structured content like education, experience, and skills. These data inputs are ingested by a predictive algorithm that deterministically outputs compatibility scores for job roles and organization fit.	Drives down time to hire, increases match quality, elevates candidate experience, decreases hiring bias
Onboarding	AI-based onboarding journeys, chatbots	AI assembles tailored onboarding plans according to job and employee characteristics. Virtual assistants walk new employees through admin and cultural onboarding, all to facilitate quicker onboarding. Integration with Learning Management System (LMS) allows learners to have access to content when they need it. (LMS is a software platform for the delivery, execution, and management of education courses or training programs.)	Drives integration, enhances first-day experience
Performance Management	Continuous behavioral analytics, real-time KPI tracking (updated automatically and constantly: instantly, in real time), feedback sentiment analysis	AI analyzes performance in real time with natural language processing (NLP), productivity metrics, and behavioral pattern recognition tools. These kinds of systems gather all kinds of feedback from multiple channels (emails, collab platforms, reviews) and look for trends like morale decline, spikes in performance, and the potential for burnout. They also raise warning flags about peer review disparities, suggesting interventions by managers that are objective.	Leads to more equitable and data-driven reviews, provides manager intelligence, practices early intervention, and fuels a culture of ongoing development and feedback.
Learning & Development	Intelligent content recommendation engines, adaptive e-learning systems	AI further suggests personalized training plans, based on performance background, future role needs, preferred learning style, and company-wide goals. These plans are adjusted in real time according to how well employees are doing at them and where the skill gaps are. AI also determines what training is most likely to be most effective per learner, maximizing training ROI, even for succession planning.	Helps with better retention of knowledge, proactive reskilling/upskilling, increased learning engagement, and a focus on what is required for business transformation.

Workforce Planning	Predictive modeling of workforce, analytics of attrition risk, forecasting skills demand	AI gathers both internal data (such as turnover history and team structure) and external trends (like the labor market and automation risk) to model what future workforce needs look like. Scenarios can also model results such as AI-driven job displacement or retirements. HR dashboards allow HR to have up-to-date strategic insight for making decisions on hiring, mobility, allocation of budget,etc. in real time.	Helps to alleviate labor shortage, minimize over-staffing and skill mix disparities, increase flexibility in human resource deployment, and facilitate more proactive strategic HR decision-making.
Employee Engagement	Sentiment analysis, micro-survey automation, morale prediction engines	AI measures feedback coming in from surveys, email, collaboration tools, and even facial expressions (where it's allowed), to follow emotional tone, levels of engagement, and patterns of communication. It can detect trends relating to disengagement, emotional fatigue, or morale changes among the staff. The system recommends interventions—coaching, rotating teams, or flexible work—that can help foster greater emotional connection to the organization.	Increments retention, tends to and creates a more inclusive and responsive work culture, acts as a conduit for proactive well-being, and increases the trust, loyalty, and sentiment through HR personalization.
Well-being Management	Stress and fatigue detection, AI-based mental health alerts, personalized wellness tracking	AI, embedded in wearables, employee apps, and productivity platforms, watches sleep patterns, workload imbalances, meeting overloads, and the signs of burnout or depression. It then serves up real-time recommendations—such as a slow-down prompt, wellness content, or HR alerts. The platform is able to link to Employee Assistance Programs (EAPs) and recommend support services appropriate for each case.	To promote staff health and to decrease absenteeism and presenteeism as well as nurture mental resilience and to confirm the care of the employer for the well-being of the employees.
Administrative HR	Robotic Process Automation (RPA), HR service chatbots, Smart self-service portals	AI chatbots manage tens of thousands of daily HR requests (for example, leave balances, benefits, payslip issues) with consistent, immediate response. RPA streamlines form fills, policy updates, and compliance reporting. AI-driven self-service HR platforms provide personalized suggestions (e.g., promotion, training paths) and empower employees to take much more responsibility in fulfilling their HR-related obligations.	Streamlines HR operations while eliminating errors and delays, increasing employee independence, and maintaining a high quality of service while reducing the HR support burden.

Source: Own study, based on: Malik et al. (2023); Prikshat et al. (2023); Basu et al. (2023).

then used in HR development and recruiting by well-known and sizable corporations like Ikea, Unilever, Intel, and Vodafone (Wilson & Daugherty). ADM is primarily motivated by the following goals: reducing risks, increasing decision certainty, improving productivity, automation, speed, and scaling, and saving money and time (McColl & Michelotti, 2019; Suen, Chen, & Lu, 2019; Woods et al., 2020). Aside from these financial considerations, businesses use ADM to reduce human biases (such as preconceptions and personal beliefs), which improves the impartiality, consistency, and equity of HR development and recruitment procedures (Langer, König, & Papathanasiou, 2019; Raghavan et al., 2020). ADM seems to be more impartial and equitable than human decision-making at first glance (Lepri et al., 2018).

AI systems trained on data reflecting historical biases can reproduce biases regarding gender, race, or age. This can further inequity, even when the software is not intentionally biased. It is important for companies to be vigilant about these biases and to attend to them when data does not fairly represent certain groups, and these biases should be checked for wherever algorithms are being used (Lambrecht & Tucker, 2019; Köchling & Wehner, 2020).

As the datasets used to train the systems do not reflect diverse candidate pools, these systems can in turn perpetuate the marginalization of minority groups. In order to guarantee that AI systems are ethical and sustainable, companies need to audit the data they use to make certain that it is diverse and not corrupted by historical biases.

Köchling and Wehner (2020) show that the historical data used to train algorithms often contain embedded biases (e.g., concerning gender, race, or age) that the algorithms can undesignedly reproduce and strengthen. The outcomes of this process originate in what has been referred to as algorithmic discrimination, in which decisions appear to be neutral, but are in fact grounded in latent biases (Raghavan et al., 2020).

And equally important is the quality and representativeness of the data that trains computer algorithms. Lambrecht and Tucker (Lambrecht & Tucker, 2019) show that the biases present in a society will be reproduced and magnified in the model if the training set is not population-representative or if historical inequality is part of it. Therefore, in order to combat algorithmic bias and make the procedure fair for all candidate groups, algorithm fairness would require that the diversity of the training data be "as representative as possible" for all the candidate groups. This includes preemptive audit of data sources, testing for bias, and having underrepresented voices involved in the design phase of the model.

The obscurity of ADM systems is another limiting factor (Delecraz et al., 2022; Leicht-Deobald et al., 2022). Decisions based on one or more AI in particular within the fields of recruitment or employees' performance review take place via "black-box" algorithms, i.e., they are not human-interpretable. This lack of visibility into roles can contribute to disgruntled employees and undermine confidence in the equity of HR processes. Organizations need to develop explainable AI systems through which the decision-making logic can be made simple so that it can be further explained to stakeholders.

The usage of AI in HR also poses ethical concerns surrounding human autonomy and moral integrity (Lepri et al., 2018; Binns, 2022). An excessive dependence on automated decision-making depersonalizes employees and HR practitioners, who may perceive they are being over-ridden by machine-based decision-making to the detriment of their own judgment. Finding the balance between AI's efficiency and human values, such as ethical judgment and empathy, is key to maintaining the moral core of the HR function.

Oversight and accountability make for another important factor to be considered (Lambrecht & Tucker, 2019). With companies turning more and more to AI to help them make crucial HR decisions, it is essential to have strident ethical frameworks and informed governance to underpin these systems. Without strong checks, it can be difficult to make AI systems accountable for errors or biases in their products. Such ethical frameworks should ensure that there is a human who is responsible for the decisions made by AI, especially in areas such as hiring and performance reviews.

Algorithmic fairness and inclusion must be a core priority (Rahman et al., 2025). AI systems must be developed to foster equality and inclusiveness in HRM practices, securing diversity and equity in the workplace. Companies must aim to make sure that their AI systems do not have the effect of accidentally excluding or disadvantaging any one particular group but rather serve to help develop a more diverse and fair-minded workforce.

The same problems are addressed by Loi relative to recruiting algorithms. The opaqueness of so-called black-box AI systems also leaves candidates in the dark about why they were rejected from a job or not, perpetuating serious concerns about procedural justice (Loi, 2020). We are of the view that ethical frameworks and transparent ADM policy guidelines are crucial to developing trust and sustained recruitment success (Rahman et al., 2025). In addition, the authors Leicht-Deobald et al. (Leicht-Deobald et al., 2022) note that ADM approaches fully replacing human decision-making can threaten the personal integrity and moral autonomy of employees.

There is a growing consensus for a conscientious, convergent process to steer ADM tool design and governance. One of the most important aspects of this approach is transparency, not just with respect to the outputs that these algorithms are producing, but also with respect to the logic and organization of the models themselves. As Delecraz et al. (Delecraz et al., 2022) state, organizations need to focus on building algorithms that are explainable to developers and end users, enabling those in HR, as well as job candidates, to comprehend how specific inputs feed into the outcome of decisions. Without this explainability, accountability becomes less clear, and stakeholders are left with few options to question, or make sense of, what the system does.

A second bedrock feature of ethical ADM is the maintenance of interactional justice in automated environments (Binns, 2022). In the case of algorithmic HR tools, that requires making it possible for candidates and employees to question or challenge decisions and ensuring that you communicate with humans. This human touch is key for organizations, to steer clear of the dehumanization that comes with opaque automation and to reinforce trust in their workflows (Lee, Lee, & Kim, 2025; Giovanola & Tiribelli, 2022).

TABLE 1.5 Examples of ethical and sustainable practices of ADM in HRM

Company name	Name of ethical and sustainable practice	Description
Unilever	Ethical video interview analysis using AI	Unilever now uses AI-driven interviewing by way of the HireVue platform to review applicants in the beginning stages of the hiring process. The system analyses facial expressions, intonation, and spoken content to measure competencies in front of relevant job criteria. But what makes Unilever's strategy different is its dedication to ethical governance and transparency. The firm insists on independent audits of its algorithmic models to avoid and reduce bias for gender, for ethnicity, or for accents of language. That way, technology works better for equity, rather than against it. One aspect of ADM that is consciously embedded with transparency and fairness is its ADM system; this is how Unilever not only improves efficiency, but also ensures its global strategy in talent acquisition is trustful and legitimate.
Microsoft	Human-in-the-loop systems; Microsoft's responsible AI governance	Microsoft uses algorithmic tools in its internal HR processes, such as performance review and career development planning, to utilize AI and provide workers with personalized recommendations drawn from employee data. But the final decisions are not automatic. Microsoft adopts a human-in-the-loop approach to its responsible AI governance, where algorithmic suggestions in HR processes like career planning are reviewed and approved by human managers. Microsoft's method strikes a balance between technological performance and human-led governance, which showcases the necessity for perpetuating human intervention side by side with AI-based insights to keep sustainability in ADM.

Source: Own study.

A sustainable perspective on ADM must reconcile technological efficiency and human-centered values—bridging the accuracy and scalability of AI with the ethical imperatives of fairness, inclusivity, and autonomy (Podgorodnichenko et al., 2022; Almarzooqi, Khan, & Khalid, 2019; Keles, 2025). Table 1.5 shows examples of ethical and sustainable practices of ADM in HRM.

REFERENCES

Ali, A., & Rafi, N. (2024). Enhancing human resource management through advanced decision-making strategies: Harnessing the power of artificial intelligence for strategic, data-driven, and judicious choices. *Journal of Human Resource Management, 21*(8), 881–889.

Almarzooqi, A. H., Khan, M., & Khalid, K. (2019). The role of sustainable HRM in sustaining positive organizational outcomes. *International Journal of Productivity and Performance Management, 68*(7), 1272–1292. Available from: www.emerald.com/insight/content/doi/10.1108/ijppm-04-2018-0165/full/pdf.

Alnamrouti, A., Rjoub, H., & Ozgit, H. (2022). Do strategic human resources and artificial intelligence help to make organisations more sustainable? Evidence from non-governmental organisations. *Sustainability, 14*(12), 7327. Available from: www.mdpi.com/2071-1050/14/12/7327.

Armstrong, M. (2006). *A Handbook of Human Resource Management Practice,* Kogan Page Publishers.

Aust, I. (2009). *Sustainable Human Resource Management. A Conceptual and Exploratory Analysis from a Paradox Perspective,* Physica-Verlag. Available from: https://ebookcentral.proquest.com/lib/kxp/detail.action?docID=450567.

Aust, I., Matthews, B., & Muller-Camen, M. (2020). Common Good HRM: a paradigm shift in Sustainable HRM? *Human Resource Management Review, 30*(3), 100705.

Bagga, T., & Srivastava, S. (2014). SHRM: alignment of HR function with business strategy. *Strategic HR Review, 13*(4/5). Available from: www.emerald.com/insight/content/doi/10.1108/shr-03-2014-0023/full/pdf?casa_token=hi28hvgdgwaaaaaa:f8mjjkwdw4df0okptg8aht45vbtybmkwxniz70zyptw-pnifhas-y89re1gft-r50ekh2_m842bq-zdhkcew425afbfcyu3t4d6uvocqheh4eyvi.

Basu, S., Majumdar, B., Mukherjee, K., Munjal, S., & Palaksha, C. (2023). Artificial intelligence–HRM interactions and outcomes: a systematic review and causal configurational explanation. *Human Resource Management Review, 33*(1), 100893.

Becker, B. E., Huselid, M. A., & Ulrich, D. (1992). The HR scorecard: linking people, strategy, and performance. *(No Title).* Available from: https://cir.nii.ac.jp/crid/1130000793710958208.

Berber, N., Susnjar, G. S., Slavic, A., & Baosic, M. (2014). Relationship between corporate social responsibility and human resource management – as new management concepts – in Central and Eastern Europe. *Engineering Economics, 25*(3), 360–369.

Binns, R. (2022). Human judgment in algorithmic loops: individual justice and automated decision-making. *Regulation & Governance, 16*(1), 197–211.

Böhmer, N., & Schinnenburg, H. (2023). Critical exploration of AI-driven HRM to build up organizational capabilities. *Employee Relations: The International Journal, 45*(5), 1057–1082.

Bondarouk, T., & Brewster, C. (2016). Conceptualising the future of HRM and technology research. *The International Journal of Human Resource Management, 27*(21), 2652–2671.

Boudreau, J. W., & Ramstad, P. M. (2005). Talentship, talent segmentation, and sustainability: a new HR decision science paradigm for a new strategy definition. *Human Resource Management, 44*(2), 129–136.

Budhwar, P., Malik, A., Silva, M. T. T. de, & Thevisuthan, P. (2022). Artificial intelligence – challenges and opportunities for international HRM: a review and research agenda. *The International Journal of Human Resource Management, 33*(6), 1065–1097.

Bujold, A., Roberge-Maltais, I., Parent-Rocheleau, X., Boasen, J., Sénécal, S., & Léger, P-M. (2024). Responsible artificial intelligence in human resources management: a review of the empirical literature. *AI and Ethics, 4*(4), 1185–1200. Available from: https://link.springer.com/article/10.1007/s43681-023-00325-1.

Butler, S. (2025). Generational differences: motivations and values of younger and older workers. *Strategic HR Review, ahead-of-print*(ahead-of-print). Available from: www.emerald.com/insight/content/doi/10.1108/shr-04-2025-0037/full/pdf?casa_token=biw7ap7fu-aaaaaa:hpslv3ysdda4kpajwts1em2y5fgijjwln2oevw6rq26693hgjxuccllw5jyn95ullafg6rbs3uiy-dbvzrjcksa95un_m7bgrkhjhflqehvp4j9o.

Chams, N., & García-Blandón, J. (2019). On the importance of sustainable human resource management for the adoption of sustainable development goals. *Resources, Conservation and Recycling, 141*, 109–122.

Cohen, E., Taylor, S., & Muller-Camen, M. (2010). HR's role in corporate social responsibility and sustainability. *SHRM Foundation.* Available from: www.researchgate.net/profile/farley-nobre/post/can_anyone_provide_suggestion_about_the_role_of_hr_function_in_implementing_corporate_sustainable_development/attachment/59d6408bc49f478072eaa55b/as%3a273788803977225%401442287745638/download/csr+exec+briefing-+final.pdf.

Delecraz, S., Eltarr, L., Becuwe, M., Bouxin, H., Boutin, N., & Oullier, O. (2022). Responsible artificial intelligence in human resources technology: an innovative inclusive and fair by design matching algorithm for job recruitment purposes. *Journal of Responsible Technology, 11*, 100041.

Deller, J., Gu, X., Choi, S. J., & Wöhrmann, A. M. (2025). Working conditions and organizational practices to support well-being of multiage workforce in Germany, USA, Japan, and South Korea. *Public Administration and Policy, ahead-of-print*(ahead-of-print). Available from: www.emerald.com/insight/content/doi/10.1108/pap-08-2024-0143/full/pdf.

DuBois, C. L. Z., & Dubois, D. A. (2012). Strategic HRM as social design for environmental sustainability in organization. *Human Resource Management, 51*(6), 799–826.

Duvnjak, B., & Kohont, A. (2021). The role of sustainable HRM in sustainable development. *Sustainability, 13*(19), 10668. Available from: www.mdpi.com/2071-1050/13/19/10668.

Ehnert, I., Parsa, S., Roper, I., Wagner, M., & Muller-Camen, M. (2016). Reporting on sustainability and HRM: a comparative study of sustainability reporting practices by the world's largest companies. *The International Journal of Human Resource Management, 27*(1), 88–108.

Farndale, E., & Paauwe, J. (2018). SHRM and context: why firms want to be as different as legitimately possible. *Journal of Organizational Effectiveness: People and Performance, 5*(3), 202–210. Available from: www.emerald.com/insight/content/doi/10.1108/joepp-04-2018-0021/full/pdf?casa_token=v2dfg0xd0_iaaaaa:vbdrvz0tjrgf78dxkhe0soo2-lo9togjej_ih4wthj89i8cprntecmgyy9uqd2isoa8m1le96c_wzrgwbge5vnyudwoml8geyzr3ctq5bfpriady.

Faugoo, D. (2024). Human capital as strategic valued assets: core drivers of organizational success in the modern-day workplace. *International Journal of Business and Technology Management, 6*(3), 617–628. https://doi.org/10.55057/ijbtm.2024.6.3.55

Figueira, A. d. S., Reis da Costa, S. R., Rampasso, I. S., & Resende, D. N. (2024). *Literature review: sustainable human resource management.* Available from: www.zbw.eu/econis-archiv/bitstream/11159/701568/1/1905672195_0.pdf#page=101.

Giovanola, B., & Tiribelli, S. (2022). Weapons of moral construction? On the value of fairness in algorithmic decision-making. *Ethics and Information Technology, 24*(1), 1–13. Available from: https://link.springer.com/article/10.1007/s10676-022-09622-5.

Gomes, G. P., Coelho, A., & Ribeiro, N. (2025). A systematic literature review on sustainable HRM and its relations with employees' attitudes: state of art and future research agenda. *Journal of Organizational Effectiveness: People and Performance, 12*(1), 37–56. Available from: www.emerald.com/insight/content/doi/10.1108/joepp-11-2023-0497/full/pdf.

Griep, Y., Hansen, S. D., Kraak, J. M., Sherman, U., & Bankins, S. (2024). Sustainable human resource management: the good, the bad, and making it work. *Organizational Dynamics, 53*(1), Article 101112. https://doi.org/10.1016/j.orgdyn.2023.101112

Imperatives, S. (1987). Report of the World Commission on Environment and Development: Our common future. *Feb*, *10*(42,427), 1–223.

Kaufman, B. E., & Association, I. R. R. (2004). *Theoretical Perspectives on Work and the Employment Relationship*, Cornell University Press.

Keles, S. (2025). Navigating in the moral landscape: analysing bias and discrimination in AI through philosophical inquiry. *AI and Ethics*, *5*(1), 555–565. Available from: https://idp.springer.com/authorize/casa?redirect_uri=https://link.springer.com/article/10.1007/s43681-023-00377-3&casa_token=bicjn-euzeyaaaaa:rlr80ojl0j58nmg2y3witbo0gr8ibw2vh5hkfhaqlbhvich0vzeqcfayntyyrvyn1apgyu-brg6oqq.

Khair, M. A., Khair, M. M., Shaheen, N., & Bindewari, S. (2025). From automation to autonomy: leveraging Oracle HCM Cloud's AI capabilities to create autonomous hr processes and decision-making. *International Journal of Research in Humanities and Social Sciences*, *13*(3), 271–288.

Köchling, A. & Wehner, M. C. (2020). Discriminated by an algorithm: a systematic review of discrimination and fairness by algorithmic decision-making in the context of HR recruitment and HR development. *Business Research*, *13*(3), 795–848.

Kramar, R. (2014). Beyond strategic human resource management: is sustainable human resource management the next approach? *The International Journal of Human Resource Management*, *25*(8), 1069–1089.

Labelle, F., Parent-Lamarche, A., Koropogui, S. T., & Chouchane, R. (2025). The relationship between sustainable HRM practices and employees' attraction: the influence of SME managers' values and intentions. *Journal of Organizational Effectiveness: People and Performance*, *12*(1), 127–144. Available from: www.emerald.com/insight/content/doi/10.1108/joepp-10-2023-0475/full/pdf?casa_token=99eencvfpleaaaaa:gedmbyrsthul8fjedpcapd5-7fdzovbupblkhbkrhqwxgfrzrotyz1ylq9mdtgtqmwlcrxi_vzhdcbqyyz5ix3rhvhlpvixrmymcbhhgmvdzwi7krq.

Lambrecht, A. & Tucker, C. (2019). Algorithmic bias? an empirical study of apparent gender-based discrimination in the display of STEM career ads. *Management Science*, *65*(7), 2966–2981.

Langer, M., König, C. J., & Papathanasiou, M. (2019). Highly automated job interviews: acceptance under the influence of stakes. *International Journal of Selection and Assessment*, *27*(3), 217–234.

Lee, B., Lee, E., & Kim, J. (2025). Analysis of factors affecting job satisfaction for sustainable workforce development: insights from IT industry employee reviews. *Sustainability*, *17*(4), 1689. Available from: www.mdpi.com/2071-1050/17/4/1689.

Leicht-Deobald, U., Busch, T., Schank, C., Weibel, A., Schafheitle, S., Wildhaber, I., & Kasper, G. (2022). The challenges of algorithm-based HR decision-making for personal integrity. In *Business and the Ethical Implications of Technology* (pp. 71–86). Springer. Available from: https://link.springer.com/chapter/10.1007/978-3-031-18794-0_5.

Lepri, B., Oliver, N., Letouzé, E., Pentland, A., & Vinck, P. (2018). Fair, transparent, and accountable algorithmic decision-making processes. *Philosophy & Technology*, *31*(4), 611–627. Available from: https://idp.springer.com/authorize/casa?redirect_uri=https://link.springer.com/article/10.1007/s13347-017-0279-x&casa_token=ayy6de_ul04aaaaa:lpbyrxd28yly-52vlooc0dvrekyskt48ytf41xfdxqbx1cvozzucybxmgqsfsbigu-j9ul5dtd5e-a.

Loi, M. (2020). *People Analytics Must Benefit The People. An Ethical Analysis of Data-Driven Algorithmic Systems in Human Resources Management*. Algorithmwatch.

Malik, A., Budhwar, P., Mohan, H., & Srikanth, N. R. (2023). Employee experience –the missing link for engaging employees: insights from an MNE's AI -based HR ecosystem. *Human Resource Management, 62*(1), 97–115.

Mariappanadar, S. (Ed.). (2019). *Sustainable Human Resource Management: Strategies, Practices and Challenges*, Bloomsbury Publishing.

McColl, R., & Michelotti, M. (2019). Sorry, could you repeat the question? Exploring video-interview recruitment practice in HRM. *Human Resource Management Journal, 29*(4), 637–656.

Moore, P. V. (2017). *The Quantified Self in Precarity: Work, Technology and What Counts*, Routledge.

Podgorodnichenko, N., Akmal, A., Edgar, F., & Everett, A. M. (2022). Sustainable HRM: toward addressing diverse employee roles. *Employee Relations: The International Journal, 44*(3), 576–608. Available from: www.emerald.com/insight/content/doi/10.1108/er-01-2019-0016/full/pdf?casa_token=smwm6aw0xfmaaaaa:35mz57yxv2vfynqybipf4ii5lfwjw6bxn_37gzihspmgbbnuhkkjtq-qsyzjyel_t8gnb5ob-wx1fp_gz7zvqyagzllylozvp81q36qd8iiydpps.

Prikshat, V., Islam, M., Patel, P., Malik, A., Budhwar, P., & Gupta, S. (2023). AI-augmented HRM: literature review and a proposed multilevel framework for future research. *Technological Forecasting and Social Change, 193*, 122645.

Raghavan, M., Barocas, S., Kleinberg, J., & Levy, K. (2020). Mitigating bias in algorithmic hiring. In *Proceedings of the 2020 Conference on Fairness, Accountability, and Transparency* (pp. 469–481). ACM.

Rahman, S. M., Hossain, M. A., Miah, M. S., Alom, M. M., & Islam, M. (2025). Artificial intelligence (AI) in revolutionizing sustainable recruitment: a framework for inclusivity and efficiency. *International Research Journal of Multidisciplinary Scope, 06*(01), 1128–1141.

Rosak-Szyrocka, J. (2024). The era of digitalization in education where do Universities 4.0 go? *Management Systems in Production Engineering, 32*(1), 54–66.

Rosak-Szyrocka, J., & Wolniak, R. (2025). *Smart Universities in Smart Cities*, Routledge. Available from: www.taylorfrancis.com/books/mono/10.4324/9781003621829/smart-universities-smart-cities-joanna-rosak-szyrocka-rados%c5%82aw-wolniak.

Rosak-Szyrocka, J., Żywiołek, J., Nayyar, A., & Naved, M. (2023). *The Role of Sustainability and Artificial Intelligence in Education Improvement*, CRC Press.

Shahid, S., Kaur, K., Patel, P., Kumar, S., & Prikshat, V. (2025). Integrating sustainable development goals into HRM in emerging markets: an empirical investigation of Indian and Chinese banks. *International Journal of Manpower, ahead-of-print*(ahead-of-print). Available from: www.emerald.com/insight/content/doi/10.1108/ijm-01-2024-0075/full/pdf.

Singh, A., Kushwaha, D., Kumari, B., Srivastava, G., & Agrawal, N. (2025). AI in HRM: Revolutionizing the future of work. *International Journal of Research in Human Resource Management, 7*(1), 267–272. https://doi.org/10.33545/26633213.2025.v7.i1c.279

Sołtysik, M., Tyrańska, M., Piwowar-Sulej, K., & Agustina, T. S. (2024). *Sustainable Human Resource Management*, Routledge.

Suen, H.-Y., Chen, M.Y.-C., & Lu, S.-H. (2019). Does the use of synchrony and artificial intelligence in video interviews affect interview ratings and applicant attitudes? *Computers in Human Behavior, 98*, 93–101.

Surugiu, C., Surugiu, M.-R., Grădinaru, C., & Grigore, A.-M. (2025). Factors motivating generation z in the workplace: managerial challenges and insights. *Administrative Sciences, 15*(1), 29. Available from: www.mdpi.com/2076-3387/15/1/29.

Thite, M., Kavanagh, M. J., & Johnson, R. D. (2012). Evolution of human resource management & human resource information systems: The role of information technology. In M. J. Kavanagh, M. Thite, R. D. Johnson (Eds.), *Human Resource Information Systems: Basics* (pp. 2–34). Applications & Directions. Available from: www.researchgate.net/publication/277249737

Thom, N., & Zaugg, R. J. (2004). Nachhaltiges und innovatives personal management. In *Nachhaltiges Innovationsmanagement* (pp. 215–245). Gabler Verlag. Available from: https://link.springer.com/chapter/10.1007/978-3-663-10862-7_11.

Tian, X., Pavur, R., Han, H., & Zhang, L. (2023). A machine learning-based human resources recruitment system for business process management: using LSA, BERT and SVM. *Business Process Management Journal, 29*(1), 202–222. Available from: www.emerald.com/insight/content/doi/10.1108/bpmj-08-2022-0389/full/pdf?casa_token=91oifxmiliwaaaaa:2tikexny3uxm6ksgnidcpke3ap7mhfnjzpjjs-b9izy-qwuhbeyu8ef4cxxw0dqepnbs16zi8-hbvbsdeclqlbxcnggy1yjvke_xgfo96epajbos.

Tripathi, S., & Rosak-Szyrocka, J. (2024). *Impact of Artificial Intelligence on Society,* CRC Press.

Ulrich, D., Brockbank, W., Johnson, D., Sandholtz, K., & Younger, J. (2010). HR competencies: mastery at the intersection of people and business. *NHRD Network Journal, 3*(4), 103–104.

Walker, J. (2012). Meet the new boss: big data. *Wall Street Journal, 20.* Available from: www.wsj.com/articles/SB10000872396390443890304578006252019616768

Wilson, H. J., & Daugherty, P. R. Human + machine: reimagining work in the age of AI. *(No Title).* Available from: https://cir.nii.ac.jp/crid/1130000796158338560.

Woods, S. A., Ahmed, S., Nikolaou, I., Costa, A. C. & Anderson, N. R. (2020). Personnel selection in the digital age: a review of validity and applicant reactions, and future research challenges. *European Journal of Work and Organizational Psychology, 29*(1), 64–77.

World Economic Forum. (2025). *The Future of Jobs Report 2023.* Available from: www.weforum.org/publications/the-future-of-jobs-report-2023/ [10 May 2025].

Zaugg, R. J., Blum, A., & Thom, N. (2001). Sustainability in human resource management. *Evaluation Report. Survey in European Companies and Institutions. Arbeitsbericht des Instituts für Organisation und Personal der Universität Bern und des eidgenössischen Personalamtes, 1*(1), 1–31.

CHAPTER 2

Theoretical Foundations of AI-Driven Sustainable HRM

2.1 AI AND ITS APPLICATIONS IN HRM

Integration of AI in HRM practices makes the organizational decision-making process faster and more efficient and further improves the overall organization performance. Leveraging AI-driven insights allows employers to sift through infinite datasets and uncover trends while generating insights HR professionals can use to help drive strategic goals (Mahade et al., 2025). IBM has realised great savings in HRM-related costs by utilizing AI and still anticipates its strategic role within the future of HR parties (Guenole & Feinzig, 2018).

Using AI in HRM transforms how employees are managed at work (Böhmer & Schinnenburg, 2023). Companies seem to have a good chance of gaining a competitive edge via unique core competencies by using AI early on, which will result in better choices, more efficient operations, and happier workers (Basu et al., 2023; Rosak-Szyrocka et al., 2023; Tripathi & Rosak-Szyrocka, 2024). AI systems can function with varying degrees of autonomy, and they can: (1) sense real and/or virtual environments using inputs from humans and/or machines; (2) create models based on this information; and (3) use the implications of these models to provide information or action options (Tambe, Cappelli, & Yakubovich, 2019). Therefore, it is conceivable to automate work processes, which might increase human expertise and perhaps replace human labor (Markoff, 2016).

Artificial intelligence (AI) could greatly transform Human Resource Management (HRM), particularly with regard to sustainable development (SD). Conventional HRM activities have frequently relied on heavy use of natural resources, including paper, and increased energy consumption for running the organization on a day-to-day basis. Organizations can leverage AI to lessen that impact by deploying more sustainable

DOI: 10.1201/9781003668282-3

solutions—social, ecological, and economical. In terms of sustainable development, AI has the potential to be an engine for not just economic growth, but also social and environmental benefits for organizations. By contributing to the well-being of employees, promoting energy efficiency, and enabling environmentally friendly practices, AI plays a crucial role in creating sustainable business for the future (Chin, Mohamad, & Lo, 2024; Demetris Vrontis et al., 2023). Table 2.1 shows the application of AI in HRM and how it results in sustainable development in social, environment, and economic contexts via the beneficial impact of using AI in HRM activities.

AI has gained prominence in HRM in order to improve processes for recruitment, for engagement of employees, and for workforce development. Approaches like machine learning (ML), natural language processing (NLP), robotic process automation (RPA), and AI-powered HR analytics play a vital role in this. They serve as a vehicle for efficiency and growth, not to mention building toward the future of the organization and the people working within it (Tian et al., 2023). Table 2.2 shows key AI technologies in HR.

These possibilities have been highlighted by recent debates around ChatGPT's natural language processing (NLP) capabilities and the potential fundamental changes to many organizational roles and tasks (Forbes, 2024).

2.2 THE CONCEPT OF SUSTAINABILITY IN HRM

SuHRM marks a sea change in organizations' sense of their responsibility to people, the community, and the environment (Jangbahadur et al., 2025; Westerman et al., 2020). SuHRM is therefore a concept directed toward value-oriented management of the workforce in relation to ethics, society, and ecology. It is rooted in the international context as well as the developing theory of HRM, both of which challenge how human capital management is conducted in the 21st century (Lopez-Cabrales & Valle-Cabrera, 2020; Westerman et al., 2020). With 169 objectives and 17 sustainable development goals (SDGs), the UN General Assembly unveiled "the 2030 Agenda for Sustainable Development" in 2015. The aims are designed to achieve the unfinished Millennium Development Goals (MDGs). Together, the 17 objectives are integrated into the economic, social, and environmental facets of sustainable development. Their foundation is based on the "five Ps": "**people, planet, prosperity, peace, and partnership**." As for "people" and "prosperity," the SDGs seek to create favorable contexts and particular circumstances that support the rise of long-term economic expansion, effective resource distribution, shared prosperity, and respectable working conditions. From a business standpoint, the ultimate goal of the SDGs is to create "sustainable, innovative, and people-oriented" economies that increase job possibilities, especially for women and the younger population. The goal of businesses is to make sure that their employees are healthy and educated and to develop the knowledge and skills necessary to produce productive workers and engaged citizens who make valuable contributions to society (Chams & García-Blandón, 2019). In this sense, HR has a significant role in transferring organizational practices in relation to the vision and mission within the sustainability context and CSR practices (Austen & Piwowar-Sulej, 2025; Ehnert et al., 2016; Ramya & Prabu, 2025). By managing talent responsibly,

TABLE 2.1 The application of AI in HRM and results in sustainable development in social, environment, and economic contexts from the beneficial impact of using AI in HRM activities

Sustainability aspect	Description of AI application	Benefits for SD	Examples
Green HRM Practices	With AI, recruitment becomes paperless to a large extent. It streamlines the application process, stores data digitally, and enables swift review of resumes and cover letters. AI also minimizes paper moving and, hence, CO_2 emission due to paper transport. AI also helps drive the efficiency of HR workloads such as staff planning and performance diagnostics, saving energy and costs.	Saves paper, lowers the CO_2 transportation emissions of documents, and reduces energy usage in HR processes.	IBM uses AI to streamline the hiring process, cutting down on paper use while increasing HR department productivity.
Social Sustainability	Algorithms from AI are also used to analyze data; then it was shown that AI can detect biases in recruitment processes and in relation evaluation. This leads to much fairer decisions being made for hiring, performance reviews, and promotion, making the labor market more diverse and inclusive. AI makes it fairer for those being recruited and assessed: it ensures that race, gender, age, or background play no part in the decision-making on a candidate.	Promotes equal opportunity, eliminates bias in hiring and employee performance evaluations, and fosters a more diverse and inclusive workplace.	Google, the company, uses machine learning techniques to strip out biases in hiring, allowing them to build a far more diverse team.
Economic Sustainability	AI will improve HR practices, including workforce planning, performance management, and churn prediction. Automation of mundane activities saves time and money, and the AI's analysis of engagement data of employees means that staff can be managed more efficiently and cost-effectively. AI improves business efficiency and reduces overhead costs.	Improves operational efficiency, saves time and money, and optimizes manpower planning and performance assessment.	The automation of McDonald's HR streamlined their backend procedures, which reduced costs in space, money, and time.
Long-Term Employee Development	AI makes personalized career growth plans by diagnosing skill gaps and providing customized training. AI can also constantly evaluate employees' progress, allowing them to adjust to the incongruities of the job market and learn new skills. By taking the long view and investing in employee development, AI can help companies cultivate a workforce that is flexible and able to tackle future challenges.	Provides an adaptable workforce, eliminates skill gaps, enhances long-term organizational results, and promotes employee success over time.	Unilever leveraged AI to personalize career development plans for its staff, fostering more engagement and operating efficiency.

Source: Own study, based on: (Liu, Yousaf, & Rosak-Szyrocka, 2024; Gupta, 2021).

TABLE 2.2 Key AI technologies in HR

AI technology	Description	Application in HRM	Application in recruitment, engagement, and development
Machine learning (ML)	Machine learning is a technology that allows AI systems to analyze data, learn from it, and then make decisions without having to program every rule. In HRM, ML is applied to predict employee turnover, examine performance data, and predict which employees are most likely to be promoted. ML-based models for predictions also allow for faster and better staffing decisions and better talent management.	The use of HRM in recruiting enables predicting the size and needs of a future workforce, the determination of HR activities to be evaluated on effectiveness, and the identification of talents. ML can also predict possible employee turnover and preempt employee dissatisfaction signals for proactive personnel management.	AI in HRM is applied to analyze application data, predict the success of candidates, or even recognize talent. It is useful in matching candidates to suitable job openings and predicting their future success. This gives companies the freedom to choose candidates with whom they fit in terms of culture and who will be most effective in their positions.
Natural Language Processing (NLP)	Natural language processing (NLP) makes it possible for software to understand, interpret, and create human text. Within HCM, NLP is employed to process CVs, cover letters, and staff communication; it is also employed in recruitment, where it aids in more accurate and quicker candidate matching. NLP assists with automating document classification and quality of communication within an organization.	The application documents of a large number of individuals can now be analyzed together through natural language processing, which reduces the time of recruitment and enhances the quality of candidate selection. It is also used to track sentiment around staff communication and analyze their feelings about the company. NLP can be used to spot issues related to employee engagement and satisfaction, with faster feedback to their requirements.	NLP enables the parsing of application documents, cover letters, and communication with employees, automatically, in the recruiting process. It is also leveraged for employee sentiment analysis, which in turn leads to better employee engagement and satisfaction. Moreover, NLP drives employee development by providing a means to analyze business feedback and employee sentiment to adapt career development programs.
Robotic Process Automation (RPA)	RPA is a technology in which routine tasks, like manual computer work, can be performed by software, and not by a human anymore. In HRM applications, RPA may include handling documents, data entry processing of leave applications, and automated processing of invoices, which minimizes human errors and enhances productivity. With RPA, processes are smarter and the time spent on repetitive tasks is reduced.	RPA is for standard, administrative parts of the recruitment process, like entering data into systems and managing the applications. This enables HR departments to concentrate more strategically on talent development and employee engagement. RPA improves the efficiency and the speed of operations and more effectively controls the internal process.	The automation of such administrative tasks as handling leave requests and personnel data management takes a load off HR employees and ensures process accuracy thanks to RPA. This allows companies to concentrate on more strategic elements of talent management and employee well-being.

(*Continued*)

TABLE 2.2 (*Continued*)

AI technology	Description	Application in HRM	Application in recruitment, engagement, and development
AI-Driven HR Analytics	AI-based HR analytics leverages sophisticated algorithms to study huge amounts of data related to the staff, their productivity, their happiness, and their engagement. Now, organizations can spot trends in how employees are engaging with their work, develop programs that promote career growth, and, ultimately, yield more optimized hiring processes in a world where talent management is increasingly competitive. AI-based HR analytics makes it possible for businesses to take a more objective, data-driven approach, ensuring that HR strategy is aligned with enterprise needs.	With HR analytics using AI, you can also make a data-oriented decision in areas including compensation, promotion, and employee development. "Powered by AI, this product enables companies to customize HR policies based on employee performance data and make real-time HR decisions for the ever-changing organizational needs." It also assists in tracking the success of HR activities by driving rapid response to changes and improvement of strategies.	HR analytics powered by AI is applied for analyzing employee data, performance, and engagement to develop customized career development programs. AI also assists in maximizing the benefits of the recruitment process by "guessing" which candidates will have the best cultural fit. And by analyzing those data, companies can more effectively customize developmental programs based on the specific needs of their employees.

Source: Own study, based on: (Tian et al., 2023).

TABLE 2.3 Approaches to defining SuHRM

Approach/Authors	Description
Environmental & Ergonomic Approach (Bolis, Brunoro, & Sznelwar, 2014; Gajšek et al., 2022; Hasanain, 2024; Zink, 2014)	SuHRM looks at how ergonomic design, quality of the workplace, and its environmental upgrading play a role with regard to employee well-being, creativity, and absence reduction. This is a win-win where employee happiness is in balance with increased organizational efficiency.
HRM Practices & Employee Engagement (Kumar & Sia, 2012; Prins, Stuer, & Gielens, 2020; Richards, 2022; Usha & Ramkumar, 2025)	SuHRM applies inclusive HR practices which enhance work-life balance, employee commitment, and inclusiveness. From work-life balance, diversity and employee involvement come HR practices that strengthen organizational commitment and performance.
Social Justice & Social Dialogue Approach (Austen & Piwowar-Sulej, 2025; Camuffo, Stefano, & Paolino, 2017; Fostervold, Koren, & Nilsen, 2018; Prins, Stuer, & Gielens, 2020)	This perspective centers on social equity, good work, and tripartism between employers, governments, and representatives of workers. It seeks to address systemic issues such as gender inequality, disability inclusion, and fair pay, for both the social impact it can have and its potential impact on the organization.
Sustainable Working Lives (Akkermans et al., 2013; Hasanain, 2024; Madero-Gómez et al., 2023; Richards, 2022)	Conceptualizes SuHRM as the opportunity to have long, healthy, and adaptable careers. Concentrates on employee resilience, lifelong learning, flexible work, and publish or perish programs and policies that ease burnout while promoting career development over the life course.

Source: Own study.

adopting inclusive practices, and providing programs for workforce development, HR departments act as the enablers of ethical business and social impact (Bujold et al., 2024; Tripathi & Rosak-Szyrocka, 2024). Table 2.3 shows approaches to defining SuHRM.

SuHRM is not only to be seen as a compliance with non-financial reporting standards like the Global Reporting Initiative (GRI) Standards, which serve as a framework for sustainability reporting, or the International Labour Organization (ILO) Decent Work Agenda, fostering decent work and fair and inclusive working conditions (Chams & García-Blandón, 2019; Ehnert et al., 2016). The Global Reporting Initiative (GRI) and the International Labour Organization (ILO) are considered to be the key contributors of operational indicators in the field of sustainable HRM. Specifically, the GRI's Labour Practices and Decent Work (LA) and Human Rights (HR) categories encompass indicators concerning the quality of work, working conditions, freedom of association, equity, and protection from discrimination. These measures draw from the foundations of the ILO Decent Work Agenda and the ILO Declaration on Fundamental Principles and Rights at Work. For instance, indicator LA4 is the percentage of employees covered by collective bargaining, which GRI regards as responsible management and stakeholder engagement. By integrating such standards into HR policies, organizations are not only capable of being compliant with ESG standards but can also proactively develop employment policies under sustainable development (Vinnikova et al., 2024).

It is increasingly being viewed by organizations and researchers as a multidimensional, long-term approach that contributes to the general advancement of the HR system, integrating ethical, social, and environmental criteria into HR practices both as an objective and a means of implementing it (Chams & García-Blandón, 2019; Ehnert et al., 2016). At its heart is the bringing together of three perspectives: caring for employee well-being, eco-responsibility, and the creation of long-term economic value—consistent with the triple bottom line approach (Lopez-Cabrales & Valle-Cabrera, 2020; Westerman et al., 2020).

In the HRM context, the "people" element is about making an organizational culture conducive to physical and mental well-being, work-life balance, diversity, and equal opportunities, as well as to employees' involvement in decision-making. The "Work and Well-being 2023" article by the American Psychological Association also stated that organizations that provide well-being see increased employee engagement and employee retention (APA, 2023). In the majority of Scandinavian countries, lower levels of burnout and less absenteeism have been found as a result of SuHRM measures, such as flexible working hours and structured social dialogue (Fostervold, Koren, & Nilsen, 2018).

A second pillar, "planet," corresponds to HR activities that explicitly aid, support, or complement environmental objectives—directly (e.g., decreasing the use of resources and digitalizing HR processes, promoting individuals' sustainable ways to commute) and indirectly (e.g., raising environmental consciousness, promoting pro-environmental behavior, recruiting for green skills). Siemens is a good example in that regard, adopting a green HR policy as part of its sustainability strategy that is fully committed to "green onboarding," workplace sustainability training, and carbon footprint measurement within HR teams (Siemens Sustainability Report, 2022). Similarly, IKEA invests in HR-initiated initiatives that drive ecological behavior and emissions reduction throughout its supply chain in its "People and Planet Positive" strategy (Alzoubi, Al-Talib, & Al Saad, 2023).

"Profit" as one of the pillars in SuHRM does not merely mean the "transitional profits" that are generated by the achievement of operational effectiveness; it rather refers to creating long-term economic value by investing in employees, building core competencies, minimizing employee turnover, and enhancing trust with employees. Research by Lee et al. (Lee, Lee, & Kim, 2025) validates the organizations which engage in sustainable HR practices to create greater job satisfaction and less employee turnover, which can obviously be considered an important source of competitive advantage and workforce stability. In its "Human Capital Trends 2023" report, Deloitte also highlights that businesses that embed sustainability into their corporate culture are more crisis-resilient and create more loyal, creative employees (Deloitte Insights, 2025).

And, importantly, HR's role is stretching beyond the realm of the organization. HR is turning into a "glue role," helping connect ESG strategies with social practice—starting local partnerships, developing civic competencies, and advocating for equal opportunity through the value chain. North American outdoor apparel retailer Patagonia (Bhatia, 2025) and global food giant Unilever are examples of this, creating internal and external (supplier- and community-driven) SuHRM programs with an emphasis on fair labor and social exclusion (Lase & Waruwu, 2025) (Unilever HRM Sustainability Model, 2021). SuHRM is, in this sense, not only an HRM model but a cultural and strategic foundation in the organization, influencing its image, the identity of the company, and its capacity to generate social value. It's a systemic, sustained, and value-based process that demands the right people processes as well as conscious and committed HR leadership.

Six of the United Nations Sustainable Development Goals (SDGs) (United Nations Department of Public Information, 2017) are directly impacted by this crucial role of SuHRM: 3 (health and well-being), 5 (gender equality), 8 (decent work and economic growth), 10 (reduction of inequality), 12 (responsible consumption and production), and 17 (implementation and revitalization of global partnerships) (UN Secretary-General, 2017). SuHRM can be linked to a company's attractiveness as an employer in terms of the sustainability of its HR practices and the level of job satisfaction, as adhering to SuHRM can, in turn, help companies attract, retain, and invest in qualified employees in the long run (Nyangoma et al., 2025; Kim, Wang, & Boon, 2021; Labelle et al., 2025; Lee, Lee, & Kim, 2025).

In the literature, a number of different types of sustainable HRM are distinguished, reflecting ways in which organizations work out social, environmental, and economic values in HRM. Each one focuses on different aspects of sustainability—reflecting the changing demands of staff, stakeholders, and society. There are four types of sustainable HRM (Table 2.4).

2.3 AI AND THE TRIPLE BOTTOM LINE (PEOPLE, PLANET, PROFIT)

According to Vinuesa et al. (Vinuesa et al., 2020), AI may contribute to the achievement of 134 objectives (79%) across the SDGs. It is this expansive reach that situates AI as a central piece of strategic sustainability thinking, including with frameworks like the triple bottom line (TBL)—People, Planet, Profit—and the environmental, social, and governance (ESG) framework for measuring impact (Ehnert et al., 2016; Fauzi, Svensson, & Rahman, 2010). AI can span both by offering up-to-the-minute information and prediction analytics around ESG from an HRM perspective, and the stakeholder account adopted in the TBL encourages an equal consideration of employee well-being, environmental stewardship, and long-run economic value. As integration of AI in HR becomes more prevalent, discussion and study on incongruities and challenges are warranted so that AI tools for sustainable development can be aligned (Ehnert et al., 2016; Tripathi & Rosak-Szyrocka, 2024).

AI applications in the "People" segment are mostly concerned with hyperfairness, well-being, and hyperlearning for the employees. In this case, hyperlearning is the application of AI systems to deliver active, personalized, and continuous learning and development experiences, individualized to employees' current role, career ambitions, and skill demands (Hess, 2020). It involves continuous unlearning, relearning, and upskilling within complex digital environments and AI-driven HR systems delivering real-time content recommendations and adaptive training that reflect changing business requirements (Manoharan, 2024).

It is AI being used to get rid of unconscious bias in recruitment and performance reviews. Machine learning algorithms can identify patterns in CVs, candidate speech, or recurring reviews and alert to potential signs of discrimination. For instance, Google used in-house AI tools to study job ad language and recruitment outcomes in order to remove wordings that might deter women and minority group applicants. IBM Watson

TABLE 2.4 Four types of SuHRM

Type		Description
I	**Socially Responsible HRM (SR-HRM)**	SR-HRM places emphasis on the incorporation of ethical business behavior in the management of employee relations. It focuses on well-being and fairness for employees around issues like diversity and inclusion, real pay, health and safety policies, and work-life balance. SR-HRM has also included the specific employee's development programs on the basis of the longer-term development of their personal and professional lives. In its pursuit of the development of socially responsible HRM practices, this approach seeks to enhance employee satisfaction and commitment and to ensure that HR practices match the social expectations of justice and fairness.
II	**Green HRM (GHRM)**	GHRM aims at injecting environmental sustainability into HR practices by utilizing the workforce as a major developmental agent to adopt eco-friendly activities within the organization. This includes incentivizing employees to change their behavior so that they engage in green activities such as saving energy, reducing their waste, and incorporating eco-friendly ways of getting to and from work. HR programs for GHRM involve the hiring of environmentally aware employees, training to develop sustainable practices, and rewarding sustainable behavior. This is aimed at cutting corporate carbon emissions, improving environmental performance, and contributing to local, regional, and national environmental targets to secure a cleaner, healthier, and more sustainable future.
III	**Triple Bottom Line HRM (TBL-HRM)**	TBL-HRM connects human resource practices with the triple bottom line (TBL) logic, which weights the three central themes: social (people), environment (planet), and financial (profit). It considers not only the financial dimension of the business but also the social and environmental effects. HR policies under this approach seek to generate the organizational conditions that benefit employees by, for example, paying fair wages, offering opportunities for development, and fostering environmental responsibility through sound business operations on the inclination that the control of knowledge can strengthen an organization's environmental performance and thus drive economic growth. TBL- HRM recognizes the connectedness of these three areas and seeks to make a balanced contribution to all.
IV	**Common Good HRM**	Common Good HRM expands the notion of sustainable HRM to encompass the collective welfare of society, the natural environment, and the organization. It calls on businesses to have a mission that goes beyond maximizing profits. This model involves companies that have incorporated community development, ethical labor practices, and environmentally friendly programs into their HR policy. They emphasize that their work has significant, enduring effects on local populations, the global environment, and the world at large. HR is a critical enabler of such a culture, in which human dignity, environmental limits, and shared prosperity serve the common good.

Sources: Aust, Matthews, & Muller-Camen (2020); Bondarouk, Parry, & Furtmueller (2017); Dyllick & Muff (2016); Strohmeier (2020).

Recruitment, however, allows the assessment of candidates′ competencies with no reference to demographic information. Another area of significance is the management of well-being and mental health of the employee. Tools like Microsoft Viva Insights dissect employees' work habits—their activity, calendar overload, the number of meetings they are in—and feed the findings to managers in the form of nudges to help avoid burnout. It can also sense dips in mood or engagement from how workers interact with corporate communication tools (Budhwar et al., 2022; Garg et al., 2022; Malik et al., 2021; Prikshat, Malik, & Budhwar, 2023b).

Although AI can be applied as an effective solution to further sustainability in the TBL framework, it is not exempted from its internal paradoxes. AI solutions that focus on being operationally efficient and economically valuable (profit) can conflict with being benign to the employee (people) or affecting the environment (planet). For example, AI systems aimed at enhancing efficiency may drive ubiquitous surveillance of employees' actions, leading to digital stress and a loss of autonomy (Barredo Arrieta et al., 2020; Budhwar et al., 2022; Mollah et al., 2024). Also, algorithms that attempt to forecast employee turnover can be biased in terms of segmentation or risk profiling when they are developed based on historic biased data. Large AI models also need a lot of computing power (especially machine learning and natural language processing) (Garcia, Rosak-Szyrocka, & Bozkurt, 2025; Garg et al., 2022; Sharma & Chanana, 2025). This implies that the increase in protocol overhead impacts this issue negatively and not positively, paradoxically leading to questioning of the environmental sustainability. Finally, there is a growing threat of technological greenwashing in the domain where AI solutions are applied to mimic sustainability indicators with no effect or transparency. As such, we expect organizations to take a critical perspective in relation to the implementation of AI in sustainable HRM. This implies not only understanding which dimensions of TBL, but also predicting trade-offs between them. This would require balancing innovation and equity, and digital transformation and ethical responsibility, and ensure that AI-led HR practices genuinely contribute to sustainable development (Ahmad Giran, Muhamad Tamyez, & Fauzi, 2025; Cesário et al., 2025; Elnakib & Gallego-Roquelaure, 2025).

Although AI has the potential to revolutionize HRM by advancing TBL objectives, it is essential to recognize and resolve any trade-offs or inconsistencies that may occur in real-world scenarios. These advantages may come at the cost of worker autonomy or mental health, even when AI systems increase productivity and lower expenses (profit) (Tripathi & Rosak-Szyrocka, 2024). Systems that monitor worker productivity and engagement via communication technologies, for example, may result in excessive digital monitoring, which raises the risk of techno-stress and job discontent. It becomes essential for sustainable HRM design to strike a balance between innovation and dignity (Fianko et al., 2023; Goldwasser, 2012; Malik et al., 2021).

There are carbon costs associated with the broad use of AI from an environmental standpoint (Gaur et al., 2023; Tamburrini, 2022). AI model training and operation need a lot of energy, especially for large-scale deep learning systems. Given that data centers and outsourced digital infrastructure may significantly increase an organization's carbon footprint, this is pertinent to the GHG Protocol's Scope 2 and Scope 3 emissions (Asif et al., 2022; Matisoff, Noonan, & O'Brien, 2013). Therefore, the energy intensity and inherent environmental cost of AI must be included in any evaluation of its contribution to the "Planet" component. AI systems may also unintentionally reinforce preexisting prejudices if they are educated on historical data that exhibits structural inequality. AI may encode and reinforce small types of prejudice even when it is used to lessen human bias (for example, in hiring) if the training datasets are not carefully selected and updated on a regular basis. The equitable objectives of the "People" pillar, which need ongoing audits and transparency procedures, are compromised by this.

Beyond efficiency and cost savings, enterprises can use multidimensional performance indicators to minimize these risks and optimize AI's alignment with TBL and ESG goals. To assess AI's effects on inclusivity and development access, measures including algorithmic fairness scores, employee well-being indices, and learning equity indicators should be used. The principle focuses on building AI tools that minimize bias in decision-making, specifically with regard to hiring, performance, and promotion. This extends the basic result found in the work of Dwork et al. (Dwork et al., 2012), who characterized fairness as treating similarly situated people alike. In practice, the achievement of algorithmic fairness relies on fairness-aware machine learning, bias audits, and the ongoing performance monitoring of AI models. For example, tools for recruitment based on AI such as IBM Watson Recruitment or Google internal systems that are designed to censor biased language in job ads demonstrate how fairness can be operationalized in HR algorithms (Yabanci, 2019). The HR sustainability audit should include emission monitoring dashboards that are connected to AI system activities, such as server and cloud energy use. In addition to standard key performance indicators (KPIs), businesses should assess the long-term value of human capital (such as resilience, creativity, and retention) as a result of AI-enhanced HR initiatives (Madanchian, Taherdoost, & Mohamed, 2023; Tripathi & Rosak-Szyrocka, 2024). A potential path is the incorporation of AI into ESG reporting systems, which would enable HR departments to take the initiative in data collecting and analysis (Mohamed Riyath & Inun Jariya, 2024). AI-powered HR analytics tools enable businesses to gather real-time sustainability metrics (such as internal mobility rates, e-learning engagement, and workforce diversity) and convert them into visual dashboards that comply with EU, International Labour Organization (ILO), or Global Reporting Initiative (GRI) taxonomy criteria. This facilitates openness on the outside as well as internal responsibility. AI may help with scenario planning for skill shortages, demographic changes, and adjustments to remote work, all of which contribute to long-term workforce sustainability (Lee, Lee, & Kim, 2025). By simulating talent requirements under future economic or environmental restrictions, for instance, algorithmic forecasting tools enable HR departments to transition from reactive staffing to strategic workforce planning (Kim, Khoreva, & Vaiman, 2025).

The integration of AI into HRM should also take governance and ethics into account. Implementing cross-functional AI ethics committees, including workers and other stakeholders in AI design, and making sure that data protection, explainability, and permission procedures are followed are all part of this. This is particularly relevant to AI technologies that affect work, performance reviews, or measures of well-being. AI is increasingly being used in organizations to personalize employee development. At Unilever, for example, staff members receive algorithm-based recommendations on career paths that use data on competencies, performance, interests, and aspirations. This also democratizes development and makes it more available to everyone who's not had access to traditional mentorship. Internal communication and employee engagement are also crucial for AI. An increasing number of organizations rely on HR chatbots to provide answers on salaries, leave, or benefits, with the added benefit of employees having access to information around the clock. In firms such as SAP and Amazon, these bots manage

TABLE 2.5 Examples of contributions of AI to the TBL in SuHRM.

TBL dimension	AI applications in HRM	Description	Examples
People	Recruitment bias detection, sentiment analysis, mental health monitoring, AI career development, AI HR support chatbots	Timely identification of burnout and stress Access to development opportunities for everyone 24/7 access to HR support	Google, IBM, Microsoft, SAP, Unilever, Amazon, Accenture, Deloitte
Planet	Paperless onboarding, greening e-learning, greening skill-matching, AI-driven analysis of workplace energy use (IOT), gamified environmental nudges	Less use of ink and paper to print due to energy wastage Environmental behavior change Tighter alignment with ESG objectives Staff involvement in green action Heightened attention to sustainability in daily work practices	Siemens, IKEA, Schneider Electric, HP, Salesforce, Patagonia, Capgemini
Profit	Attrition and workforce planning predictive analytics, adminstrative task automation, hiring for culture fit, performance forecasting	Savings from reduced staff turnover More productivity and process efficiency Increased cultural and skill fit when hiring Scalable talent management Reliable HR investments	IBM, McDonald's, Hilton, PepsiCo, Nestlé, PwC, L'Oréal, General Electric

Source: Own study, based on: Mahade et al. (2025); Sova et al. (2023).

thousands of queries per month, thereby relieving the HR department of the stress and also enhancing the employee experience. Table 2.5 shows examples of the contribution of AI to the TBL in SuHRM.

The TBL model's "Planet" component is becoming more or less permeated in HR practices due to the establishment of the green HRM concept. Artificial intelligence could be used to great effect to this end, by streamlining administrative processes and influencing employee pro-environmental behavior. One of the top examples is applying AI to digitize HR processes—for example, replacing paper-based recruitment, automating documents, and shifting on-site training to the web (Murugesan et al., 2023). Siemens, for instance, cut CO_2 emissions stemming from business travel through deploying remote AI-based onboarding and training (Siemens report 2024). The organization also tracks the carbon emissions caused by HR actions such as office energy use and document printing.

In the recruitment and development space, many companies are increasingly leveraging AI to spot "green skills"—skills that are related to sustainable development goals (Anshima et al., 2025). AI solutions can rank the candidature with respect to environmental sensitivity, pro-ecological preparedness, and experience in CSR projects (Fioravante, 2024; Ozkan). IKEA, for example, through its "People and Planet Positive" approach, applies AI to identify candidates with corresponding environmental attitudes, seeking to raise employees' awareness of ecology (Inter IKEA Group, 2025). AI is also used to provide tailored e-learning modules to promote environment-friendly behavior at the workplace (e.g., minimizing energy consumption, sustainable means of transport).

AI can also review information fed back from sensors in the IoT (e.g., in office buildings) on energy use (e.g., in that building) and suggest ways to save energy (Mehmood et al., 2019; Rosak-Szyrocka & Wolniak, 2025). HR applications that gamify sustainability challenges create employee involvement with environmental efforts. Although AI in HRM can promote social and environmental values, its relevance for corporate performance and economic value creation is critical (Fenwick, Molnar, & Frangos, 2024). The "Profit" category of the TBL model extends beyond immediate profitability to create long-term economic value through sustainable human capital practices. AI supports more robust prediction of real-time work demands, insights regarding turnover analysis and labor efficiency, and optimized cost-per-hour. With predictive analytics, companies could build HR planning scenarios and manage possible skill gaps. For example, IBM used AI to analyze employment, training, and performance data to forecast which employees could be expected to leave—and even proposed remedies (Guenole & Feinzig, 2018). It also helps to automate the routine administrative HR work like creating contracts, implementing leave, and scheduling work hours. It helped to reduce the HR request processing time by more than 70%, along with increased accuracy, at McDonald's (Barrett, 2024). Another use is to optimize recruitment fit through better matching of candidates, which in turn is essential to reducing attrition, coordinating a smooth onboarding, and improving productivity (Gimenez, Sierra, & Rodon, 2012; Gryncewicz, Zygała, & Pilch, 2023; Varma, Dawkins, & Chaudhuri, 2023). Hiring algorithms developed by the likes of Hilton Inc. offer a more specific measure of fit—not just for the job's requirements, but for the corporate culture (What's next is everything, 2025).

2.4 ETHICAL AI AND HUMAN-CENTRIC HR PRACTICES

With the advent of AI-based tools in short order, HR departments around the world are increasingly looking at systems supporting personnel decisions (Rosak-Szyrocka & Wolniak, 2025; Tripathi & Rosak-Szyrocka, 2024). Everything from hiring, to promotions, to performance management, to predicting voluntary turnover can be automated (Garcia, Rosak-Szyrocka, & Bozkurt, 2025; Rosak-Szyrocka et al., 2023). However, as Binns (Binns, 2018) has argued, the application of machine learning in one way or another impacting human lives carries immediate implications for fairness, transparency, and bias.

Ethical debates around discrimination have traditionally focused on the motives of human decision-makers (Dignum, 2019; Giannoccaro et al., 2025). But algorithmic systems don't have intent or consciousness—yet they can unwittingly perpetuate systemic inequalities that are built into the data used to train them. Such injustices do not result from malicious algorithms but rather from the way in which the classifications are built into the deep fabric of society—even more dangerous, as they are more difficult to detect and challenge (Binns, 2018).

Here ethics is not a luxury addition, but a prerequisite of the application of AI in HR (Garcia, Rosak-Szyrocka, & Bozkurt, 2025; Binns, 2018). It's not just about following the law, it's about making responsible design choices—what variables to consider, what are the best classification rules, and helping ensure you are treating everyone equally even if they're part of a protected group. For one, various definitions of "fairness" (for example, equal opportunity, outcome parity, or error balance) are often in tension, that is, mutually incompatible, so we end up having to make trade-offs—normative decisions with real impact on lives (Floridi & Cowls, 2022; Binns, 2018).

These normative challenges are not specific to artificial intelligence, but their impact is multiplied when deployed at scale, particularly in high-stakes HR settings. But HR departments need to do more than just recognize these tensions—they need to operationalize ethics in a manner that combines technical and human judgment. This means moving from abstract ethical ideals to practice of governance. Instead of plastering fairness, transparency, or accountability on top of the system and hoping they will remain once the model is deployed, responsible AI in HR is about baking those principles into the systems, workflows, and boundaries of the decision.

Recent studies emphasize that ethics should be taken into account not only after model deployment but already in initial stages including dataset composition, feature selection, and use case definition (Bujold et al., 2024; Fenwick, Molnar, & Frangos, 2024).

In the context of the growing influence of artificial intelligence on personnel processes, the human-centric approach has become a fundamental pillar of responsible human resource management. Human-centric HR practices are not merely an ethical add-on; they are a prerequisite for realizing ethical AI. Without incorporating the voice, interests, and well-being of employees, even formally fair algorithms risk reinforcing feelings of alienation and powerlessness.

Human-centered AI-based HRM reinstates employee dignity, participation, and rights at the very core of every algorithm-supported process. The goal of the human-centered AI development idea is to take into account and include human needs and viewpoints into the AI development process and beyond (Auernhammer, 2020; Friedrich et al., 2024). To ensure that the final product adheres to certain principles of human-centered AI, such as explainability, transparency, ethical standards, fairness (e.g., non-discriminatory decision-making), trustworthiness, responsibility, and sustainability, human-centeredness must continue after an AI-based technology has been trained and put into use. This requires taking into account the entire AI lifecycle (Hartikainen et al., 2022).

In practice, the human-centric approach is implemented through a series of concrete actions. First, employee subjectivity must be ensured; employees should have the right to appeal algorithmic decisions and the ability to understand them. Transparency in AI-supported decisions is not only a system function (such as through Explainable AI, or XAI) but also a communicative obligation: the logic behind decisions must be accessible and understandable (Eisbach, Langer, & Hertel, 2023; Gerdes, 2024; Janssen et al., 2022). Second, employee participation and co-design are essential. Employees, as end-users of AI systems, should be engaged as early as the design and testing stages, a process referred to as co-creation (Tripathi & Rosak-Szyrocka, 2024). This both enhances the quality of the tools and fosters trust and acceptance of new technologies. A third key pillar is fairness and equality (Vraňaková, Gyurák Babeľová, & Chlpeková, 2021). AI must not replicate structural inequalities; therefore, bias audits, robust data quality controls, and the exclusion of so-called proxy variables (e.g., ZIP code as a substitute for socio-economic or ethnic background) are critical (Murikah, Nthenge, & Musyoka, 2024).

Equally important is the control of personal data aligned with the principles of purpose limitation and proportionality. HR systems should not collect excessive data (e.g., emotional metrics, behavioral tracking at the computer) unless it is strictly justified and voluntarily accepted by employees (Garcia, Rosak-Szyrocka, & Bozkurt, 2025). Workers should have access to their data, the right to correct it, and the option to deny its use for specific purposes. Human-centric HRM cannot exist without empathy and relationality. Even the most advanced algorithm cannot replace a meaningful, empathetic conversation with a supervisor or a two-way developmental evaluation (Audretsch & Kariv, 2025). AI can support the identification of skill gaps and training needs, but final decisions must be rooted in human relationships (Napier & Wada, 2024).

This lifecycle approach recasts AI from an unbiased tool to a socially embedded system—one that is formed by the priorities, culture, and power dynamics of the organization. It also underscores the importance of shared responsibility across roles; HR professionals, data scientists, compliance officers, and impacted employees all must have a say in the design and governance of AI systems.

In order to reflect this complexity into practice, the ethical principles have to be translated into specific HRM practices. Human-centered AI-based HRM reinstates employees' dignity, involvement, and rights at the core of any automated process. It's not just about preventing harm, but about building trust, autonomy, and well-being in workers through transparent, supportive, and participative systems (Rezaev & Tregubova, 2025).

Yet, in practical terms, human-centricity in AI-driven HRM is an ethic that is actually translated into certain operative behaviors. It involves empowering employee subjectivity, facilitating contestability of algorithmic outputs, embedding transparency not only as a technical feature but also as a communicative obligation, and fostering inclusive design through employee engagement. People-focused AI HRM returns dignity, inclusiveness, and rights to the very heart of every algorithm-driven process. The goal is not to avoid harm, but to construct trust, autonomy, and employee well-being using transparent, dialogical systems. Instead of being an ultimate authority, AI becomes a collaborator, a tool in the hands of humanity (Basnet, 2024; Boehmer & Schinnenburg, 2023).

The principle of fairness is perhaps about more than simply looking for discriminatory outcomes; it's about reconsidering what counts as a legitimate input into hiring or promotion decisions (Majrashi, 2025; Zaidi et al., 2025). Explainability is not just a technical feature; it is meant to guarantee that when employees have concerns, they can understand and question why an algorithm spat out a decision (Barredo Arrieta et al., 2020; Nuseir

TABLE 2.6 Link between ethical values and HRM activities

HRM Domain	Ethical AI Principle	Description
Recruitment & selection	Fairness/Anti-Bias—Machine learning programs must be designed and tested to ensure they do not perpetuate social, gender, or racial disparities. Justice is equality of opportunity for all people in society.	Consider the demographic impact when developing models; train models with rebalanced data; remove proxy variables, like ZIP code, that may be associated with protected attributes.
Performance evaluation	Explainability—Decisions made by AI should be comprehensible, understandable, and justifiable to the employee. Explanations need to be actionable and grounded in transparent metrics.	Employ interpretable models (such as SHAP or LIME); produce dashboards that display the key performance factors affecting assigned scores; enable managers to verify AI-generated scores.
Career development	Human Agency—AI must amplify, not replace, human decisions. Workers need to have the freedom and ability to challenge any algorithmic recommendations that could impact their advancement or trajectories.	Establish formal recourse mechanisms for AI-driven promotion decisions; allow for opt-out functionality of algorithmic recommendations; engage employees in the logic of goal-setting.
Retention prediction	Non-maleficence—Model outputs should not create harmful assumptions (e.g., "likely to churn") without context. Systems can't incriminate workers due to a mere inference.	Don't have punitive names for algorithms (like "blacklists"); notify employees when behavior tracking is used; check algorithmic predictions using qualitative manager feedback before any HR decision.
Data governance	Privacy & Consent—Temperature and other data about employees (furnished, behavioral, emotional, biometric) should be collected and utilized as little as possible, with informed consent and strict purpose limitation.	General Data Protection Regulation (GDPR); opt-out practices; explicit employee consent; purpose limitation.

Source: Own study, based on: Prikshat et al. (2023a); Reuben Binns (2018).

et al., 2024). And human agency means that while algorithmic recommendations can exist, they can only ever be just that: recommendations, with the ultimate control held by humans (Schuster & Lazar, 2025; Yeung, 2018). The link between ethical values and HRM activities is demonstrated in Table 2.6.

As the new moral elements surface, implanting AI in HR systems, from a human lens, is getting complicated. Reports like the World Economic Forum's Future of Jobs 2023 highlight the increasing recognition by executives of the ethical considerations surrounding AI in talent management (World Economic Forum, 2025a, 2025b). Likewise, research quoted in Deloitte's Human Capital Trends 2023 shows that 41% of employees need to confirm that AI-generated HR decisions are reviewed by human beings before they trust them, drawing attention to the importance of AI co-review processes and design features that are transparent (Deloitte, 2023).

REFERENCES

Ahmad Giran, A. H., Muhamad Tamyez, P. F., & Fauzi, M. A. (2025). The paradoxes of sustainable HRM: insights through the perspective of common good, green, social responsibility, and triple bottom line. *Human Systems Management, 44*(4), 691–709.

Akkermans, J., Brenninkmeijer, V., Huibers, M., & Blonk, R. W. B. (2013). Competencies for the contemporary career. *Journal of Career Development, 40*(3), 245–267.

Alzoubi, A., Al-Talib, M., & Al Saad, W. K. (2023). Sustainability as a competitive advantage: IKEA as a case study. In *Proceedings of the International Conference on Industrial Engineering and Operations Management*. IEOM Society International.

American Psychological Association (APA). (2023). *Work and Well-Being Survey: Findings from the 2023 American Workforce Survey*. American Psychological Association. Available from www.apa.org/pubs/reports/work-in-america/2023-workplace-health-well-being

Anshima, A., Bhardwaj, B., Sharma, D., & Chand, M. (2025). Ensuring sustainability through green HRM practices: a review, synthesis and research avenues. *Journal of Organizational Effectiveness: People and Performance, 12*(1), 57–90. Available from: www.emerald.com/insight/content/doi/10.1108/joepp-10-2023-0493/full/pdf?casa_token=z-0halg4sb0aaaaa:rs4xcb3x4z7dljriatln98jk_0ehblchvs_g-2qupx64ljbhdh45pyik2ovz1vygpj-s4vffm09ntnhqyzox9ukcvdfny78jo_znown_l-aygp0e

Asif, M. S., Lau, H., Nakandala, D., Fan, Y., & Hurriyet, H. (2022). Case study research of green life cycle model for the evaluation and reduction of scope 3 emissions in food supply chains. *Corporate Social Responsibility and Environmental Management, 29*(4), 1050–1066.

Audretsch, D. B., & Kariv, D. (2025). Emotional resources and knowledge management: a gender perspective on human-centric innovation amidst crises. *Journal of Knowledge Management* (ahead-of-print). Available from: www.emerald.com/insight/content/doi/10.1108/jkm-02-2024-0235/full/pdf?casa_token=qk7v8yjrwuyaaaaa:gvklmfjrmzr9j776fvk2ilelpo4u8wsuz6xvtaa5obrs2wjxtlbflfje2zdp6erki-mwig-wsjg5vhun36dxveznmtcfs-waphf65i1f2u9aimcd.

Auernhammer, J. (2020). Human-centered AI: The role of human-centered design research in the development of AI. In S. Boess, M. Cheung, & R. Cain (Eds.), *Synergy - DRS International Conference 2020*, 11–14 August. https://doi.org/10.21606/drs.2020.282

Aust, I., Matthews, B., & Muller-Camen, M. (2020). Common Good HRM: a paradigm shift in Sustainable HRM? *Human Resource Management Review, 30*(3), 100705.

Austen, A., & Piwowar-Sulej, K. (2025). Addressing big societal challenges: towards Common Good HRM. *Organizacja i Kierowanie, 197*(1), 23–37. Available from: https://econjournals.sgh.waw.pl/oik/article/view/4368

Barredo Arrieta, A., Díaz-Rodríguez, N., Del Ser, J., Bennetot, A., Tabik, S., Barbado, A., et al. (2020). Explainable Artificial Intelligence (XAI): Concepts, taxonomies, opportunities and challenges toward responsible AI. *Information Fusion, 58*, 82–115.

Barrett, S. (2024, March 19). *How McDonald's is using AI to boost efficiency and workflows*. AI Magazine. https://aimagazine.com/articles/how-mcdonalds-is-using-ai-to-boost-efficiency-and-workflows

Basnet, S. (2024). Navigating the AI/ML-driven future of HRM: Balancing technological innovation with human collaboration. *International Journal of Research and Review, 11*(10). Available from: www.ijrrjournal.com. E-ISSN: 2349-9788; P-ISSN: 2454-2237

Basu, S., Majumdar, B., Mukherjee, K., Munjal, S., & Palaksha, C. (2023). Artificial intelligence–HRM interactions and outcomes: a systematic review and causal configurational explanation. *Human Resource Management Review, 33*(1), 100893.

Bhatia, S. (2025) Sustainability: ecological organizational performance and Green Human Resource Management (GHRM). In *Implementing ESG Frameworks Through Capacity Building and Skill Development* (pp. 195–218). IGI Global Scientific Publishing; IGI Global.

Binns, R. (2018). Fairness in machine learning: lessons from political philosophy. *Conference on Fairness, Accountability and Transparency*, 149–159. PMLR from https://proceedings.mlr.press/v81/binns18a.html.

Böhmer, N., & Schinnenburg, H. (2023). Critical exploration of AI-driven HRM to build up organizational capabilities. *Employee Relations: The International Journal, 45*(5), 1057–1082, from www.emerald.com/insight/content/doi/10.1108/er-04-2022-0202/full/pdf.

Bolis, I., Brunoro, C. M., & Sznelwar, L. I. (2014). Mapping the relationships between work and sustainability and the opportunities for ergonomic action. *Applied Ergonomics, 45*(4), 1225–1239.

Bondarouk, T., Parry, E., & Furtmueller, E. (2017). Electronic HRM: four decades of research on adoption and consequences. *The International Journal of Human Resource Management, 28*(1), 98–131.

Budhwar, P., Malik, A., Silva, M. T. T. de, & Thevisuthan, P. (2022). Artificial intelligence – challenges and opportunities for international HRM: a review and research agenda. *The International Journal of Human Resource Management, 33*(6), 1065–1097.

Bujold, A., Roberge-Maltais, I., Parent-Rocheleau, X., Boasen, J., Sénécal, S., & Léger, P.-M. (2024). Responsible artificial intelligence in human resources management: a review of the empirical literature. *AI and Ethics, 4*(4), 1185–1200, from https://link.springer.com/article/10.1007/s43681-023-00325-1.

Camuffo, A., Stefano, F. de, & Paolino, C. (2017). Safety reloaded: lean operations and high involvement work practices for sustainable workplaces. *Journal of Business Ethics, 143*(2), 245–259, from https://idp.springer.com/authorize/casa?redirect_uri=https://link.springer.com/article/10.1007/s10551-015-2590-8&casa_token=uka0bu6gpp4aaaaa:0mtmgwladhyh0hcss-bmkak_smycdjq9j3bfabtbhmatzgqh659osxofe6-vupvvdurs_u0cth2m8g.

Cesário, F., Sabino, A., Palma-Moreira, A., & Pinto-Coelho, M. (2025). Exploring links between Green HRM, greenwashing, and sustainability: the role of individual and professional traits. *Sustainability, 17*(4), 1764, from www.mdpi.com/2071-1050/17/4/1764.

Chams, N., & García-Blandón, J. (2019). On the importance of sustainable human resource management for the adoption of sustainable development goals. *Resources, Conservation and Recycling, 141*, 109–122.

Chin, Y. S., Mohamad, A. A., & Lo, M. C. (2024). Harnessing the power of artificial intelligence (AI): a paradigm shift in HRM practices for employee sustainable performance. *Global Knowledge, Memory and Communication*. https://doi.org/10.1108/GKMC-06-2024-0355

Deloitte. (2023). *2023 Global Human Capital Trends: New Fundamentals for a Boundaryless World*. Deloitte Insights. Retrieved from https://www2.deloitte.com/us/en/insights/focus/human-capital-trends/2023.html

Deloitte Insights. (2025). *2023 Global Human Capital Trends*. Retrieved May 15, 2025, from https://www2.deloitte.com/us/en/insights/focus/human-capital-trends/2023.html.

Dignum, V. (2019). *Responsible artificial intelligence: how to develop and use AI in a responsible way* (Vol. 2156). Springer.

Dwork, C., Hardt, M., Pitassi, T., Reingold, O., & Zemel, R. (2012). Fairness through awareness. In S. Goldwasser (Ed.), *Proceedings of the 3rd Innovations in Theoretical Computer Science Conference* (pp. 214–226). ACM.

Dyllick, T., & Muff, K. (2016). Clarifying the meaning of sustainable business. *Organization & Environment, 29*(2), 156–174.

Ehnert, I., Parsa, S., Roper, I., Wagner, M., & Muller-Camen, M. (2016). Reporting on sustainability and HRM: a comparative study of sustainability reporting practices by the world's largest companies. *The International Journal of Human Resource Management, 27*(1), 88–108.

Eisbach, S., Langer, M., & Hertel, G. (2023). Optimizing human-AI collaboration: effects of motivation and accuracy information in AI-supported decision-making. *Computers in Human Behavior: Artificial Humans, 1*(2), 100015.

Elnakib, A., & Gallego-Roquelaure, V. (2025). Sustainable human resources management in small-medium enterprises in developing countries: a systematic literature review. *Employee Relations: The International Journal, ahead-of-print*(ahead-of-print), from www.emerald.com/insight/content/doi/10.1108/er-09-2024-0527/full/pdf?casa_token=59qwyrhlsssaaaaa:jqiijfdvnb6m5jpwcxprn8d_0fmjsw64tkbndj6ssvs7yytnrtxgmrp8rlp-loehkykhhyuqjcu7jc1bg_nh7cbdxrxmaalrioofyuzwwtaykve_.

Fauzi, H., Svensson, G., & Rahman, A. A. (2010). "Triple Bottom Line" as "Sustainable Corporate Performance": a proposition for the future. *Sustainability, 2*(5), 1345–1360.

Fenwick, A., Molnar, G., & Frangos, P. (2024). The critical role of HRM in AI-driven digital transformation: a paradigm shift to enable firms to move from AI implementation to human-centric adoption. *Discover Artificial Intelligence, 4*(1), 1–16, from https://link.springer.com/article/10.1007/s44163-024-00125-4.

Fianko, A. O., Essuman, D., Boso, N., & Muntaka, A. S. (2023). Customer integration and customer value: contingency roles of innovation capabilities and supply chain network complexity. *Supply Chain Management: An International Journal, 28*(2), 385–404.

Fioravante, R. (2024). Beyond the business case for responsible artificial intelligence: strategic CSR in light of digital washing and the moral human argument. *Sustainability, 16*(3), 1232, from www.mdpi.com/2071-1050/16/3/1232.

Floridi, L., & Cowls, J. (2022). A unified framework of five principles for AI in society. In *Machine Learning and the City* (pp. 535–545). John Wiley & Sons, Ltd.

Forbes. (2024). *ChatGPT and Generative AI: what this technology means for today's CIO.* Retrieved May 14, 2025, from www.forbes.com/councils/forbestechcouncil/2023/03/02/chatgpt-and-generative-ai-what-this-technology-means-for-todays-cio/.

Fostervold, K. I., Koren, P. C., & Nilsen, O. V. (2018). Defining sustainable and "decent" work for human factors and ergonomics. In *Ergonomics and Human Factors for a Sustainable Future* (pp. 47–76). Palgrave Macmillan.

Friedrich, J., Brückner, A., Mayan, J., Schumann, S., Kirschenbaum, A., & Zinke-Wehlmann, C. (2024). Human-centered AI development in practice—insights from a multidisciplinary approach. *Zeitschrift für Arbeitswissenschaft, 78*(3), 359–376, from https://link.springer.com/article/10.1007/s41449-024-00434-5.

Gajšek, B., Draghici, A., Boatca, M. E., Gaureanu, A., & Robescu, D. (2022). Linking the use of ergonomics methods to workplace social sustainability: the Ovako Working Posture Assessment System and Rapid Entire Body Assessment Method. *Sustainability, 14*(7), 4301, from www.mdpi.com/2071-1050/14/7/4301.

Garcia, M. B., Rosak-Szyrocka, J., & Bozkurt, A. (2025). *Pitfalls of AI integration in education: skill obsolescence, misuse, and bias: skill obsolescence, misuse, and bias*, IGI Global.

Garg, S., Sinha, S., Kar, A. K., & Mani, M. (2022). A review of machine learning applications in human resource management. *International Journal of Productivity and Performance Management, 71*(5), 1590–1610, from www.emerald.com/insight/content/doi/10.1108/ijppm-08-2020-0427/full/pdf.

Gaur, L., Afaq, A., Arora, G. K., & Khan, N. (2023). Artificial intelligence for carbon emissions using system of systems theory. *Ecological Informatics, 76*, 102165.

Gerdes, A. (2024). The role of explainability in AI-supported medical decision-making. *Discover Artificial Intelligence, 4*(1), 1–7, from https://link.springer.com/article/10.1007/s44163-024-00119-2.

Giannoccaro, I., Garcia, M. B., Rosak-Szyrocka, J., & Bozkurt, A. (2025). *Pitfalls of AI integration in education*, IGI Global.

Gimenez, C., Sierra, V., & Rodon, J. (2012). Sustainable operations: their impact on the triple bottom line. *International Journal of Production Economics, 140*(1), 149–159.

Goldwasser, S. (Ed.). (2012). *Proceedings of the 3rd Innovations in Theoretical Computer Science Conference*. ACM.

Gryncewicz, W., Zygała, R., & Pilch, A. (2023). AI in HRM: case study analysis. Preliminary research. *Procedia Computer Science, 225*, 2351–2360.

Guenole, N., & Feinzig, S. (2018). *The business case for AI in HR: with insights and tips on getting started.* IBM Publishing, from https://research.gold.ac.uk/id/eprint/33662/.

Gupta, M. (2021). The role of artificial intelligence in adopting Green HRM practices. In *Reinventing Manufacturing and Business Processes Through Artificial Intelligence* (pp. 1–18). CRC Press.

Hartikainen, M., Väänänen, K., Lehtiö, A., Ala-Luopa, S., & Olsson, T. (2022). Human-centered AI design in reality: a study of developer companies' practices. In *Nordic Human-Computer Interaction Conference* (pp. 1–11). ACM.

Hasanain, B. (2024). The role of ergonomic and human factors in sustainable manufacturing: a review. *Machines, 12*(3), 159, from www.mdpi.com/2075-1702/12/3/159.

Hess, E. D. (2020). *Hyper-Learning: how to adapt to the speed of change*, Berrett-Koehler Publishers.

Inter IKEA Group. (2025, January 27). *IKEA Sustainability Report FY24*. IKEA. www.ikea.com/global/en/images/IKEA_Sustainability_Report_FY_24_2025_01_27_2c35989733.pdf

Jangbahadur, U., Ahlawat, S., Rozera, P., & Gupta, N. (2025). The effect of AI-enabled HRM dimensions on employee engagement and sustainable organisational performance: fusion skills as a moderator. *Evidence-based HRM: a Global Forum for Empirical Scholarship, 13*(1), 85–107, from www.emerald.com/insight/content/doi/10.1108/ebhrm-02-2023-0038/full/pdf?casa_token=5076fqxbw9waaaaa:aj-5zmjjfss5zslsjz5as0m3x5knwe-didcyhx8dd-3lp8o5ap2twlvtmamhzxb76clrffo0_sqtgqici3dbvjmn18oxadaf3qhzcubsozefd0ua.

Janssen, M., Hartog, M., Matheus, R., Yi Ding, A., & Kuk, G. (2022). Will algorithms blind people? the effect of explainable AI and decision-makers' experience on AI-supported decision-making in government. *Social Science Computer Review, 40*(2), 478–493.

Kim, S., Khoreva, V., & Vaiman, V. (2025). Strategic human resource management in the era of algorithmic technologies: key insights and future research agenda. *Human Resource Management, 64*(2), 447–464.

Kim, S., Wang, Y., & Boon, C. (2021). Sixty years of research on technology and human resource management: looking back and looking forward. *Human Resource Management, 60*(1), 229–247.

Kumar, R., & Sia, S. K. (2012). Employee engagement. *Management and Labour Studies, 37*(1), 31–43.

Labelle, F., Parent-Lamarche, A., Koropogui, S. T., & Chouchane, R. (2025). The relationship between sustainable HRM practices and employees' attraction: the influence of SME managers' values and intentions. *Journal of Organizational Effectiveness: People and Performance, 12*(1), 127–144, from www.emerald.com/insight/content/doi/10.1108/joepp-10-2023-0475/full/pdf?casa_token=d7iygczehvuaaaaa:ykis4mliasn76tpaomcsbr5oxglmrhriktljrp8s65afrj1lwmsw9wtzky8csecrchcxxug9scnqqlzgzbhl1yz5jwqw2qnppa8tbs45vftxsyya.

Lase, D., & Waruwu, E. (2025). Corporate Social Responsibility in Management Human Resources (HRM) 2.0. In *Sustainable Management Practices for Employee Retention and Recruitment* (pp. 103–126). IGI Global Scientific Publishing; IGI Global.

Lee, B., Lee, E., & Kim, J. (2025). Analysis of factors affecting job satisfaction for sustainable workforce development: insights from IT industry employee reviews. *Sustainability, 17*(4), 1689, from www.mdpi.com/2071-1050/17/4/1689.

Liu, D., Yousaf, Z., & Rosak-Szyrocka, J. (2024). Environmental performance through green supply chain management practices, green innovation, and zero waste management. *Sustainability, 16*(24), 11173, from www.mdpi.com/2071-1050/16/24/11173.

Lopez-Cabrales, A., & Valle-Cabrera, R. (2020). Sustainable HRM strategies and employment relationships as drivers of the triple bottom line. *Human Resource Management Review, 30*(3), 100689.

Madanchian, M., Taherdoost, H., & Mohamed, N. (2023). AI-based human resource management tools and techniques; a systematic literature review. *Procedia Computer Science, 229*, 367–377.

Madero-Gómez, S. M., Rubio Leal, Y. L., Olivas-Luján, M., & Yusliza, M. Y. (2023). Companies could benefit when they focus on employee wellbeing and the environment: a systematic review of Sustainable Human Resource Management. *Sustainability, 15*(6), 5435, from www.mdpi.com/2071-1050/15/6/5435.

Mahade, A., Elmahi, A., Alomari, K. M., & Abdalla, A. A. (2025). Leveraging AI-driven insights to enhance sustainable human resource management performance: moderated mediation model: evidence from UAE higher education. *Discover Sustainability, 6*(1), 1–22, from https://link.springer.com/article/10.1007/s43621-025-01114-y.

Majrashi, K. (2025). Employees' perceptions of the fairness of AI-based performance prediction features. *Cogent Business & Management, 12*(1).

Malik, A., Silva, M. T. de, Budhwar, P., & Srikanth, N. R. (2021). Elevating talents' experience through innovative artificial intelligence-mediated knowledge sharing: evidence from an IT-multinational enterprise. *Journal of International Management, 27*(4), 100871.

Manoharan, P. (2024). A review on AI Driven HR systems: revolutionizing HR systems and talent management. *Scholars Journal of Engineering and Technology, 12*(06), 179–184.

Markoff, J. (2016). *Machines of loving grace: the quest for common ground between humans and robots*, HarperCollins Publishers. https://dl.acm.org/doi/abs/10.5555/2994165.

Matisoff, D. C., Noonan, D. S., & O'Brien, J. J. (2013). Convergence in environmental reporting: assessing the carbon disclosure project. *Business Strategy and the Environment, 22*(5), 285–305.

Mehmood, M. U., Chun, D., Zeeshan, Han, H., Jeon, G., & Chen, K. (2019). A review of the applications of artificial intelligence and big data to buildings for energy-efficiency and a comfortable indoor living environment. *Energy and Buildings, 202*, 109383.

Mohamed Riyath, M. I., & Inun Jariya, A. M. (2024). The role of ESG reporting, artificial intelligence, stakeholders and innovation performance in fostering sustainability culture and climate resilience. *Journal of Financial Reporting and Accounting, ahead-of-print*(ahead-of-print), from www.emerald.com/insight/content/doi/10.1108/jfra-10-2023-0621/full/pdf?casa_token=eftev-r8pu0aaaaa:-n3bvtcctv2dy21nzqh9k3tys6dylkg7lowuzxte8omdaskhflbnrbc8-mpojqs60dud6toxemklymysq9uushe2rakoajndmxwquryoobroug8z.

Mollah, M. A., Rana, M., Amin, M. B., Sony, M. M. A. A. M., Rahaman, M. A., & Fenyves, V. (2024). Examining the role of AI-Augmented HRM for sustainable performance: key determinants for digital culture and organizational strategy. *Sustainability, 16*(24), 10843.

Murikah, W., Nthenge, J. K., & Musyoka, F. M. (2024). Bias and ethics of AI systems applied in auditing – a systematic review. *Scientific African, 25*, e02281.

Murugesan, U., Subramanian, P., Srivastava, S., & Dwivedi, A. (2023). A study of artificial intelligence impacts on human resource digitalization in Industry 4.0. *Decision Analytics Journal, 7*, 100249.

Napier, P., & Wada, T. (2024). Bridging the skills gap: the design education landscape with AI and experiential learning. *Design Management Journal, 19*(1), 19–30.

Nuseir, M. T., Alshurideh, M. T., Alzoubi, H. M., Al Kurdi, B., Hamadneh, S., & AlHamad, A. (2024). Role of Explainable Artificial Intelligence (EAI) in Human Resource Management System (HRMS). *Cyber Security Impact on Digitalization and Business Intelligence, 117*, 249–263, from https://link.springer.com/chapter/10.1007/978-3-031-31801-6_15.

Nyangoma, D., Adaga, E. M., Sam-Bulya, N. J., & Achumie, G. O. (2025). Long-term employer-talent partnerships: A conceptual model for reducing workforce turnover and enhancing retention. *International Journal of Social Sciences and Management Research, 11*(3), 195–209. E-ISSN 2545-5303 P-ISSN 2695-2203. Available from: www.iiardjournals.org

Ozkan, B. (Ed.). (2024). *Responsible Firms: CSR, ESG, and Global Sustainability*, Emerald Publishing Limited.

Prikshat, V., Islam, M., Patel, P., Malik, A., Budhwar, P., & Gupta, S. (2023a). AI-augmented HRM: literature review and a proposed multilevel framework for future research. *Technological Forecasting and Social Change, 193*, 122645.

Prikshat, V., Malik, A., & Budhwar, P. (2023b). AI-augmented HRM: antecedents, assimilation and multilevel consequences. *Human Resource Management Review, 33*(1), 100860.

Prins, P. de, Stuer, D., & Gielens, T. (2020). Revitalizing social dialogue in the workplace: the impact of a cooperative industrial relations climate and sustainable HR practices on reducing employee harm. *The International Journal of Human Resource Management, 31*(13), 1684–1704.

Ramya, M., & Prabu, G. (2025). Unveiling the synergy: exploring the forces driving CSR and sustainable performance through GHRM practices. In *Digital Transformation and Sustainability of Business* (pp. 618–621). CRC Press.

Rezaev, A. V., & Tregubova, N. D. (2025). Looking at human-centered artificial intelligence as a problem and prospect for sociology: an analytic review. *Current Sociology, 73*(1), 120–138.

Richards, J. (2022). Putting employees at the centre of sustainable HRM: a review, map and research agenda. *Employee Relations: The International Journal, 44*(3), 533–554.

Rosak-Szyrocka, J., & Wolniak, R. (2025). *Smart universities in Smart Cities: shaping the future of education and urban innovation*, Taylor & Francis.

Rosak-Szyrocka, J., Żywiołek, J., Nayyar, A., & Naved, M. (2023). *The role of sustainability and artificial intelligence in education improvement,* CRC Press.

Schuster, N., & Lazar, S. (2025). Attention, moral skill, and algorithmic recommendation. *Philosophical Studies, 182*(1), 159–184, from https://link.springer.com/article/10.1007/s11098-023-02083-6.

Sharma, C., & Chanana, N. (2025). The intersection of artificial intelligence and human resources: transforming journey using natural language processing. *Iran Journal of Computer Science*, 1–16, from https://idp.springer.com/authorize/casa?redirect_uri=https://link.springer.com/article/10.1007/s42044-025-00261-9&casa_token=l6b0a9ese4uaaaaa:ca4ndt-gavlrr35oxpgg4btwhlk8n4vwv5h5yjllxlqnawavc5wg62gs0ptcbtlfbvgfayeg20jhcw.

Siemens AG. (2022). *Sustainability Report 2022.*

Siemens AG. (2024). *Sustainability report 2024.* www.siemens.com/global/en/company/investor-relations/events-publications-ad-hoc/annualreports.html

Sova, O., Bieliaieva, N., Antypenko, N., & Drozd, N. (2023). Impact of artificial intelligence and digital HRM on the resource consumption within sustainable development perspective. *E3S Web of Conferences, 408*, 1006.

Strohmeier, S. (2020). Digital human resource management: a conceptual clarification. *German Journal of Human Resource Management: Zeitschrift für Personalforschung, 34*(3), 345–365.

Tambe, P., Cappelli, P., & Yakubovich, V. (2019). Artificial intelligence in Human Resources Management: challenges and a path forward. *California Management Review, 61*(4), 15–42.

Tamburrini, G. (2022). The AI carbon footprint and responsibilities of AI scientists. *Philosophies, 7*(1), 4, from www.mdpi.com/2409-9287/7/1/4.

Tian, X., Pavur, R., Han, H., & Zhang, L. (2023). A machine learning-based human resources recruitment system for business process management: using LSA, BERT and SVM. *Business Process Management Journal, 29*(1), 202–222.

Tripathi, S., & Rosak-Szyrocka, J. (2024). *Impact of artificial intelligence on society,* CRC Press.

UN Secretary-General (2017). *Activities of the Department of Public Information:: news services: report of the Secretary-General:* UN.

Usha, M., & Ramkumar, N. (2025). Happy workers, healthy business: The impact of sustainable human resource management and workplace happiness on employee engagement of women employees in tea plantations. *Sustainability (2071-1050), 17*(3), 1047.

Varma, A., Dawkins, C., & Chaudhuri, K. (2023). Artificial intelligence and people management: a critical assessment through the ethical lens. *Human Resource Management Review, 33*(1), 100923.

Vinnikova, I. S., Prokhorova, M. P., Krylova, T. V., Shkunova, A. A., & Zhulkova, J. N. (2024). Human Resource Management tools for companies based on ESG guidelines. In *Sustainable development of the agrarian economy based on digital technologies and smart innovations* (pp. 191–197), from https://link.springer.com/chapter/10.1007/978-3-031-51272-8_32.

Vinuesa, R., Azizpour, H., Leite, I., Balaam, M., Dignum, V., Domisch, S., et al. (2020). The role of artificial intelligence in achieving the Sustainable Development Goals. *Nature Communications, 11*(1), 233.

Vraňaková, N., Gyurák Babeľová, Z., & Chlpeková, A. (2021). Sustainable Human Resource Management and generational diversity: the importance of the age management pillars. *Sustainability, 13*(15), 8496, from www.mdpi.com/2071-1050/13/15/8496.

Vrontis, D., Christofi, M., Pereira, V., Tarba, S., Makrides, A., & Trichina, E. (2023). Artificial intelligence, robotics, advanced technologies and human resource management: a systematic review. In *Artificial Intelligence and International HRM* (pp. 172–201). Routledge.

Westerman, J. W., Rao, M. B., Vanka, S., & Gupta, M. (2020). Sustainable human resource management and the triple bottom line: Multi-stakeholder strategies, concepts, and engagement. *Human Resource Management Review, 30*(3), 100742.

What's Next is Everything. (2025). *How Hilton and Wendy's are using AI to improve customer interactions — What's Next is Everything.* Retrieved May 25, 2025, from www.whatsnextiseverything.com/blog/2024/9/28/how-hilton-and-wendys-are-using-ai-to-improve-customer-interactions.

World Economic Forum. (2025a). *The Future of Jobs Report 2023.* Retrieved May 27, 2025, from www.weforum.org/publications/the-future-of-jobs-report-2023/.

World Economic Forum. (2025b). *The Future of Jobs Report 2024.* Geneva: World Economic Forum.

Yabanci, O. (2019). From human resource management to intelligent human resource management: a conceptual perspective. *Human-Intelligent Systems Integration, 1*(2-4), 101–109, from https://idp.springer.com/authorize/casa?redirect_uri=https://link.springer.com/article/10.1007/s42454-020-00007-x&casa_token=oj2qgekeb94aaaaa:wmbgvcyxyhxxkcuvqcd8-r6srckvriwfzf_bkqn1u9_ztcstwhmoalmk1ho7xor8wxslflha2htrpg.

Yeung, K. (2018). Algorithmic regulation: a critical interrogation. *Regulation & Governance, 12*(4), 505–523.

Zaidi, S. Y. A., Aslam, M. F., Mahmood, F., Ahmad, B., & Tasaddque, S. (2025). Accomplishing the SDGs through Green HRM practices: insights from industrial sustainability experts. *Global Business and Organizational Excellence, 44*(5), 19–45. https://doi.org/10.1002/joe.22294

Zink, K. J. (2014). Designing sustainable work systems: the need for a systems approach. *Applied Ergonomics, 45*(1), 126–132.

II

AI-Powered HRM Practices for Sustainability

CHAPTER 3

AI in Talent Acquisition and Recruitment

3.1 AI-POWERED HIRING PROCESSES

According to Lovelock et al. (2018), the artificial intelligence (AI) market was estimated to be worth a whopping $1.2 trillion in 2018, and 61% of companies were allegedly using AI in some capacity inside their organizations (Narrative Science, 2018). Profitability might be considerably increased by 30% thanks to AI (Purdy & Daugherty, 2017). Global investment in AI and cognitive solutions is expected to reach USD 57.6 billion by 2021, growing at a compound annual growth rate (CAGR) of 50.1% (Kumar, 2020).

According to research by Accenture, AI may increase profitability by an average of 38% by 2035 and generate an additional $14 trillion in economic growth across 16 sectors in 12 countries by that time (Purdy & Daugherty, 2017). In this new age, with the power of AI, the recruitment industry is empowering employers to meet recruitment challenges. With AI, recruiters can process volumes of data to find suitable candidates. AI can scan social media data to assess the candidate's values, beliefs, and attitudes. With AI, recruiters are getting clues on personality traits and suitability that go beyond the traditional resumes. AI is unbiased and screens resumes fairly by giving equal weight to all candidates (Upadhyay & Khandelwal, 2018).

Organizations struggle to find the proper personnel, and HR managers play a critical role in talent acquisition (TA) (Huang et al., 2002). According to a study by Alexander Mann Solutions, 96% of HR experts think AI can help in talent acquisition (Nair, 2017). TA is the primary indicator of organizational efficiency in this fiercely competitive, international market (Allen, Mahto, & Otondo, 2007; Huang et al., 2002; Phillips-Wren, Doran, & Merrill, 2016). The TA role entails a significant financial outlay for the recruitment, selection, and training of newly recruited personnel (Pillai & Sivathanu, 2020). Because human resources are crucial to the efficient operation of the company, HR managers must

DOI: 10.1201/9781003668282-5

be very careful when choosing the best applicants (Singh, 2018; Das and Kodwani, 2018). The advent of the Internet and technology that makes it easier for HR managers to contact possible job applicants has intensified competition for talent acquisition. HR managers will be able to enhance the effectiveness of the HR department's performance and talent acquisition function by using AIT for TA ((Upadhyay & Khandelwal, 2018). Benefits of the AIT for TA include enhanced recruiter performance, reduced repetitious resume-screening activities, enhanced applicant attractiveness, and better candidate experience (McDonald, Fisher, & Connelly; van Esch, Black, & Ferolie, 2019). To remain successful in the modern tech-driven economy, HR managers must use AI technologies for talent acquisition (Rosak-Szyrocka et al., 2025; Walker & Larson, 2025).

Three degrees of AI have arisen for human resource management: assisted intelligence, augmented intelligence, and autonomous intelligence (Charlier et al. 2017). AI has become more important in this regard (Pillai & Sivathanu, 2020; Rosak-Szyrocka, 2024; Tripathi & Rosak-Szyrocka, 2024). Table 3.1 shows levels of AI in HRM with applications in talent acquisition.

Companies are starting to realize that they need to actively seek talent instead of depending only on conventional job advertising, much as talent managers are recognizing the shifting views of their prospective workforce. Social media tactics provide businesses with the chance to connect with today's job searchers via new forms of interaction, such as customization and direct contact (Phillips-Wren, Doran, & Merrill, 2016). Table 3.2 presents applications of AI in recruitment processes.

3.2 REDUCING BIAS AND PROMOTING DIVERSITY THROUGH AI

The process of acquiring talent entails intricate exchanges between prospective employees and the companies hoping to hire them. However, research on millennials, or those born between the early 1980s and 2000, shows that they are a sizable group of individuals looking for work right now and that one of their traits is value orientation, or the desire for their occupations and businesses to change the world.

AI's ability to improve decision-making efficiency and expedite recruiting procedures has led to a significant increase in its use in recruitment (Yanamala, 2022).

But this move toward automation has not been without its difficulties, especially when it comes to prejudice and justice. Numerous studies have shown that AI-based hiring algorithms are biased, often reflecting or even exaggerating the biases found in the historical data that these systems are trained on. One of the most well-known examples is the AI hiring tool that Amazon discontinued when it was shown to be discriminatory against women (Dastin, 2022). After ten years of processing applications, the algorithm learnt to prioritize male applicants over female ones, especially for technical positions. This happened because most of the resumes in the training sample were from males; therefore, the AI penalized resumes that included phrases relating to women, such as women's groups or women's universities.

But as AI deployment spreads, there are rising worries that these systems' conclusions may be swayed by the prejudices of model creators or organizational staff, as shown by a number of events (Mujtaba & Mahapatra, 2019). Men were shown high-paying

TABLE 3.1 Levels of AI in HRM with applications in talent acquisition

AI level	Function in HRM	Examples	Impact on TA
Assisted intelligence	This tier is about automating predictable, repeatable tasks with clear rule-based logic that don't need sophisticated data interpretation. That includes answering basic HR questions through chatbots, scheduling interviews, submitting documents, and organizing employee information. The idea is to take HR people out of burdensome admin, which will allow them to focus on strategic activities.	Chatbots for initial candidate screening, scheduling automation tools and reminders for several hiring stages.	Dramatically speeds up early-stage candidate screening, relieves administrative burden, and gives recruiters an edge. It also ensures consistent and uniform communication with candidates.
Augmented intelligence	This level supports HR professionals to make better decisions by blending human judgment with AI-powered recommendations. It's technology that understands behavior data, personalizes experiences for candidates, and provides decision support for candidate selection and experience. The emphasis is on a partnership between humans and machines, with AI enabling the humans and not replacing them.	Conversational bots for scheduling interviews, answering candidates' questions, and helping recruiters identify candidate potential.	Customization for personalized touch, instant communication capability, and employer branding functionality to enhance the candidate's experience. It's about forming authentic, scalable relationships in a digital context.
Autonomous intelligence	This is the ultimate layer, where the AI operates autonomously using highly sophisticated data analysis and ongoing learning. That involves such functions as ranking candidates, predicting workforce needs, assessing turnover risks, and automating compliance processes. Such systems are designed to be primarily autonomous, with weak or infrequent interventions, learning from data (supervised/unsupervised/reinforcement) over time.	Unbiased candidate assessment, algorithmic job-candidate matching using performance data, AI-driven predictive hiring tools.	Promotes objectivity, increases precision of candidate-job matching, and makes room for scaling data-driven hiring practices. It minimizes bias, accelerates the hiring process, and enables organizations to make more informed, consistent decisions.

Source: own study, based on: (Albert, 2019).

job posts more often than women in 2015, for example, demonstrating gender bias in Google's employment suggestion algorithm (Miller, 2015). This case, and others like it from Google and Facebook, demonstrates how bias introduced through training data can become absorbed and replicated by automated systems on a vast scale.

The serious danger that AI systems may inherit and reinforce preexisting biases in data is highlighted by this instance, especially in areas like hiring where historical inequalities and discriminatory practices can influence algorithmic decision-making (Bergelson, Tracy, & Takacs, 2022; Chen, 2023; Mokhtech et al., 2022b). Systems that combine and

TABLE 3.2 Applications of AI in recruitment processes

AI application area/AI intelligence level	AI function description in recruitment process	Function in AI recruitment	Benefits
Automation of Repetitive Tasks/Assisted intelligence	In recruitment, AI handles mundane or time-consuming work like conducting initial screenings of applicants, collecting and sorting resumes, or answering FAQs through chatbots. These are systems that evaluate the incoming data and send only the most qualified candidates to more advanced processes. Therefore, recruiters can concentrate on strategic work. Examples: automated CV screener, FAQ bots like Mya and Xor	AI automates mundane and time-consuming duties, ranging from reducing the burden of an initial screening and resume filtering, to chatbots responding to FAQs and handling candidate documents. These are simple systems that evaluate base data and message the best potential candidates to include them in the subsequent stages in the process.	Decreases admin work, cuts down the time from hire to hire, allows recruiters to work on more strategic tasks, and boosts overall hiring process productivity
Data Analysis and Candidate Matching/ Augmented intelligence	Advanced algorithms analyzing CVs, social media, and competency tests are used to compare this information to the demands of individual jobs. It allows for a better matching between a candidate's resume and the job offer. The industry is rewarded with higher-quality hires, lower attrition, and happier candidates and employers. Examples of tools: SmartRecruiters, Ideal, HireVue predictive	AI analyzes information from CVs, psychometric tests, social media, and ATS platforms to match with job descriptions. Predictive analytics and matching algorithms help it to determine if a candidate is likely to be a right fit and to succeed.	It helps to improve the landing accuracy of the candidate role, promote the quality of recruitment, minimize the employee turnover rate, and improve the satisfaction of the employer and the candidate.
Chatbots and AI Assistants/ Assisted intelligence	Virtual assistants in the form of chatbots answer candidate queries, remind them of interviews, and also conduct preliminary recruitment interviews. Candidates are virtually guided through the process and feel valued as their questions are addressed in real time—driving greater attention and a more enjoyable experience. This is especially useful where there are large numbers of applications and the recruiter is interested in concentrating on the most promising candidates, and leaving the initial filtering process to the system. Example of tools: Olivia chatbot, AllyO virtual assistant	Chatbots powered by AI interact with candidates to answer their questions, help them through the application process, schedule interviews, and keep them informed at each stage of the hiring process.	Enhances candidates' user experience, increases engagement, facilitates real-time communication, and unburdens the HR team in a personal way.

TABLE 3.2 (*Continued*)

AI application area/AI intelligence level	AI function description in recruitment process	Function in AI recruitment	Benefits
Bias Detection and Reduction/ Autonomous intelligence	Artificial intelligence (AI) algorithms are engineered to bypass private, possibly prejudiced data, like gender, age, or ethnicity. What they do, instead, is judge candidates purely by their experience and their qualifications. This results in a more equitable and unbiased recruitment process, encourages diversity, and removes the possibility of bias. Examples of tools: Pymetrics for blind hiring, Textio for bias	By using algorithms, we can code out potentially prejudiced data (like gender, age, ethnicity, and education) when considering applicants and instead assess them based on their skills and how well they fit in with a job.	Encourages diversity and objectivity, supports a more inclusive environment, enhances employer image, and decreases exposure to legal risk from discriminatory practices.
Personalization and Feedback/ Augmented intelligence	Rejection letters can be automatically sent via AI, which can offer explanations for rejections and even suggest areas for improvement. Because of this, candidates feel respected—and your company develops a professional and responsible employer image. It would also make it more likely that those candidates would have a go at applying again later. Examples of tools: LinkedIn feedback plugins	AI can respond in real time to applicants, letting them know how they are faring in the application process and where they fall short and, sometimes, offering potential paths for reskilling.	Increases transparency, strengthens the employer brand, and motivates declined candidates to reapply in the future by making candidates feel respected and well-informed.
Optimization of Time-to-Hire/ Assisted intelligence	Automation systems that screen and reach out to potential applicants shave down a few ticks of the clock between the vacancy and when it gets filled. Companies that implement solutions such as these are better positioned to quickly adapt to hiring requirements and save on the cost associated with lengthy hiring processes. This is responsible for more flexible and cost-efficient processes of recruitment. Examples of tools: Beamery AI for outreach, Entelo for prequalifications	And for candidates, AI accelerates the process of their assessment and communication, thereby allowing them to move faster through the recruiting funnel. Perfect fits are fast-tracked to interviews or offers.	Drives faster time-to-fill, lowers hiring costs, and enhances flexibility to address staffing demands of the business.

(*Continued*)

TABLE 3.2 (*Continued*)

AI application area/AI intelligence level	AI function description in recruitment process	Function in AI recruitment	Benefits
Strategic Support/ Augmented intelligence	AI can assume the tactical work and HR can focus on strategic projects such as workforce planning, building organizational culture, and shaping the employee experience. This serves to elevate the position of HR to that of a partner in the business. Examples of tools: Workday Talent Insights	AI can help HR to become more strategic and responsive to business needs by removing transactional work like workforce planning, culture creation, or ensuring the best employee experience.	Enhances the strategic role of the HR function, strengthens decision-making, and ensures greater alignment with long-term business objectives.
High-Volume, High-Touch Recruitment Model/ Augmented intelligence	AI empowers high-volume hiring and doesn't erode the quality of communication with applicants. This architecure enables companies to scale their recruiting while keeping the process as personalized as needed. This enables companies to run big hiring campaigns and take care of candidates' experience at high volume. Examples of tools: HireVue Engage, Jobpal AI recruitment	AI brings the ability to handle a lot of candidates but still maintain high-quality individualized communication through automated messaging and engagement technology.	Supports scalable recruiting while maintaining a personalized touch, improves the efficacy of high-volume recruiting campaigns, and delivers a positive candidate experience at scale.

Source: own study, based on: (Albert, 2019; Upadhyay & Khandelwal, 2018).

evaluate inputs from many modalities, including text, pictures, and structured data, in order to make choices are referred to as multimodal AI. Multimodal AI systems may evaluate a candidate's video interview, social media profiles, CV, and even audio inputs in the context of hiring. A more thorough and all-encompassing view of a candidate's potential might be produced by integrating several data kinds (Cheng et al., 2020; Parcalabescu, Trost, & Frank, 2021). The aim to improve applicant assessments' precision and depth has fueled the usage of multimodal AI in hiring (Fauria et al., 2020; Tripathi & Rosak-Szyrocka, 2024). While text analysis of a CV might highlight pertinent experiences and talents, video interview analysis can provide information about a candidate's emotional intelligence and communication abilities. Quantitative comparisons of applicants may be made using structured data, such as employment history and educational background. Multimodal AI systems may provide a more comprehensive and nuanced evaluation than conventional single-modality systems by integrating these diverse input sources. But the intricacy of multimodal AI also brings with it special difficulties, especially with regard to bias. Every modality may have a unique set of biases, and the likelihood of compounding or crossing biases grows when they are combined. For example, linguistic trends in text-based analysis may introduce gender bias, while variations in face recognition accuracy may cause picture analysis to be biased against certain ethnic groups.

Recruitment bias may take many different forms, including discrimination against certain groups of applicants based on their gender, race, age, and socio-economic background (Soleimani et al., 2021). Because they are often ingrained in the historical data used to train AI models, these biases may be especially harmful. For example, if a company's employment history indicates that it prefers applicants from a certain demographic, an AI system educated on this data may unintentionally reproduce and reinforce similar prejudices in its recruiting recommendations. Furthermore, many AI algorithms are black-box, which adds an additional level of complexity. These systems often function in ways that are not entirely clear or intelligible to their human users, which makes bias detection and correction challenging. This lack of openness presents serious legal problems in addition to ethical ones, especially in areas with strong anti-discrimination legislation.

In Deloitte's 2024 report on enterprise generative AI adoption, 44% of organizations surveyed said that ethical considerations, including bias and fairness, were one of their three biggest concerns when expanding AI efforts (Deloitte United States, 2025).

Meanwhile promoting diversity by ensuring equal opportunities in recruitment is not only a social responsibility but also a business advantage. Companies in the top quartile for gender diversity on executive teams were 25% more likely to have above-average profitability than companies in the fourth quartile, according to a 2019 diversity report by McKinsey (2025).

For example, companies must make sure that their automated decision-making processes do not result in discriminatory consequences under the General Data Protection Regulation (GDPR) of the European Union. Reducing prejudice in AI hiring practices requires a multifaceted strategy that incorporates ethical and legal issues with technological progress. Conventional methods for reducing bias often include pre-processing strategies, such as balancing datasets or eliminating sensitive features, and post-processing strategies, which modify the AI model's outputs to guarantee equity. These techniques do have certain drawbacks, however. The efficacy of the hiring process may be jeopardized by post-processing modifications that result in choices between accuracy and fairness, while pre-processing methods may miss intricate, underlying biases in the data. Developing adaptive bias reduction strategies that can dynamically adapt to the data as the AI system processes it is becoming more and more popular in light of these difficulties (Crawford & Calo, 2016; Crawford & Paglen, 2021; Fauria et al., 2020; Paramita, Okwir, & Nuur, 2024; Roppelt et al., 2024). Adaptive procedures are not dependent on static modifications made either before or after the model is trained, as is the case with conventional methods. On the contrary, they continually observe the outputs of the system, identify biases in real time, and modify the model's decision-making process as necessary. In recruiting, where data might range significantly across various applicant pools and job responsibilities, this dynamic method enables more responsive and sophisticated bias reduction (Brooks et al., 2025; Science, 2018).

Many AI systems, such as facial recognition software, use machine learning algorithms that have been trained on labeled data. Algorithmic discrimination has been observed lately in algorithms trained on biased data (Bolukbasi et al., 2016; Caliskan, Bryson, & Narayanan, 2017). Even the well-known word embedding space, Word2Vec, was shown by Bolukbasi et al. to encode gender prejudices in society. An analogy generator that fills in the blanks in analogies was trained by the authors using Word2Vec (Ahmad et al., 2025).

The preconception that programming is connected with males and homemaking with women was confirmed by the comparison of a woman to a computer programmer and a man to a housewife. Therefore, any system that employs this embedding is likely to be affected by the biases in Word2Vec (Ahmad et al., 2025; Taneja, Vashishtha, & Ratnoo, 2025).

A variety of face perception tasks, such as face detection (Mathias et al., 2014; Zafeiriou, Zhang, & Zhang, 2015; Bai & Ghanem, 2017), face classification (Reid et al., 2013), and face recognition (Ranjan et al., 2017), are described by automated facial image analysis. Companies like Google, Microsoft, IBM, and Face++ have produced commercial software that does automated facial analysis, and the majority of smartphones now come with face recognition software built in. For instance, academics and firms like Affectiva (Aectiva) try to determine emotions from photos of people's faces (Dehghan et al., 2017).

The Israeli business Faception and Wu and Zhang (Wu & Zhang, 2017) have created software that claims to be able to identify a person's traits (such as IQ, terrorism, or predisposition toward crime) based just on their face. These instances underscore how AI models trained on biased data, far from mitigating such stereotypes, may in fact mirror and even perpetuate them. Therefore, the AI applied to recruitment must be ethically and transparently designed (Buolamwini & Gebru, 2018; Balasubramaniam et al., 2023; Felzmann et al., 2020; Rigotti & Fosch-Villaronga, 2024).

To mitigate these risks, an increasing number of AI applications in recruiting have been created from the ground up with the goal of ensuring they're bias-free and supporting diversity and inclusion (Guizzardi et al., 2020; Shams, Zowghi, & Bano, 2025). Table 3.3 presents AI applications that support diversity and fair hiring.

3.3 ETHICAL CHALLENGES IN AI-DRIVEN RECRUITMENT

Data shows that the use of AI in hiring and recruitment decisions is growing significantly (Mujtaba & Mahapatra, 2025). According to a 2019 industry survey, 88% of organizations worldwide have experimented with AI in recruitment activities; 41% of these have used AI-based chatbots for candidate engagement, 44% have used AI to identify candidates using public data and social media, and 43% have used AI to recommend training (Gong, Fan, & Bartram, 2025).

AI is transforming the way hiring is done in many organizations, promising greater efficiency, objectivity, and scalability in candidate assessment (Tripathi & Rosak-Szyrocka, 2024; Rahman et al., 2025). All of this can be done very quickly at scale by algorithmic systems which process thousands of applications at a time, look for patterns, and make

TABLE 3.3 AI applications supporting diversity and fair hiring

AI application area	AI function description	Function in recruitment process	Benefits
Bias Detection and Mitigation	AI screens recruitment data in a manner that is devoid of personal characteristics, such as, for example, gender, age, race, or ethnicity. Algorithms are taught to consider talent based on merit, experience, role, and role fit alone. Methods involve "blind screening" and analysis of gender-neutral language.	Removes factors that promote unintentional discrimination, enabling equal evaluation of all candidates. Assists HR with conducting a fair and equitable selection process.	Advances a level playing field of opportunity and decreases bias in hiring. Makes the team more diverse, improves the reputation of the employer, and mitigates legal exposure over discriminatory practices.
Job Ad Language Analysis	AI tools analyze job posting language to identify and recommend alternatives to exclusionary or stereotypical language that could discourage people from some groups (women, older candidates).	Supports ambitions to make job descriptions gender-neutral and inclusive, in order to not inadvertently limit the applicant pool.	Expands both the variety and number of applications. Reduce bias at the first stage of hiring, strengthen an equal employer image.
Algorithm Transparency and Explainability	AI systems provide "explainability" functions that allow traces to be made of algorithmic decisions—like say, why a candidate was turned down. How decisions were made could be understood by both recruiters and candidates.	Provides fine-grained control over algorithms and feedback for candidates through objective-based feedback.	Both the number and diversity of applications are increased. Reduces bias in initial hires and strengthens an employer brand that is pro-inclusivity.
Anonymized Applications	Before recruiters review applications, AI systems scrub any clues to your identity—name, age, photo, school—and evaluate only qualifications and experience.	Removes potential for recruitment bias and focuses on that which is of most value on an application.	Provides improvements in selection fairness that allow for diverse teams to be comprised based on merit, not bias.
Cultural Add Value Analysis	Some tools can even determine whether a candidate will add value through diverse viewpoints rather than merely being another cog in the existing wheel.	Hires candidates who will expand, not replicate, the current organizational culture.	Fosters cognitive and cultural diversity for greater innovation and team effectiveness.

Source: own study, based on: (Bergelson et al., 2022; Ferrara, 2024; Mokhtech et al., 2022b; Mokhtech et al., 2022a).

predictions of fit for candidates to jobs. But a range of international organizations and researchers are increasingly stressing that the development of such technology raises major ethical issues that cannot be ignored. Amongst the most frequently discussed pitfalls is the potential reproduction of systemic biases inherent in data in algorithms that end up biased in favor of particular groups of candidates and against others, contravening the principle of equal treatment (Chang, 2024).

According to the European Commission with its draft AI Act (European Commission, 2021), AI in HR is considered "high-risk" and necessitates human oversight, data quality control, and explainable decision-making. Research in academia warns that misuse of AI may cause teams to homogenize, since AI could prioritize "typical" profiles and filter out unconventional candidates who could bring innovation and diversity (Ajunwa, 2020, 2024). Table 3.4 presents ethical challenges in AI-driven recruitment.

3.4 CASE STUDIES OF AI IN FAIR HIRING PRACTICES

As companies scramble to revamp their hiring pipelines, here's a hiring disruptor and driver of change: artificial intelligence (AI). No longer a part of some sci-fi prognostication, AI is now directly implicated in the way companies are screening, evaluating, and interacting with candidates—in a volume that's scaled and with an accuracy that's grown more refined. However, even though the efficiency and objectivity promised are capturing the imagination of many, the proof will be in the fairness (John-Mathews, Cardon, & Balagué, 2022). Table 3.5 presents case studies of AI in fair hiring practices.

TABLE 3.4 Ethical challenges in AI-driven recruitment

Ethical challenge	Description
Bias and Discrimination	AI systems are trained on historical data which could contain implicit or explicit human prejudices. These biases can work their way into algorithms and contribute to systemic discrimination by gender, age, race, or socio-economic class. Plenty of qualified individuals could, therefore, be unfairly disqualified, running the risk of lawsuits and damage to the employer's brand.
Lack of Transparency and Explainability	Decisions made by AI are often complex and opaque. Candidates do not know why they have been chosen or rejected, so they cannot question the result. This is damaging to both trust and legal defensibility.
Data Privacy and Consent	AI tools process tons of personal data—including the traditional application materials as well as behavioral data (social media profiles, facial expression, voice tone, and so on). This creates very serious issues with privacy, informed consent, and compliance with privacy laws such as GDPR.
Lack of Human Oversight and Accountability	When the hiring process becomes too automated, no one can see who is responsible (and potentially accountable) for bad or unfair hiring decisions. At the same time, with vendors in the loop, accountability can become fuzzy, and any ethical breaches can go uncorrected. Human monitoring is essential to maintain justice and sensibility.

TABLE 3.4 (*Continued*)

Ethical challenge	Description
Negative Candidate Experience and Vendor Oversight	Too much automation and the hiring process becomes impersonal and opaque, leaving candidates who are rejected without an explanation. This does nothing but damage the employer brand on Glassdoor or LinkedIn, and creates a terrible candidate experience. The dependence on third-party vendors also dissolves lines of accountability for biased or unfair results. Unethical behavior may be overlooked or left unaddressed, particularly when there is no obvious human in the loop to provide oversight. Maintaining openness and human control is critical for preserving trust and fairness.
Absence of Ethical Guidelines in HR AI	The law and ethical norms have not kept pace with the rapid adoption of AI in the recruitment process. Without such norms, organizations may feel free to operate in gray zones, risking abuse and trust decay.
Erosion of Public Trust	Without transparency, fairness, and accountability in AI-powered hiring, public skepticism could increase. Unfair treatment hurts employers' reputations and may undermine applicants' trust in these HR technologies.
Asymmetry of Knowledge	Candidates, and sometimes even HR people, don't know in detail how AI tools work, creating an information gap. This end-runs around informed consent and has the potential to shift the balance of power in favor of organizations.
Lack of Ethical Auditing Mechanisms	Most organizations do not have established independent or periodic ethical auditing of AI systems. Without oversight, biases or errors may go unnoticed and unaddressed.
Ethical Risks in Vendor Procurement	Businesses can purchase AI tools from third parties and thus lack visibility into how the tools are built, the places from which the data is pulled, and the testing protocols. This creates hidden ethical liabilities—even though employees' actions may not be illegal, they can still potentially reflect poorly on the organization's reputation.

Source: own study, based on: (Alp, 2025; Chang, 2024; Sánchez-Monedero, Dencik, & Edwards, 2020).

TABLE 3.5 Case studies of AI in fair hiring practices.

Case study	Solution/ tools used	Description
IBM – AI for BiasFree Talent Acquisition	**Use of predictive systems based on algorithms**	Algorithms help the recruiter make plans using smarter data analysis, prioritize the candidates, and identify inconsistencies in the job and the resume, thereby enhancing consistency and objectivity in the assessment and selection of candidates.
	AI Fairness 360	The open-source tool box AI Fairness 360 has been developed as a dedicated tool to identify and mitigate algorithmic bias in data and prediction models, particularly with respect to protected attributes such as sex, race, and age. It complies with global anti-discrimination norms such as those in place for the Equal Employment Opportunity Commission (EEOC) in the USA and the European Union's General Data Protection Regulation (GDPR).

(*Continued*)

TABLE 3.5 (*Continued*)

Case study	Solution/ tools used	Description
Unilever—key features AI-Powered Fair Hiring Through Gamification and Video Interviews	There are the following recruitment stages:**1.Gamified preselection**	Unilever, the FMCG behemoth, has taken the lead in using artificial intelligence to amend the way it recruits people, which promises to revolutionize the way we hire, as new technology emerges to help us with hiring better and treating people more fairly and to speed up the process of hiring. With more than 1.8 million job applications every year from 190 or so countries, the company wanted to rethink its hiring model. As a result, it has rolled out a three-stage AI-powered system that makes use of gamification, video analysis, and human-led final review. An elimination of about 70,000 person-hours spent on interviewing and applicant evaluation is proof enough of Unilever's success in AI-driven recruiting innovation (Hu, 2023). The process starts with neuroscience-based psychometric games designed by Pymetrics. These games assess cognitive and emotional traits in candidates—things like empathy, decision-making, focus, and how you react to risk. The results are then automatically compared to the profiles of Unilever's high-flying employees; the company can find out how suitable a candidate is without any reference to demographic information (or anyone's CV). Most importantly, each candidate receives bespoke feedback, promoting transparency and communication.
	2. AI-assisted video interviews	In this part, candidates are asked to record themselves answering a set of structured interview questions, thanks to AI platform HireVue. The algorithm evaluates speech patterns, facial expressions, tone, and language structure to develop multidimensional personality and competency profiles. AI provides recommendations but doesn't make final choices, acting as decision support for recruiters. This has allowed Unilever to reduce recruiter time in interviews by more than 50,000 hours per year and improve the consistency of candidate evaluation across international offices. It reduced the time taken to select a winner by 75%; it was more fair and much, much quicker. The intuitive and modern user interface (UI) was praised by applicants as the process was also faster and more transparent.
	3. Final human-led evaluation	Shortlisted candidates are invited to participate in group exercises, simulations, and interviews with hiring managers. Final decisions are made based on a holistic assessment that combines AI-generated insights with human judgment of soft skills, motivation, and cultural fit. This ensures that empathy and personal connection remain integral to the hiring process.
Hilton Hotels—AI in High-Volume Hiring to Ensure Fairness	**Integration of AI-powered assessments and interviews facilitated by platforms like HireVue**	As one of the planet's largest employers in the hospitality industry, Hilton Hotels has an ongoing requirement to source a high volume of hires—particularly for positions like housekeeping, guest services, event coordination, and food and beverage. To address these requirements, accelerate fair hiring, and maintain a high-performance workforce, Hilton has implemented AI-enhanced recruiting solutions enabling them to recruit fast, consistently, and fairly at scale around the world. The recruitment process will start with an online aptitude test consisting of numerical reasoning, verbal reasoning, logical reasoning, and a personality questionnaire. Such tests screen applicants on objective cognitive and behavioral measures and minimize human bias in early rounds.

TABLE 3.5 (*Continued*)

Case study	Solution/ tools used	Description
	A structured, asynchronous video interview	Using a computer program from HireVue, the interview is analyzed on measures like how animated candidates are when they speak, their tone of voice, and even the complexity of their language. The AI uses consistent rubrics to evaluate the responses, but, of course, each candidate is given an equivalent but separate amount of time (e.g., 30 seconds to prepare and then 90 to respond per question). The candidate profiles generated as a result are then forwarded to human recruiters who maintain full control over final hiring decisions.
	Approach "human-in-the-loop"	AI is a tool to help, not replace, recruiters. This hybrid model guarantees AI can be used to make things more efficient, fairer, and standardized, while human judgment remains the heart of the last mile.
Amazon—Lessons Learned from AI Bias in Hiring	**Machines don't have inherent bias—they acquire it from humans**	Amazon's botched AI recruiting experiment was a wake-up call to the HR tech world. It stimulated essential introspection that serves as a basis for the creation of ethical AI systems in hiring. Algorithms are based on historical data to the extent that they include previous decisions and company behavior. That's the case with a dataset; it's a document of people's behavior and if it includes—perhaps unconsciously or due to systemic bias—preferences toward employees of a specific gender, let's say, or those with a certain level of education, the algorithm will replicate those preferences. In Amazon's specific situation, it was not difficult for the CV-ranking algorithm to screw women over, since the ten years of hiring data had been benefiting male applicants in the category of "more suitable" by huge margins.
	The significance of constructing fair and diverse datasets	Amazon's model was based only on internal hiring data and, thus, lacked external viewpoints and more diversified samples of competencies and candidate backgrounds. This constrained the model's learning signal and in fact made it quite "blind" to a range of professional types.
	Outdated old logic in the algorithm	Amazon taught its system on resumes over a ten-year period; standards of inclusivity and soft and technical skills have changed a lot in that time, as have expectations about how you format your résumé. The AI, in that case, kept to the old way instead of the forward-looking approach one would expect from the most cutting-edge hiring technology.
	Transparency and accountability	Despite the flop, Amazon didn't hide the tool's limitations. Instead, by publicly admitting the problem, the company played a role in forcing an industrywide reckoning. This openness marked a turning point and led to serious discussions about ethical design, testin,g and governance of AI-powered recruiting systems.
	Semantic AI	The industry has learned, thanks to these experiences, and created more responsible ways of applying AI for hiring. These are used for semantic analysis and context comprehension, rather than merely for elementary keyword matching, which provides limited utility in supporting qualified candidates who have been unfairly disadvantaged for an extended period. Operating at the semantic level of understanding rather than the text level, semantic AI provides better, fairer assessments.

(*Continued*)

TABLE 3.5 (*Continued*)

Case study	Solution/ tools used	Description
	Human-in-the-loop systems	Bring about a model that functions as a hybrid model; AI supports, but does not replace, human decision-making. Especially in final hiring decisions, human supervision is still necessary to ensure ethical judgment, empathy, and alignment with the company culture.
Contextual validation	New algorithms are now trained to identify how a word is used depending on the context (e.g., "leadership" as a skill vs. the name of a course). It improves the precision of candidate evaluations and decreases misclassification.	
Open-source ethical frameworks	Such as IBM's AI Fairness 360. These software tools have proliferated and been adopted as a new class of industry standards for auditing, bias, and mitigation and fairness in algorithmic systems.	
Google—AI-Driven Fair Hiring	**Structured interviews**	The company uses a hybrid model with artificial intelligence and predictive analytics in a well-structured selection process. Not only have they done so in the hopes of being more efficient in their hiring, but they have also done it in a fair and consistent manner for all candidates, no matter what their background, gender, or style of communication is. Structured interviews are based on a standard set of questions asked to all job applicants. Received responses are scored directly against clear scoring rubrics. This standardization enables apples-to-apples comparisons, eliminates any unconscious bias, and ensures decisions are made based on job-related factors—and not how well the person interviews, or whether or not they are someone you want to have a beer with.
	Multirater evaluation system	No one recruiter or manager decides who gets hired. After interviews, the evaluations are sent to a hiring committee—a group of impartial evaluators who score the candidate as a whole. It is a committee-based exercise that ensures accountability, minimizes subjectivity, and brings greater transparency to hiring decisions.
	Predictive data analytics to determine the characteristics	Based on an analysis of data on employee performance, they have boiled it down to four key areas to assess performance: general cognitive ability, role-related knowledge, leadership potential, and cultural fit (called "Googleyness"). All of those are evaluated and rewarded with behavioral questions and data-informed metrics.
	A human-in-the-loop model	Technology complements—rather than the other way around—human recruiters. Even if algorithms do assist in shortlisting candidates or identifying matches for skills, the ultimate decision to hire (or not) is made by people. The corporation also regularly reviews its recruitment practices to evaluate efficacy, identify bias, and make changes in response to feedback and data.

TABLE 3.5 (*Continued*)

Case study	Solution/ tools used	Description
PepsiCo—AI-Powered Chatbots for Fair Hiring	**Hired Score platform**	Machine learning-driven overlay that plugs directly into the company's applicant tracking systems, candidate relationship management systems, and internal HR databases. Its flagship feature, called "Fetch," is designed to automatically search across all available candidate profiles—including both external candidates and people who already work with the company—to find only the best people for a specific role. This two-sided strategy makes it possible to unearth not just new talent but also internal candidates who might be left behind with traditional methods. Hired Score is a "glass-box" supplier with transparent, auditable, and explainable algorithms to enable compliance monitoring and adverse impact analysis and to document ethical accountability.
	Spotlight Screening	Enables prospective active candidates to be assessed and rated against the job profile. This speeds up the screening process and offers more precise, data-based recruitment decisions, minimizing subjectivity and improving decision-making uniformity.
	Hiring Manager Hub	Provides hiring managers with historical analytics on similar positions, time-to-fill averages, and sourcing recommendations, to better align their hiring plans with company objectives.
	AI-powered chatbots	PepsiCo used chatbots enabled by AI to manage those early conversations with candidates. These bots give details, respond to frequent questions, and walk the applicants through every phase. This makes for a much cleaner, candidate-friendly experience and lightens the communication load on HR, freeing up time to do more critical thinking and interaction.
McDonald's—AI for Fair Hiring in Fast-Food Workforce Recruitment	**McHire platform**	McDonald's made a strategic improvement to their process by using the AI recruitment platform McHire, which the company developed with Paradox. With the adoption of McHire in the US, Canada, & now UK & Ireland, McDonald's is establishing a global gold standard of responsible, human-centric, and scalable AI in high-volume hiring. This strategic initiative was designed to improve the candidate experience, optimize the hiring process, and decrease time to hire, especially in high-volume environments such as the quick-service restaurant industry. McHire mirrors precisely the way conversational AI can overhaul fairness, speed, and scalability in recruiting without giving up on candidate satisfaction. The front-line recruiter is an AI assistant, Olivia, engaging candidates in natural conversation in 24/7 mode. Instead of completing static application forms, candidates are led through an active and engaging process in which they respond to prescreening questions and take an assessment. This data autocompletes the application form and enables the AI to evaluate fit and automatically schedule in-person interviews for eligible candidates at appropriate restaurant locations.

(*Continued*)

TABLE 3.5 (*Continued*)

Case study	Solution/ tools used	Description
		The McHire model has produced notable outcomes. Time to hire dropped by almost 65%, meaning less of an operational headache for restaurant managers and recruiters. Furthermore, candidate completion was also up by 20% and 85.9% of applicants rated their experience a four or five out of five in December 2022. Recruiters also reclaimed 3–5 hours per week to focus on onboarding and training new hires—a key element in keeping talent and improving customer service within demanding restaurant environments. To facilitate the rollout, McDonald's created a People Technology Team. This cross-functional team worked together with the Enfuse Group to make the tool integration seamless and fit for purpose at a local business level. The team designed an extensive training program, with over 30 face-to-face workshops for 2,000 users, provided hands-on testing environments, and set up a staged pilot across 29 restaurants. These actions facilitated valuable user adoption and iterative user-guided enhancements beyond launch. The key, however, is that the approach to change management embraced people-centered change. The aim was to empower franchisees and staff with tech that feels intuitive and useful, not disruptive. Feedback loops and ongoing dialogue were critical; the team logged over 20 post-launch feature enhancements driven by restaurant feedback. McDonald's, for example, created transparent guidelines, legal compliance practices, and modular training for various audiences, such as recruiters, people managers, and franchisees. In its focus on inclusivity and process transparency, McHire has become not only an instrument of operating efficiency but also an emblem of ethical, AI-enabled hiring. It tackles fairness by using explainable AI techniques and auto pre-screening logic to treat all candidates equally without human bias in the early stages of hiring.

Source: own study, based on Guenole and Feinzig (2018); Al-Alawi et al. (2021); Malhotra, Maurya, & Maniam (2024); HRD, (2024); Hu (2023); IMD business school for management and leadership courses (2022); Toolify (2024); Jeffrey Dastin (2022).

REFERENCES

Ahmad, S., Javed, U., Sharma, C., & Siddiqui, M. S. (2025). Green human resource management: analyzing sustainable practices and organizational impact through a Word2Vec approach. *Green Technologies and Sustainability*, *3*(4), 100224. https://doi.org/10.1016/j.grets.2025.100224

Ajunwa, I. (2024). AI and captured capital. *Yale LJF*, *134*, 372. https://heinonline.org/HOL/Page?handle=hein.journals/yljfor134&div=13&g_sent=1&casa_token=9mn2ZzGCWxkAAAAA:Ofwrvg4y6WfNORdwJuAodeIEkmTLJUK8KlCX2y4ZcEwVp-ICJOkV9EEC9bIuE_YdCxn7OG8&collection=journals.

Ajunwa, I. (2020). The "black box" at work. *Big Data & Society, 7*(2).

Al-Alawi, A. I., Naureen, M., AlAlawi, E. I., & Naser Al-Hadad, A. A. (2021). The role of artificial intelligence in recruitment process decision-making. In *2021 International Conference on Decision Aid Sciences and Application (DASA)* (pp. 197–203). IEEE.

Albert, E. T. (2019). AI in talent acquisition: a review of AI-applications used in recruitment and selection. *Strategic HR Review, 18*(5), 215–221, from www.emerald.com/insight/content/doi/10.1108/shr-04-2019-0024/full/.

Allen, D. G., Mahto, R. V., & Otondo, R. F. (2007). Web-based recruitment: effects of information, organizational brand, and attitudes toward a web site on applicant attraction. *The Journal of Applied Psychology, 92*(6), 1696–1708.

Alp, T. (2025). *7 ethical considerations in AI-driven recruitment.* Retrieved May 30, 2025, from https://alp.consulting/ethical-considerations-in-ai-driven-recruitment/.

Bai, Y., & Ghanem, B. (2017). Multi-scale fully convolutional network for face detection in the wild. In *Proceedings of the IEEE Conference on Computer Vision and Pattern Recognition Workshops* (pp. 132–141). IEEE. https://openaccess.thecvf.com/content_cvpr_2017_workshops/w33/papers/Bai_Multi-Scale_Fully_Convolutional_CVPR_2017_paper

Balasubramaniam, N., Kauppinen, M., Rannisto, A., Hiekkanen, K., & Kujala, S. (2023). Transparency and explainability of AI systems: From ethical guidelines to requirements. *Information and Software Technology, 159*, 107197.

Bergelson, I., Tracy, C., & Takacs, E. (2022). Best practices for reducing bias in the interview process. *Current Urology Reports, 23*(11), 319–325, from https://link.springer.com/article/10.1007/s11934-022-01116-7.

Bolukbasi, T., Chang, K. W., Zou, J. Y., Saligrama, V., & Kalai, A. T. (2016). Man is to computer programmer as woman is to homemaker? Debiasing word embeddings. *Advances in Neural Information Processing Systems, 29*, 1–9.

Brooks, N. E., French, J. C., Lipman, J. M., & Prabhu, A. S. (2025). To blind or not to blind: evaluating the impact of withholding scores and grades from interviewers in general surgery resident recruitment. *Journal of Surgical Education*, 103463. https://doi.org/10.1016/j.jsurg.2025.103463

Buolamwini, J., & Gebru, T. (2018). Gender shades: intersectional accuracy disparities in commercial gender classification. *Conference on Fairness, Accountability and Transparency*, 77–91, from http://proceedings.mlr.press/v81/buolamwini18a.html?mod=article_inline&ref=akusion-ci-shi-dai-bizinesumedeia.

Caliskan, A., Bryson, J. J., & Narayanan, A. (2017). Semantics derived automatically from language corpora contain human-like biases. *Science, 356*(6334), 183–186.

Chang, K. (2024). Ethical and operational challenges in AI-empowered employee recruitment: insights and suggestions to the managers and managerial practitioners. *Innovations in Business and Strategic Management, 2*(1), 29–32, from https://repository.uel.ac.uk/item/8y1q7.

Charlier, R., & Kloppenburg, S. (2017). *Artificial intelligence in HR: A no-brainer.* PwC Netherlands.

Chen, Z. (2023). Ethics and discrimination in artificial intelligence-enabled recruitment practices. *Humanities and Social Sciences Communications, 10*(1), 1–12.

Cheng, J., Dai, Y., Yuan, Y., & Zhu, H. (2020). A simple analysis of multimodal data fusion. In *2020 IEEE 19th International Conference on Trust, Security and Privacy in Computing and Communications (TrustCom)* (pp. 1472–1475). IEEE.

Crawford, K., & Calo, R. (2016). There is a blind spot in AI research. *Nature, 538*(7625), 311–313, from www.nature.com/articles/538311a.

Crawford, K., & Paglen, T. (2021). Excavating AI: the politics of images in machine learning training sets. *AI & SOCIETY, 36*(4), 1105–1116, from https://idp.springer.com/authorize/casa?redirect_uri=https://link.springer.com/article/10.1007/s00146-021-01162-8&casa_token=ffbpq7abl3saaaaa:m0dglcxrmg9sy__-juv0fjc7hqumjwsoaghmpk35npnpdo-c3n7yde6ntobrzo26ndgpa5b54b_jeq.

Das, R., & Kodwani, A. D. (2018). Strategic human resource management: a power based critique. *Benchmarking: An International Journal, 25*(4), 1213–1231. https://doi.org/10.1108/BIJ-09-2016-0143

Dastin, J. (2022). Amazon scraps secret AI recruiting tool that showed bias against women*. In *Ethics of data and analytics* (pp. 296–299). Auerbach Publications.

Dehghan, A., Ortiz, E. G., Shu, G., & Masood, S. Z. (2017). *DAGER: Deep Age, Gender and Emotion Recognition using Convolutional Neural Network.*

Deloitte United States. (2025). *State of Generative AI in the Enterprise 2024.* Retrieved May 29, 2025, from https://www2.deloitte.com/us/en/pages/consulting/articles/state-of-generative-ai-in-enterprise.html.

European Commission. (2021). *Proposal for a regulation of the European Parliament and of the Council laying down harmonised rules on artificial intelligence (Artificial Intelligence Act) and amending certain Union legislative acts* (COM/2021/206 final). EUR-Lex. https://eur-lex.europa.eu/legal-content/EN/TXT/?uri=CELEX:52021PC0206

Fauria, K., Forcano, L., Knezevic, I., Minguillón, C., Menezes-Cabral, S., Gispert, J. D., et al. (2020). PENSA study: study design, recruitment profiles and participant inclusion in multimodal intervention studies. *Alzheimer's & Dementia, 16*(S10), e045074.

Felzmann, H., Fosch-Villaronga, E., Lutz, C., & Tamò-Larrieux, A. (2020). Towards transparency by design for artificial intelligence. *Science and Engineering Ethics, 26*(6), 3333–3361, from https://link.springer.com/article/10.1007/s11948-020-00276-4.

Ferrara, E. (2024). Fairness and bias in artificial intelligence: a brief survey of sources, impacts, and mitigation strategies. *Sci, 6*(1), 3, from www.mdpi.com/2413-4155/6/1/3.

Gong, Q., Fan, D., & Bartram, T. (2025). Integrating artificial intelligence and human resource management: a review and future research agenda. *The International Journal of Human Resource Management, 36*(1), 103–141.

Guenole, N., & Feinzig, S. (2018). The business case for AI in HR. *With insights and tips on getting started.* IBM Smarter Workforce Institute, IBM Corporation

Guizzardi, R., Amaral, G., Guizzardi, G., & Mylopoulos, J. (2020). *Ethical Requirements for AI Systems* (pp. 251–256). Springer.

HRD. (2024). *Inside 'McHire': How AI reduced McDonald's time-to-hire by 65% – HRD.* Retrieved June 01, 2025, from www.hrdconnect.com/casestudy/inside-mchire-how-ai-helped-mcdonalds-drop-time-to-hire-by-65/.

Hu, Q. (2023). Unilever's practice on AI-based recruitment. *Highlights in Business, Economics and Management, 16*, 256–263.

Huang, G. Z., Roy, M. H., Ahmed, Z. U., Heng, J. S., & Lim, J. H. (2002). Benchmarking the human capital strategies of MNCs in Singapore. *Benchmarking: An International Journal, 9*(4), 357–373, from www.emerald.com/insight/content/doi/10.1108/14635770210442699/full/pdf?casa_token=0zt0w4siraqaaaaa:tggudyfo4_raucnjglu96knwmqpwqgb8tbwyl6-7bfyx_mssxutut0ycagdyyq1ayqhinro1eotvcslhxqnvooptb5nfg9ln1syv8uvd08ocq_mi.

IMD Business School for Management and Leadership Courses. (2022, October 25). *Amazon's sexist hiring algorithm could still be better than a human.* IMD. www.imd.org/research-knowledge/digital/articles/amazons-sexist-hiring-algorithm-could-still-be-better-than-a-human/

John-Mathews, J.-M., Cardon, D., & Balagué, C. (2022). From reality to world. a critical perspective on AI fairness. *Journal of Business Ethics, 178*(4), 945–959, from https://link.springer.com/article/10.1007/s10551-022-05055-8.

Kumar, A., 2020. *National Strategy for Artificial Intelligence: India's Approach*, National Institution for Transforming India (NITI Aayog). India. Retrieved from https://coilink.org/20.500.12592/77cgrk on 09 Aug 2025. COI: 20.500.12592/77cgrk.

Lovelock, J. D., Hare, J., Woodward, A., & Priestley, A. (2018). Forecast: The business value of artificial intelligence, worldwide, 2017-2025. *Gartner.(ID G00348137).*

Malhotra, A., Maurya, A., & Maniam, B. (2024). Smart HR with smart technologies. In *Artificial intelligence-enabled businesses* (pp. 121–135). John Wiley & Sons, Ltd.

Mathias, M., Benenson, R., Pedersoli, M., & van Gool, L. (2014). Face detection without bells and whistles. In D. Fleet, T. Pajdla, B. Schiele, & T. Tuytelaars (Eds.), *Computer Vision – ECCV 2014: 13th European Conference, Zurich, Switzerland, September 6–12, 2014, Proceedings, Part IV* (pp. 720–735). Springer.

McDonald, K., Fisher, S., & Connelly, C. E. (Eds.). *Electronic HRM in the Smart Era,* Emerald Publishing Limited.

McKinsey. (2025). *How diversity, equity, and inclusion (DE&I) matter.* Retrieved May 29, 2025, from www.mckinsey.com/featured-insights/diversity-and-inclusion/diversity-wins-how-inclusion-matters.

Miller, C. C. (2015). When algorithms discriminate. *The New York Times, 9*(7), 1.

Mokhtech, M., Jagsi, R., Vega, R. M., Brown, D. W., Golden, D. W., Juang, T., et al. (2022). Mitigating bias in recruitment: attracting a diverse, dynamic workforce to sustain the future of radiation oncology. *Advances in Radiation Oncology, 7*(6), 100977.

Mujtaba, D. F., & Mahapatra, N. R. (2019). Ethical considerations in AI-based recruitment. In *2019 IEEE International Symposium on Technology and Society (ISTAS).* IEEE.

Mujtaba, D. F., & Mahapatra, N. R. (2025). *Fairness in AI-driven recruitment: challenges, metrics, methods, and future directions.* (Version 3) [Preprint]. arXiv. https://doi.org/10.48550/arXiv.2405.19699

Nair, P. (2017). The rise of the AI recruiter: Is HR tech the next to challenge human intuition. *Digital Policy, Regulation and Governance, 22*(3), 245–257. https://doi.org/10.1108/DPRG-03-2017-0015

Narrative Science. (2018). *Artificial intelligence (AI) adoption grew over 60% in the last year.* GlobeNewswire. / www.globenewswire.com/news-release/2018/01/17/1295827/0/en/Artificial-Intelligence-AI-Adoption-Grew-Over-60-in-the-Last-Year.html

Paramita, D., Okwir, S., & Nuur, C. (2024). Artificial intelligence in talent acquisition: exploring organisational and operational dimensions. *International Journal of Organizational Analysis, 32*(11), 108–131, from www.emerald.com/insight/content/doi/10.1108/ijoa-09-2023-3992/full/pdf.

Parcalabescu, L., Trost, N., & Frank, A. (2021). *What is multimodality?* (Version 3) [Preprint]. arXiv. https://doi.org/10.48550/arXiv.2103.06304

Phillips-Wren, G., Doran, R., & Merrill, K. (2016). Creating a value proposition with a social media strategy for talent acquisition. *Journal of Decision Systems, 25*(sup1), 450–462.

Pillai, R., & Sivathanu, B. (2020). Adoption of artificial intelligence (AI) for talent acquisition in IT/ITeS organizations. *Benchmarking: An International Journal, 27*(9), 2599–2629, from www.emerald.com/insight/content/doi/10.1108/bij-04-2020-0186/full/pdf.

Purdy, M., & Daugherty, P. (2017). *How AI boosts industry profits and innovation.* Accenture. https://www.accenture.com/fr-fr/_acnmedia/36DC7F76EBAB444CAB6A7F44017CC3997.p

Rahman, S. M., Hossain, M. A., Miah, M. S., Alom, M. M., & Islam, M. (2025). Artificial Intelligence (AI) in revolutionizing sustainable recruitment: a framework for inclusivity and efficiency. *International Research Journal of Multidisciplinary Scope, 6*(1), 1128–1141. DOI: 10.47857/irjms.2025.v06i01.02698

Ranjan, R., Sankaranarayanan, S., Castillo, C. D., & Chellappa, R. (2017). An all-in-one convolutional neural network for face analysis. In *2017 12th IEEE International Conference on Automatic Face & Gesture Recognition (FG 2017)* (pp. 17–24). IEEE.

Reid, D. A., Samangooei, S., Chen, C., Nixon, M. S., & Ross, A. (2013). Soft biometrics for surveillance: an overview. In *Handbook of statistics* (pp. 327–352). Elsevier.

Rigotti, C., & Fosch-Villaronga, E. (2024). Fairness, AI & recruitment. *Computer Law & Security Review, 53*, 105966. https://doi.org/10.1016/j.clsr.2024.105966

Roppelt, J. S., Greimel, N. S., Kanbach, D. K., Stubner, S., & Maran, T. K. (2024). Artificial intelligence in talent acquisition: a multiple case study on multi-national corporations. *Management Decision, 62*(10), 2986–3007, from www.emerald.com/insight/content/doi/10.1108/md-07-2023-1194/full/pdf.

Rosak-Szyrocka, J. (2024). The role of artificial intelligence in digital education. *Zeszyty Naukowe. Organizacja i Zarządzanie / Politechnika Śląska, 2024*(195), 477–499, from https://yadda.icm.edu.pl/baztech/element/bwmeta1.element.baztech-60b404c0-03e1-43cb-a14a-535b6138e365.

Rosak-Szyrocka, J., Tripathi, S., Garcia, M. B., Festa, G., & Launer, M. A. (2025). *Reskilling and upskilling in the age of AI: a practical guide to workforce transformation* (1st ed.), Chapman & Hall/CRC. https://doi.org/10.1201/9781003611677

Sánchez-Monedero, J., Dencik, L., & Edwards, L. (2020). What does it mean to 'solve' the problem of discrimination in hiring? In *Proceedings of the 2020 Conference on Fairness, Accountability, and Transparency* (pp. 458–468). ACM.

Shams, R. A., Zowghi, D., & Bano, M. (2025). AI and the quest for diversity and inclusion: a systematic literature review. *AI and Ethics, 5*(1), 411–438, from https://link.springer.com/article/10.1007/s43681-023-00362-w.

Singh, N. (2018). Strategic human resource practices for innovation performance: an empirical investigation. *Benchmarking: An International Journal, 25*(9), 3459–3478. https://doi.org/10.1108/BIJ-08-2017-0215

Soleimani, M., Intezari, A., Taskin, N., & Pauleen, D. (2021). Cognitive biases in developing biased artificial intelligence recruitment system. In *Proceedings of the Annual Hawaii International Conference on System Sciences.* Hawaii International Conference on System Sciences.

Taneja, K., Vashishtha, J., & Ratnoo, S. (2025). Fraud-BERT: transformer based context aware online recruitment fraud detection. *Discover Computing, 28*(1), 1–16, from https://link.springer.com/article/10.1007/s10791-025-09502-8.

Toolify. (2024, February 21). *Revolutionizing talent acquisition in HR: PepsiCo's AI success story.* Toolify. www.toolify.ai/ai-news/revolutionizing-talent-acquisition-in-hr-pepsicos-ai-success-story-1824380

Tripathi, S., & Rosak-Szyrocka, J. (2024). *Impact of artificial intelligence on society,* CRC Press.

Upadhyay, A. K., & Khandelwal, K. (2018). Applying artificial intelligence: implications for recruitment. *Strategic HR Review, 17*(5), 255–258, from www.emerald.com/insight/content/doi/10.1108/shr-07-2018-0051/full/pdf?casa_token=inaiuysb0g8aaaaa:tkwzcfnptbedro-_wirjfre3ygzqn9d7hijayravtnhb6rzpubqmo364p9nl5tu0pqxhhfd34ydg89_yale_-zddihnl7wuxmi7lwaw2fhu5zqtc.

van Esch, P., Black, J. S., & Ferolie, J. (2019). Marketing AI recruitment: the next phase in job application and selection. *Computers in Human Behavior, 90*, 215–222.

Walker, D. O., & Larson, M. (2025). Leveraging generative artificial intelligence (AI) for human resource management: The AI job description assignment. *Journal of Management Education*, *49*(1), 113–141.

Wu, X., & Zhang, X. (2017). *Responses to critiques on machine learning of criminality perceptions (Addendum of arXiv:1611.04135).*

Yanamala, K. K. R. (2022). Dynamic bias mitigation for multimodal AI in recruitment ensuring fairness and equity in hiring practices. *Journal of Artificial Intelligence and Machine Learning in Management*, *6*(2), 51–61.

Zafeiriou, S., Zhang, C., & Zhang, Z. (2015). A survey on face detection in the wild: past, present and future. *Computer Vision and Image Understanding, 138*, 1–24.

CHAPTER 4

Employee Experience, Well-Being, and AI

4.1 AI FOR EMPLOYEE ENGAGEMENT AND SATISFACTION

Staff satisfaction and motivation have also long been the key to organizational success. Over the last few decades, forward-thinking organizations have shifted their attention from the solely output-driven measures toward a more holistic approach to employee health, motivation, and affective commitment to work (Rulandari & Silalahi, 2025). Into this changing world comes artificial intelligence (AI), not just as a tool to automate and optimize, but also as a disruptor that remakes the way employees come to experience work. AI is increasingly used to monitor, measure, and optimize employee satisfaction and engagement—areas that were once deemed too human and qualitative to mess with algorithmically (Vashishth et al., 2025). Earlier, organizations tracked satisfaction and engagement the traditional way, with the approach of taking an annual survey or holding exit interviews—methods plagued with bias, brevity, and delayed feedback. AI-driven systems are preemptive and real-time. Sentiment analysis, machine learning, and NLP examine employee feedback collected from multiple sources—messages in internal chat forums, performance reviews, surveys, and e-mails—to detect emerging patterns that may indicate low morale, frustration, or even burnout (Sweiss & Yamin, 2024).

These instruments also produce engagement heat maps by department, which will lead to the detection of risk teams or members by their managers. AI can detect nuanced signs—like meeting attendance decline or tone of communication shift—that would likely slip through the cracks for a human. The idea is that it doesn't usurp human judgment but adds managerial oversight with an insight built on data (Vijayakanthan et al., 2024; Shah et al., 2024).

DOI: 10.1201/9781003668282-6

Predictive analytics is truly effective at anticipating employee turnover. Connecting dots from data points like absence, work hours, and engagement indicators, AI processes can anticipate an employee's imminent departure. This allows HR to react in advance—perhaps with a chat, giving fresh challenges, or rebalancing workload assignments (Pillai et al., 2024).

Yet another potent application of AI to enhancing employee satisfaction lies in personalization. Where consumer-facing technology platforms personalize experiences to the individual, workplace AI is beginning to do the same for learning, development, and communication. AI-driven LMS can analyze an employee's skill set, job performance, and career goals and recommend customized learning paths or mentorship. Such systems create an environment where employees feel monitored and cared for—not as anonymous units of labor, but as aspiring professionals. It is a part of continuous interaction (Chakraborty et al., 2023; Kaur & Kaur, 2023). Intelligent virtual assistants are automating routine administrative work, from calendar management to HR requests.

By removing friction from routine tasks, AI allows employees to focus more on purposeful, creative, or strategic work. Satisfaction rises in low-friction, high-assistance environments. Onboarding is one of the spaces that are transforming (Pratt et al., 2021). AI-driven tools can make adjustments to the onboarding process to accommodate the pace, learning, and history of new employees so that they become comfortable and confident sooner. Effective, tailored induction to the workplace can create a lasting positive impression and promote belongingness (Ruan & Mezei, 2022). Employee recognition is a satisfaction and engagement driver that is well understood. AI can be used to provide more equitable and timely recognition. The system can use performance information and peer reviews to reward star performers, even the poor self-marketers. This eliminates the potential for favoritism and unconscious bias and generates a culture of earned and equitably distributed recognition (Tummalapalli et al., 2025).

Real-time feedback loops can also be driven by AI. Rather than ad hoc performance reviews, some are using AI platforms to collect and compile real-time feedback. Such platforms make goal-setting more elastic and mid-course correction possible, which enhance a worker's feelings of control and comprehension with regard to expectations. AI-driven chatbots can collect anonymous feedback on a regular beat so that psychological safety is practiced. The workers will probably vent their frustration or suggestions anonymously on the internet, and AI technologies can convert such inputs into actionable feedback to be acted upon by the management (Aulia & Lin, 2025; Marvi, Foroudi, & AmirDadbar, 2025; Vashishth et al., 2025).

Table 4.1 summarizes the key applications of AI for employee engagement and satisfaction, along with concise descriptions of each application area and its potential benefits.

The primary applications of AI in the above domains include predictive analytics and sentiment analysis that rely on machine learning algorithms and natural language processing (NLP) for analyzing and monitoring staff conversation, behavioral activity, and survey feedback. These applications may detect disengagement metrics, unhappiness, or emotional conflict by looking for patterns of tone, levels of communication, attendance,

TABLE 4.1 Applications of AI for employee engagement and satisfaction

AI Application Area	Description	Key Benefits
Sentiment analysis & NLP	Uses natural language processing to analyze employee communication (email, chat, survey response) and detect mood, tone, and emotional trends	Real-time awareness of morale, detection of early burnout or dissatisfaction
Predictive analytics	Analyzes historical data to predict employee turnover, disengagement, or performance degradation	Enables early intervention and retention strategies
AI-powered surveys and feedback systems	Intelligent survey tools customize questions to prior responses and analyze results for actionable insights.	Enhances quality responses, continuous feedback, better decision-making
Personalized learning and development	Recommends customized training modules or career paths based on employee objectives, competency, and performance data	Increases motivation, career satisfaction, and skills alignment
Virtual assistants and chatbots	AI-driven bots that answer HR questions, facilitate onboarding, and handle administrative tasks	Automates employee empowerment, reduces wait times, streamlines HR and onboarding processes
Recognition algorithms	Identifies high- or low-recognized employees by performance and peer feedback	Enables fair recognition, boosts morale, removes bias from performance reviews
Real-time performance monitoring	Employees' productivity and engagement are measured in real time through embedded metrics and behavioral signals.	Enables responsive goal-setting, timely coaching, and early intervention
AI for culture and diversity analysis	Inclusivity and workplace culture are tracked through analysis of language usage and demographic trends in feedback data.	Enables equity, exposes cultural disparity, propels diversity and inclusion initiatives.
Workload optimization	Workload optimization through AI-powered detection of overwork or inefficiencies and suggested task reassignment	Prevents burnout, enhances team productivity and satisfaction
Employee lifecycle analytics	Maps the entire employee experience (recruitment to exit) to identify pain points and dips in engagement	Enhances whole employee experience, enables strategic HR planning
AI-enhanced coaching platforms	Offers personalized coaching recommendations and micro-learning modules based on real-time behavioral insights.	Enables self-managed development, leverages strengths, fosters engagement
Anonymous reporting tools	Enables employees to report concerns or feedback anonymously via AI interfaces, which aggregate and interpret the information	Encourages authenticity, heightens psychological safety, makes leaders aware of unfiltered insight.

Source: Author's own work.

and reduced meeting participation. Predictive models even predict oncoming burnout or turnover, and human resources can react ahead of time accordingly. Stepping toward predictive management of employee engagement allows companies to catch budding issues before they materialize, finally leading to better job satisfaction and employee retention as a whole (Jangbahadur et al., 2025; Herlina & Iskandar, 2025).

The second area where AI is adding value is continuous development and customization. Today, AI platforms are already giving employees tailored development and learning strategies dependent on performance in the past, career desire, and employee profile. AI platforms can suggest training modules, suggest internal job postings, or suggest mentors to individuals to render development engaging and worthwhile. Similarly, chatbots and virtual AI assistants perform similar administrative tasks—welcoming, receiving, or booking HR requests and new employee induction—so that the employees are free to perform more productive work. These frictionless and customized experiences not only remove drudgery from repetitive work but also resonate with the company's values of wellness and individual achievement (Elbadawi, 2025; Alzeiby et al., 2025).

Lastly, AI is increasingly being utilized to give feedback, appreciation, and culture metrics at the workplace. AI-driven automated tools collect real-time multi-channel feedback and convert it into leadership actions. With anonymous reporting and tracking of diversity metrics, AI makes promotion of diversity and psychological safety for teams simple. AI-based recognition systems can identify contributions that would otherwise go unnoticed and drive fair, data-driven recognition of achievement. Further, AI allows managers to keep their finger on the pulse of company culture at every moment, spot strengths, and foresee issues even before they show up. Implemented ethically and transparently, such an approach not only improves organizational consciousness but also enables a more human, just, and sympathetic workplace culture (Gupta & Raheja, 2025; Lenka & Chanda, 2025).

4.2 AI-POWERED PERSONALIZED LEARNING AND DEVELOPMENT

The last decade or so has witnessed the development of artificial intelligence for use in educational and professional training begin to reshape how people learn and acquire competencies. AI-driven personalized learning is far greater than automation. It is a shift from the one-size-fits-all type of learning designs to highly individualized, adaptive, data-based learning paths and development (Coban et al., 2025).

Personalized learning involves pedagogies that customize learning experiences to the unique needs, interests, and ambitions of individual students. Previously, this was the domain of exceptional teachers in small, close-knit environments. But with AI, this degree of personalization is now feasible at scale for populations and institutions of any size (Jeong et al., 2025).

AI systems have the ability to filter through huge sets of student data such as scores, patterns of behavior, interaction levels, and even physiological signals and dynamically adjust content, pace, and mode of study. To put it simply, a system can determine, for example, that a student is deficient in abstract reasoning but proficient in visual-spatial operation. It may then branch out further by using interactive simulations rather than text modules or by re-presenting core content in game-like format for maximum levels of motivation and retention (Lyu & Salam, 2025; Mammas & Mamma, 2025).

The implications for corporate learning and development are no less powerful. Organizations already leverage AI tools to examine skill gaps, suggest customized upskilling paths, and monitor progress in real time. Not only does this optimize ROI on training investment, but it also builds a more engaged and future-ready workforce (Agatova & Latipova, 2025). No longer are employees fungible units but human beings with their life trajectories—each of them having a smart system that can guide them to their potential. AI can universalize quality learning (Vorobyeva et al., 2025). With natural language processing, adaptive feedback, and multilingual user interfaces, the systems are able to reach out to students with different backgrounds, geographies, and skills. This is how geography, language, or mental style are not barriers anymore (Tao & Pan, 2025).

Table 4.2 presents an overview of the main characteristics of AI-powered personalized learning and development, including components, functionality, benefits, and potential drawbacks. The table can be used in reports, presentations, or strategy-planning reports.

The personalization engine is a robust algorithmic centerpoint that renders learner information into responding content delivery, learning pace, and difficulty in real time. Supporting this are adaptive learning paths, which allow every student to take an adaptive journey based on their shifting capability (Tanchuk & Taylor, 2025). AI systems also consist of real-time feedback loops, where students receive instant, context-dependent feedback to eliminate confusion and validate progress. Collectively, all these technologies

TABLE 4.2 AI-powered personalized learning and development

Component	Description
Personalization engine	AI algorithms track student behavior, preference, levels of performance, and engagement patterns and adjust content and modes of learning accordingly.
Adaptive learning pathways	Learning modules adjust themselves in terms of difficulty level, mode, and sequence based on the student's own speed and emerging capabilities.
Real-time feedback systems	AI provides real-time, context-specific feedback to students, which can be utilized to fix errors, improve learning, and activate learners.
Intelligent content delivery	Content is aligned and made available according to relevance, student profile (visual, auditory, kinesthetic), and past interaction.
Skill gap analysis	AI systems identify at the team or individual level a lack in skill or capability and suggest gap-based development options.
Career and learning recommendations	To internal and external inputs (e.g., internal talent marketplaces, skills trends), AI suggests courses or experiences aligned with learning aims and interests.
Multimodal support	AI platforms integrate voice, text, video, VR/AR, and simulation to allow interaction with various learning environments and modes.
Scalability and accessibility	AI enables individualized learning paths at scale, often with support in multiple languages, devices, and accessibility modes (e.g., visually impaired).
Learning analytics and dashboards	AI-driven visual dashboards provide learners, teachers, and managers with immediate snapshot views of progress, strength, and areas for improvement.
Automation of administrative tasks	The above tasks can be automated using AI to carry out routine L&D activities like reporting, certifying, tracking against goals, and scheduling.

Source: Author's own work.

revolutionize learning as a dynamic, active process rather than a passive, one-way transfer of information (Shidganti et al., 2025; Akpabio, Akpabio, & Akpabio, 2025).

Enriching the experience are other abilities such as smart content delivery and analysis of skill gaps, which enable learners to be given exactly what they need exactly when they need it. From recommending visualization simulation to cementing abstractions to identifying missing capability for a new role, this AI ability maximizes utility and usefulness. Career and learning recommendations most often employ large datasets, like analysis of labor markets, which allow AI systems to not only aid users in their immediate contexts but guide them toward as-yet-distant destinations. Concurrently, multimodal support through VR, voice, text, or interactive media enables accessibility and inclusivity among various types of learners and learning environments. (Ragab, 2025)

The focus on accessibility and scalability as primary defining characteristics is a reference to one of the greatest advantages of AI: its capacity to deliver tailored experiences to enormous numbers of people. Features such as learning analytics dashboards and automated admin capabilities also confer operational advantages, streamlining everything from learner evaluation to certification administration. Together, each forms a strong foundation that not only individualizes learning but also hones more strategic organizational and institutional decision-making. However, as the table continues to reflect, the potential of AI must be tapped into with ethical delicacy so that individualization doesn't come at the expense of equity, privacy, or human dignity (Mishra, Ara, & Mishra, 2025; Waladi, Lamarti, & Khaldi, 2025).

The advantage of AI-based personalized learning is a transformation in the way learning, knowledge transmission, and memory take place (Table 4.3). The most significant advantage is the capacity to provide tailored learning experiences. Conventional education models, normally bound by rigid curricula and rigid pacing, have wrestled for decades with serving learners with varying capabilities, interests, and objectives. AI accomplishes this differently, by tracking the activity of every learner continuously and adjusting the presentation of material accordingly. Not only does this enable a better understanding and longer-term memory but it also facilitates a higher level of responsibility and investment

TABLE 4.3 Benefits and considerations of AI-powered personalized learning

Benefit	Explanation
Individualized learning	Students learn at their own pace and in their own learning style, increasing understanding and enjoyment.
Higher engagement	Personalized, interactive material is more captivating and less exhausting than static modules.
Increased ROI in L&D	Organizations can more effectively use resources by focusing development on where it is most required.
Workforce agility	AI can reskill or upskill workers faster as a reaction to market and technology changes.
Inclusive learning	Students with a variety of backgrounds or students who are especially gifted can be instructed through variable, inclusive learning experiences.

Source: Author's own work.

in learning. Students learn at their own pace, receive material in a way most suitable to them—visual, auditory, or kinesthetic—and are likely to be more engaged and confident (Barbudhe, Zanjat, & Karmore, 2025; Khaldi, 2025).

Secondarily, there is a second-order benefit in organizational ROI and performance to learning and development. AI environments enable organizations and institutions to accurately pinpoint skill gaps at the team and individual levels and apply training budgets effectively. Rather than releasing generic programs, L&D professionals can target specific competencies via strategic goals or marketplace needs. Not only is this more pertinent training, but it leads to more responsive and foresighted workforces that are able to adapt to technological change as well as a shifting industry landscape. Shortening learning cycles as well as reducing the time spent on learning irrelevant material also saves firms money and boosts productivity (John, 2025; Barbude, Zanjat, & Karmore, 2025).

Of perhaps even greater importance, though, is the universalizing nature of AI-enabled learning. Intelligent systems have the ability to bridge gaps in access for decades-excluded students—by disability, language, or distance. With features such as live translation, adaptive text-to-speech, and personalized navigation of content, AI enables education for populations that were otherwise excluded. Such leveling of access is not a technical advantage in itself; it is a social imperative. With learning and continuous reskilling becoming the condition for being able to cooperate fully in the digital economy, AI can also level the playing field—providing an equal opportunity for each of them to learn, progress, and benefit society (Khaldi, 2025).

There are certain quite serious challenges and implications of personalized learning on AI, as compared in Table 4.4. The most prominent among them is the challenge of ensuring data security and privacy. AI technologies rely on the ongoing collection and processing of user data—ranging from learning activity to biometric signals—which understandably raises concerns over consent, transparency, and security. If left untamed, such systems also promise to encroach on peoples' rights or leak confidential information for misuse. Aside from this, bias by algorithms is also a very real threat to equity. AI systems that have been trained on biased or homogeneous historic datasets will most likely recreate

TABLE 4.4 Challenges and considerations of AI-powered personalized learning

Challenge	Description
Data privacy and security	Sensitive student information should be kept secure under protocols such as GDPR or HIPAA.
Bias in algorithms	Biases may be transmitted by AI systems if they were trained on unrepresentative or biased data.
Dependence on technology	Over-reliance reduces vital human factors such as direction and emotional quotient.
Implementation costs	Advanced AI systems can require enormous investments in infrastructure and training.
Change management	A transition to AI-supported learning patterns can be opposed by traditional teachers and managers.

Source: author's own work.

present imbalances involuntarily, especially in evaluation, recommendation, or adaptive streams. And so, personalization can be exclusionary rather than empowering unless the deep-seated prejudices are addressed.

A second challenge is obtaining balance between human and machine functions in instruction and development. No matter how carefully AI is engineered to maximize content delivery and administrative effectiveness, it is bereft of the empathetic sentiment, moral judgment, and relational depth found in human teachers and mentors. Excessive reliance on automated systems threatens to undercut these valuable human variables and simplify the learning process to a cold transaction. Furthermore, neither can ease of implementation and cost be eliminated—especially at smaller schools or smaller colleges with fewer technological facilities. Adoption does require spending money, however, not just on software but also on training, change management, and maintenance. Finally, the cultural shift which adoption of AI requires is usually resisted by teaching staff and faculty, who experience redundancy or loss of pedagogical control. If the AI is allowed to fulfill its learning potential, then its implementation must be followed by open government, open dialogue, and unbreakable commitment to design ethics.

With more and more developments in AI, the use of AI in education and training is no longer hypothetical—it's increasingly real in the world today. In education systems and industries, institutions are deploying AI-powered personalized learning platforms that revolutionize how individuals learn, gain skills, and engage in lifelong learning. These case studies reflect a variety of implementations and not only technological feasibility but also strategic and cultural feasibility.

Duolingo, the global language learning platform, uses machine learning to tailor learning to individuals. It adapts the difficulty level of lessons based on user response and performance. The platform uses spaced repetition and error prediction algorithms to customize review sessions to occur at precisely that moment when learners are most likely to forget. The result is a game-like learning experience that subtly adapts in real time to each learner's language abilities and weaknesses. By taking AI to its innermost nucleus, Duolingo has achieved what no other educational software had managed to do before: democratized access to individually tailored education across the globe.

IBM's SkillsBuild program is an excellent illustration of AI-driven learning in the business environment. In order to offer employees and job seekers the most in-demand digital and soft skills, SkillsBuild uses AI to determine individuals' learning profiles—i.e., existing skills, career goals, and past interaction history—and then builds individualized learning pathways accordingly. Microlearning modules, badges, and adaptive feedback loops comprise the system. Organizations that have implemented it report decreased time taken to onboard employees, knowledge retention, and higher levels of employee motivation. Most significantly, AI has made learning at scale for IBM resemble one-to-one mentoring.

Squirrel AI Learning, a Chinese education technology company, is at the forefront with AI educators supplemented with traditional education. Squirrel AI uses knowledge space theory and Bayesian networks to detect the conceptual gaps and misconceptions of each student and then offers hyper-targeted guidance to fill the gaps. Teachers are not replaced but augmented: AI is applied to teach and diagnose in order to free up human teachers for mentoring, emotional intelligence, and higher-order thinking. Pilot classroom results have shown dramatic gains in learning outcomes, especially for students lagging behind on them. The case contends that AI, deployed strategically, can enhance both equity and efficiency.

In collaboration with Microsoft, Coursera also developed AI-powered learning assistants to guide adult learners through challenging course material. These virtual learning coaches evaluate students' progress and provide feedback based on behavior, time spent, and career aspirations. Even the platform itself can learn and recommend courses based on future-proofed careers in the career marketplace—allowing users to upskill or reskill based on future-proofed careers. One of the biggest effects is reduced dropout rates in long-form certification programs, which were a longstanding issue with online education.

Arizona State University has also been at the forefront of using AI to drive student success. Through tools such as "eAdvisor" and "MyPath2ASU," the university uses predictive analytics to identify at-risk students and suggest tailored interventions, such as tutoring or adaptive learning paths. AI is also being used to streamline class scheduling, customize curriculum delivery, and enhance academic advising. ASU has seen quantifiable gains in student retention through these applications, with specific success for minority and first-generation students. This shows how AI can be used to support strategic goals for inclusion and educational equity.

Table 4.5 shows a summary form of key case studies of AI-driven personalized learning and development. This kind of format is best for analytical comparison, strategic review, or executive briefing.

4.3 WORK-LIFE BALANCE AND REMOTE WORK OPTIMIZATION

Historically, work-life balance had been a stringent ideal—most often articulated as ascetic timetables and a dichotomous separation of working and household space. Currently, AI is reshaping this dynamic through learning-based adaptive systems based on an individual's behavioral patterns, preferences, and cycles of thinking. Intelligent calendars, digital assistants, and well-being platforms employ machine learning algorithms to recommend best practice scheduling of work, breaks, and even physical exercise in terms of biometric feedback or assumed productivity rhythms (Gao & Zamanpour, 2024).

Software such as Microsoft Viva or Google Workspace has included AI functionality that encourages employees to schedule "focus time," clock out during off-work hours, or avoid meeting overload. These are not merely ergonomic suggestions but algorithmically optimized interventions based on a person's own workflow. AI applications also help employers detect early warning signs of burnout by analyzing tone of communication, response behavior, or behavioral change in online channels without compromising the anonymity of the users. By utilizing such preventive analysis, organizations can act positively and build well-being instead of waiting for crises to erupt.

TABLE 4.5 Applications of AI for employee engagement and satisfaction

Case Study	Organization / Platform	Description	Key Features	Outcomes / Impact
Language learning at scale	Duolingo	Utilizes computer intelligence to change language courses based on the user's performance as well as that of each learner	Adaptive difficulty, error anticipation, spaced repetition, gamified interface	Increased participation and retention; learning accessible to millions worldwide
Workforce reskilling	IBM SkillsBuild	AI-based reskilling site for employees and job applicants with customized learning paths and micro-credentials	Tailored learning paths, skill assessments, micro-learning, progress tracking	Accelerated learning; enhanced learning retention; focused upskilling due to demand in the job market
AI teachers in classrooms	Squirrel AI (China)	Utilizes AI to offer one-to-one customized learning by invoking cognitive diagnostics in the K-12 setting	Knowledge gap analysis, real-time adaptation, hybrid model with human teachers	Improved student learning; capacity for servicing struggling students; adaptive education at scale
Adult education and career	Coursera + Microsoft	Provides AI-powered virtual learning guides to assist users in navigating complex upskilling courses and recommend career-focused content	AI coaches, career-focused suggestions, analytics of progress	Fewer students drop out; more courses passed; synchronization of learning pathways with career opportunities

Source: Author's own work.

Emotional well-being is maintained by AI through sentiment analysis and online guidance. Mood tracking, mindfulness cues, and stress-reduction exercises can be offered through virtual well-being coaches. This integration of AI into routines of mental care and self-care transforms work-life balance from a vague desire to a constantly tracked and optimized state of balance (Bisht & Uniyal, 2024).

One of the consequences of AI is that it can potentially render flexible work a reality. Hybrid and remote work schemes are based on technologies with the capability to create dynamic change toward decentralized teams, asynchronous work schedules, and varying individual capabilities. AI makes this possible through facilitating intelligent scheduling, workflow prioritization, and duplicate task automation. Consider AI-based scheduling tools such as Clockwise or Reclaim, for instance, which synchronize calendars at the team level while accommodating people's time preference, workload, and location. They not just schedule meetings automatically but also provide a new type of temporal justice that allows individuals more control over when and how they work (Arnold et al., 2025; Jonek-Kowalska & Wolniak, 2023; Jonek-Kowalska & Wolniak, 2025).

AI is also used for workflow automation. For tasks involving routine or rule-based work, i.e., sorting emails, generating reports, processing routine requests, and so on, AI frees employees from being occupied with routine and repetitive tasks to perform higher-level, creative, strategic, or human-intensive tasks. Such a cognitive load distribution enhances flexibility much more. Employees with work segmented can take their work outside of traditional hours without becoming disconnected from their teams or objectives. Notably, AI can even recommend work segmentation. For example, machine learning applications may recognize optimal blocks of deep work time, cluster similar tasks for cognitive optimization, or even recommend a break from observations of keystrokes or screen time. Thus, AI is assisting not with where things are getting done but with how, when, and in what mindset they are optimally done (Gao & Zamanpour, 2024; Sharma et al., 2024).

In all likelihood, the most contentious implication of AI for the contemporary workplace is in measuring productivity. The early iterations of such tools often veered into invasive territory—monitoring screen time, keystrokes, or click rates with little regard for context or trust. Today, however, more ethical and nuanced approaches are emerging, driven by AI's capacity for intelligent insight rather than blunt measurement. Today's productivity software is increasingly being designed not to spy on but to support. For example, AI functionality in project management software like Asana, Monday.com, or Jira delivers analytics of task completion rates, bottlenecks, and the distribution of workload. Rather than punishing low productivity, they can be used to identify the underlying cause, prevent overloading, or redistribute the work. They offer a strategic dashboard to team leaders for those who wish to lead performance but not micromanage (Levin, Naimi, & Saban, 2024; Bhattacharya et al., 2024).

AI productivity tools are starting to be capable of capturing qualitative output. Natural language processing (NLP) enables tools to monitor the quality of written content or creative work, as opposed to quantity. With sentiment analysis and co-operative metadata, these kinds of tools can build rich, human-centered profiles of people's working styles and areas of strength and weakness. Goal alignment is an application with very high potential. AI systems are able to track individual contributions back to the higher organizational purposes, which makes employees see their work in context and with meaning. This connection boosts motivation and eliminates the isolation that too frequently happens in remote or blended environments. In essence, these types of systems must be transparent and consent-based in order to maintain ethical integrity, which the future generation of workplace AI is beginning to do more effectively (Zeghouani et al., 2024; Patki & Abhyankar, 2024).

The crisis precipitated by remote work underscored the potential and limits of virtual collaboration. While collaboration technologies like Zoom, Slack, and Teams energized organizations, they too frequently sacrificed spontaneity, conviviality, and casual sharing in the process. AI is now re-shaping such collaboration spaces into making digital interactions more authentic, intelligent, and inclusive (Stecuła & Wolniak, 2022a, 2022b; Wolniak & Stecuła, 2024; Kordel & Wolniak, 2021).

AI-powered communication technology enables real-time transcription, translation, and summarization, making meetings more actionable and accessible. For instance, AI capability can automatically take action items on the call, automatically assign them, and generate short-form meeting notes that are instantly shareable. These capabilities cut through meeting fatigue and prevent ideas getting lost in electronic noise. Apart from meetings, AI is enabling ambient collaboration—software that operates silently in the background to keep teams on track without requiring constant check-ins. Co-operative AI applications may mark unnecessary effort, suggest co-workers based on interest in content, or initiate cross-functional acquaintance on mutual project interests. They mimic the "water cooler effect" but virtually, bridging the gap between formalized work and unplanned cooperation (Miao et al., 2024).

AI can be an impartial team relationship mediator. By observing interaction patterns, conversational turn-taking, or communication tone, AI systems can indicate imbalances, patterns of exclusion, or communication failure—always with respect to privacy boundaries. Leveraged judiciously, this information facilitates more inclusive, psychologically healthier team cultures. AI-powered virtual workplaces are also expanding into immersive spaces. Through the convergence of AI and XR, teams can work together virtually in areas where avatars, AI agents, and real-time visualizations converge. Such virtual offices facilitate scattered groups to become co-present, allowing increased creativity, interaction, and cross-border innovation (Kaur et al., 2024; Wolniak & Jonek-Kowalska, 2022; Rosak-Szyrocka & Wolniak, 2025).

At least for now, AI is not taking away the human work experience—it's changing it. Through enabling smarter scheduling, actual flexibility, moral productivity analysis, and greater collaboration, AI is helping to align professional requirements with individual rhythms. It is creating space for performance and presence, efficacy and compassion. With wise deployment, AI is less of a chore tool and more of a scaffold for human flourishing. The organizations that thrive in the coming decades will not be those that use AI the most aggressively, but those that use it the most wisely—to work better, live fuller, and connect deeper (Bisht & Uniyal, 2024; Wolniak et al., 2024; Wolniak & Stecuła, 2024).

Table 4.6 summarizes on AI's role in optimizing work-life balance, showing the core AI functionalities and the practical benefits they bring to individuals and organizations.

Table 4.7 has classified AI as productivity measure by observation. Cognitive task and workflow analysis through AI identifies inefficiencies and suggests real-time realignment for enhancing progress. Workload forecasting aids planning and resource management more effectively, and natural language processing quantifies amount and, most importantly, quality of work output, re-emphasizing attention to quality contribution. AI applications provide people with real-time productivity boards that separate work of high and low value and enable greater awareness and time management. Sentiment analysis detects warning signs of burnout or disengagement and links well-being to productivity.

TABLE 4.6 AI's role in optimizing work-life balance

AI functionality	Description / Applications	Benefits for work-life balance
Smart scheduling and focus time allocation	AI takes user behavior, calendar routines, and task types into account in attempting to recommend best-fit blocks of time for deep work, meetings, and rest. Software programs like Microsoft Viva and Reclaim. ai autonomously schedule blocks of time for deep work as well as perform overload-blocking of calendars.	Helps to reduce distractions, protect mental focus, and ensure time for non-work activities
Automated break and disconnection reminders	Intelligent systems monitor daily workloads and remind users to take a break or log off when work is done. Integrated into products like Google Workspace and Microsoft Outlook, reminders are timely and tailored to the event.	Encourages work boundaries, reduces screen fatigue, and helps to recover during the day
Stress and burnout detection	AI may even detect changes in behavior such as delayed response times for emails or increased activity outside the fundamental work hours that could be a sign of stress. Monitoring of activity and sentiment is utilized by some of the workplace analytics tools to set up early warning signs.	Enables proactive care, reduces the risk of chronic overwork, and supports employee care systems
Health monitoring via wearables	Smartwatches use AI to track biometric data such as heart rate, sleep, and physical exercise, which could be synchronized with work activity as a way of automating activity.	Encourages alignment of physical health with work performance, with a supportive impact on general well-being
Mindfulness and well-being recommendations	Health applications such as Calm or Headspace use AI technology to recommend brief breathing, meditation, or relaxation sessions specific to a user's task and emotional cycles.	Helps with mental clarity, reduces worry, and ensures seamless transitions between tasks
Workload forecasting and capacity management	AI applications monitor future and current work to help users and managers know how to expect peak workload hours and reschedule activities prior to them. It is integrated in the likes of tools such as Jira and Trello.	Establishes realistic expectations, avoids last-minute pressure, and distributes team workload evenly
Emotional feedback and sentiment analysis	Emotion-tracking software such as AI-powered Grammarly Business or Slack bots can monitor emotional tone in messaging to enable one to identify patterns of stress over time.	Enhances emotional intelligence, helps teams have healthy interpersonal relationships
AI chatbots for mental health support	Counseling bots like Woebot or Wysa provide conversational therapy, mood tracking, and stress management coping techniques, allowing for a subtle and easy way of psychological counseling.	Delivers confidential emotional support, reduces stigma, and provides immediate access to care resources

Source: Author's own work.

TABLE 4.7 AI's role in productivity-tracking

AI functionality	Description / Applications	Benefits for productivity management
Intelligent task and workflow analysis	AI capabilities within apps like Asana, Trello, or Monday.com monitor work completion, time spent, and project dependencies to identify trends in performance. The apps are able to suggest dynamic re-prioritization of tasks or warn managers about delays.	Provides instant transparency of workflow effectiveness, allowing for timely adjustment and smoother handoff of tasks
Predictive workload forecasting	AI programs analyze historical trends of work done, deadlines, and capacity utilization of the teams to foresee times of workload increase or resource shortage. Tools like Jira or ClickUp implement such analytics on project boards.	Helps managers plan, distribute tasks more equitably, and avoid members getting overloaded
Quality and content evaluation	With natural language processing (NLP), AI is able to estimate not only the volume but the quality of documents, reports, or letters. It is especially useful in knowledge work areas.	Promotes focus on contribution quality over quantity, boosting overall work worth.
Real-time productivity insights	Computer-generated software such as ActivTrak or Time Doctor (in privacy modes) provides time dashboards of activity on tasks, distinguishing between productive and unproductive work.	Makes individual awareness easier, enhances responsibility, and helps optimize time strategies.
Sentiment and engagement monitoring	AI monitors tone, response time, and online activity for indications of fatigue, disengagement, or conflict. AI identifies lurking productivity killers.	Enables psychological safety and prevents productivity loss due to mismanaged emotional exhaustion.
Goal alignment and progress visualization	AI links one's or one's team's work to larger strategic objectives through automated tracking and visual goalboards, which are often paired with OKR software.	Boosts motivation, creates meaningful work, and helps identify personal contribution toward bigger goals.
Automation of routine reporting	AI generates automated project status reports, task reminders, or weekly activity reports, often aggregating data from many different tools and platforms simultaneously.	Saves administrative update time and allows employees to focus on high-value tasks.
Personalized productivity recommendations	AI can suggest tips to optimize time management, suggest task switching for peak brain function, or suggest workflow automation software based on usage patterns.	Makes continuous improvement easier and helps to build more productive work habits.

Source: Author's own work.

AI bridges day-to-day work and organizational objectives at scale with automatic visualization of progress and linking of OKRs, providing people with a sense of purpose. By facilitating automatic reporting and tailored suggestions for improvement, AI reduces administrative burden and encourages employees to defend their work habits in the here and now. Together, these two activities constitute a participatory mechanism where productivity is tracked, judiciously tuned, and aligned with people potential and strategic intent (Arnold et al., 2025; Sharma et al., 2024).

4.4 AI'S ROLE IN MENTAL HEALTH AND EMPLOYEE WELL-BEING

The application of AI in mental health can, on the surface, appear to be paradoxical. How, one may ask, can a system that is artificial, devoid of human experience, be able to deliver effective interventions for emotional distress? And yet this apparent paradox is being resolved on the ground. AI does not replace the therapist or mimic the subtlety of human empathy but augments human action, bridging the demand and supply of timely, scalable, and precise responses. One of the most powerful and straightforward applications of AI is early identification. AI can look for depression, anxiety, burnout, or other issues in text, speech, biometrics, or even social media (Cayol, 2025; Higgins & Wilson, 2025). Natural language processing, for example, can detect very slight variations in words used and tone that could signal emotional distress. Applied in organizational communication networks such as email or messaging software, the models can detect vulnerable individuals and trigger unobtrusive contact in their interests by healthcare or HR staff. Most significantly, it's not eavesdropping but allows companies to enter nascent well-being crises before crises become emergencies (Cecil et al., 2025; Jiang & Yang, 2025; Skubis, Wolniak, & Grebski, 2024; Wolniak et al., 2024).

AI chatbots are also increasingly being included as a default part of employee well-being initiatives. They reside on employees' desks 24/7 as a stigma-free, low-threshold portal to mental healthcare. They may provide evidence-based cognitive behavior therapy (CBT) exercises, mindfulness interventions, or a chance to vent or just talk (Goel, Yadav, & Verma, 2025). No one will propose that a chatbot is ever going to replace clinical intervention, but it can be an emergency responder of a sort—a form of triage system—de-stressing and referring users to more human assistance where and when needed (Zelenka, 2025). AI has proven to be useful in personalizing wellness programs to meet the individual's unique needs. Legacy EAPs are also afflicted with one-size-fits-all thinking, providing cookie-cutter content or services that fail to resonate with multivariate workforces. AI can do better and provide interventions that are guided by user preference, behavior, and even physiological cycles. A good system will have the ability to decide when an employee will practice mindfulness, what stress reduction content is best suited for them, or what activity is best suited to their motivational style. Personalization generates more engagement and longer-term behavior change (Zhang et al., 2025; Daungupawong & Wiwanitkit, 2025).

Of potentially greater significance, though, is how AI influences the organizational climate itself. Predictive analytics might allow companies to uncover root causes of low mental well-being—e.g., manager bullying, overloading, or communication breakdowns. By aggregating and anonymizing employees' feedback, AI technology can generate dashboards of team morale, psychological safety, and risk of burnout (Widyaswari, Nikat, & Sari, 2025; Widyaswari & Farhrudin, 2025). This will allow leaders to make data-informed, rather than intuition-based, decisions regarding workload redistribution,

TABLE 4.8 AI's role in mental health and employee well-being

Area of application	Examples of technologies / Tools	Potential benefits	Risks and challenges
Early detection of issues	Natural language processing (NLP), email and chat behavioral analytics	Early detection of depression, anxiety, and burnout; averting mental health emergencies	Privacy concerns, likelihood of false positives, need for consent from the user
First-line support tools	Mental health chatbots (e.g., Woebot, Wysa, Youper)	24/7 access, stigma-free, lower human counselor workload	Poor emotional intelligence, lack of adequate crisis management
Personalized interventions	AI recommendation systems, usage pattern analysis	Tailorable mental health content, greater user interaction, better outcomes	Risk of over-automation, sensitivity of user information
Workplace climate monitoring	Sentiment analysis, collective feedback analysis, mood-tracking tools for employees	Instant pulse on morale, burnout likelihood, and team functioning; data-informed HR decisions	Ethical issues, misinterpretation of information, scope for abuse
Scalable mental health programs	AI-curated wellness plans, digital CBT platforms	Accessibility at scale, quality of care consistency, cost savings	Fewer people interacting, cannot manage complex psychological cases
Supporting HR and management	Predictive analytics, burnout prediction, stress level-tracking	Data-informed leadership, proactive interventions, cultural adaptation	Reliance on data quality, threat of managerial overextension

Source: Author's own work.

cultural intervention, or leadership coaching. Application of AI to this sensitive domain must be carried out with extreme caution and ethical gravity (Soman, Judy, & Abou, 2025). Data privacy is of utmost importance. Employees should be convinced that their chat or biometric information will never be tampered with, used as a weapon against them, or sold without their complete awareness. Transparancy should be the default regarding how AI models work, why they work the way they do, and how far they can push. Human judgment cannot be put on trial as well. AI will show risk indicators but never ultimate authority over an individual's mental status or his/her professional reputation (Imkome et al., 2025).

Table 4.8 is an overview of AI contribution to employees' health and well-being. It spans wide areas of application, example technologies, expected benefits, and risks or challenges involved.

REFERENCES

Agatova, O., & Latipova, L. (2025). Exploring AI-powered personalized learning in universities. *International Journal of Evaluation and Research in Education*, *14*(2), 837–848.

Akpabio, E., Akpabio, I., & Akpabio, I. (2025). Leveraging AI for personalized English language learning: tailoring instruction to individual needs. In *AI Applications for English Language Learning* (pp. 385–414). IGI Global Scientific Publishing.

Alzeiby, E. A., Islam, N., Shaik, A. S., & Yaqub, M. Z. (2025). AI adoption in enterprises for enhanced strategic human resource management practices: benefiting the employee engagement and experience. *Journal of Enterprise Information Management*. www.emerald.com/jeim/article-abstract/doi/10.1108/JEIM-05-2024-0249/1252301/AI-adoption-in-enterprises-for-enhanced-strategic?redirectedFrom=fulltext

Arnold, L., Aryal, S., Hong, B., Su, W., & Piaggio, D. (2025). A systematic literature review of eye-tracking and machine learning methods for improving productivity and reading abilities. *Applied Sciences (Switzerland)*, *15*(6), 3308.

Aulia, S. R., & Lin, W.-S. (2025). Embracing the digital shift: leveraging AI to foster employee well-being and engagement in remote workplace settings in the Asia Pacific region. *Asia Pacific Management Review*, *30*(3), 100339.

Barbudhe, V., Zanjat, S. N., & Karmore, B. S. (2025). The application of AI and machine learning in personalized wellness and preventive care. In *Harnessing AI and machine learning for precision wellness* (pp. 131–147). IGI Global Scientific Publishing.

Bhattacharya, A., Misra, B., Majumder, S., Chakraborty, S., & Dey, N. (2024). Understanding the role of working style in shaping work-life balance: an XAI-based investigation of private sector employees. In *Frontiers in Artificial Intelligence and Applications* (Vol. 391, pp. 1–12).

Bisht, R., & Uniyal, A. K. (2024). Smart workspaces: integrating IoT and AI to foster work-life balance. In *Proceedings of the IEEE 2024 1st International Conference on Advances in Computing, Communication and Networking (ICAC2N 2024)* (pp. 1224–1229). IEEE.

Cayol, A. (2025). Rethinking mental health care in the age of AI | Repenser la prise en charge de la santé mentale à l'ère de l'IA. *Médecine et Droit*, *2025*(191), 53–55.

Cecil, J., Kleine, A.-K., Lermer, E., & Gaube, S. (2025). Mental health practitioners' perceptions and adoption intentions of AI-enabled technologies: an international mixed-methods study. *BMC Health Services Research*, *25*(1), 556.

Chakraborty, M., Singh, R. K., Hussein, T. M., Khan, S., & Mishra, S. (2023). Maslow's hierarchy-inspired AI-driven employee satisfaction improvement. In *Proceedings of the International Conference on Technological Advancements in Computational Sciences (ICTACS 2023)* (pp. 987–993). IEEE.

Coban, A., Dzsotjan, D., Küchemann, S., Kuhn, J., & Hoyer, C. (2025). AI support meets AR visualization for Alice and Bob: personalized learning based on individual ChatGPT feedback in an AR quantum cryptography experiment for physics lab courses. *EPJ Quantum Technology*, *12*(1), 15.

Daungsupawong, H., & Wiwanitkit, V. (2025). Comment on "Ai-Aun Chatbot: a pilot study on the effectiveness of an artificial intelligence intervention for mental health among Thai older adults." *Nursing and Health Sciences*, *27*(2), e70121.

Elbadawi, M. A. (2025). Exploring the impact of AI on employee engagement and productivity in human resource management. In *Studies in Big Data* (Vol. 158, pp. 541–550).

Gao, K., & Zamanpour, A. (2024). How can AI-integrated applications affect the financial engineers' psychological safety and work-life balance: Chinese and Iranian financial engineers and administrators' perspectives. *BMC Psychology*, *12*(1), 555.

Goel, P. K., Yadav, S. P., & Verma, S. (2025). Building trust in AI-driven mental health tools: addressing bias and fairness in NLP models. In *Demystifying the role of natural language processing (NLP) in mental health* (pp. 51–69). IGI Global.

Gupta, R., & Raheja, S. (2025). Enhancing employee engagement through AI. In *Human Resource Management and artificial intelligence: automating and optimizing processes* (pp. 44–71). Routledge.

Herlina, M. G., & Iskandar, K. (2025). Integrating sustainable HRM, AI, and employee well-being to enhance engagement in Greater Jakarta: an SDG 3 perspective. In *E3S Web of Conferences* (Vol. 601, 00020).

Higgins, O., & Wilson, R. L. (2025). Integrating artificial intelligence (AI) with workforce solutions for sustainable care: a follow up to artificial intelligence and machine learning (ML) based decision support systems in mental health. *International Journal of Mental Health Nursing, 34*(2), e70019.

Imkome, E.-U., Soonthornchaiya, R., Lakanavisid, P., Suebnukarn, S., & Matthews, A. K. (2025). Ai-Aun Chatbot: a pilot study on the effectiveness of an artificial intelligence intervention for mental health among Thai older adults. *Nursing and Health Sciences, 27*(2), e70093.

Jangbahadur, U., Ahlawat, S., Rozera, P., & Gupta, N. (2025). The effect of AI-enabled HRM dimensions on employee engagement and sustainable organisational performance: fusion skills as a moderator. *Evidence-Based HRM, 13*(1), 85–107.

Jeong, I., Kong, S., Kim, Y., Kim, J.-W., & Lee, H. (2025). Personalized health prediction AI models using transfer learning and strategic overfitting on wearable device data. *Journal of Medical Systems, 49*(1), 45.

Jiang, J., & Yang, Y. (2025). GymBuddy and Elomia, AI-integrated applications, effects on the mental health of the students with psychological disorders. *BMC Psychology, 13*(1), 350.

John, A. (2025). Revolutionizing STEAM education: harnessing the power of AI and digital technology to deliver personalized learning experiences. In *Integrating personalized learning methods into STEAM education* (pp. 143–168). IGI Global.

Jonek-Kowalska, I., & Wolniak, R. (2023). *Towards sustainability and a better quality of life?*, Routledge.

Jonek-Kowalska, I., & Wolniak, R. (2025). *Exclusion in Smart Cities assessment and strategy for strengthening resilience*, Routledge.

Kaur, R., & Kaur, H. (2023). The repercussion of AI tools for professionals in the term of compensation and leadership on the employee retention and job satisfaction. In *Lecture Notes in Networks and Systems* (Vol. 588, pp. 203–214).

Kaur, R., Kaur, H. J., Seth, N., Bawa, S. S., & Panday, S. (2024). AI-enhanced bleisure: analyzing the social dynamics of work-leisure integration in multicultural contexts. In *Proceedings of the 2024 IEEE 4th International Conference on ICT in Business Industry and Government (ICTBIG 2024)* (pp. 1–7). IEEE.

Khaldi, M. (2025). *Supporting personalized learning and students' skill development with AI* (pp. 1–472). IGI Global Scientific Publishing.

Kordel, P., & Wolniak, R. (2021). Technology entrepreneurship and the performance of enterprises in the conditions of Covid-19 Pandemic: the fuzzy set analysis of waste to energy enterprises in Poland. *Energies, 14*(13), 3891.

Lenka, R., & Chanda, R. (2025). Generative AI for predicting employee engagement in HR analytics: a bibliometric analysis. In *Lecture Notes in Networks and Systems* (Vol. 1162, pp. 201–209).

Levin, C., Naimi, E., & Saban, M. (2024). Evaluating GenAI systems to combat mental health issues in healthcare workers: an integrative literature review. *International Journal of Medical Informatics, 191*, 105566.

Lyu, W., & Salam, Z. A. (2025). AI-powered personalized learning: enhancing self-efficacy, motivation, and digital literacy in adult education through expectancy-value theory. *Learning and Motivation, 90*, 102129.

Mammas, C. S., & Mamma, A. S. (2025). AI and machine learning computational modeling that takes into consideration gut microbiota for a personalized decision support preoperative planning for an optimum liver regeneration after partial hepatectomy. *Studies in Health Technology and Informatics, 323*, 55–60.

Marvi, R., Foroudi, P., & AmirDadbar, N. (2025). Dynamics of user engagement: AI mastery goal and the paradox mindset in AI–employee collaboration. *International Journal of Information Management, 83*, 102908.

Miao, J., Thongprayoon, C., Valencia, O. G., Craici, I. M., & Cheungpasitporn, W. (2024). Navigating nephrology's decline through a GPT-4 analysis of internal medicine specialties in the United States: qualitative study. *JMIR Medical Education, 10*, e57157.

Mishra, M., Ara, A., & Mishra, S. (2025). Exploring human-AI collaboration in higher education: an investigation into AI-enabled personalized learning. In *Prompt engineering and Generative AI applications for teaching and learning* (pp. 483–501). IEEE.

Patki, S. M., & Abhyankar, S. C. (2024). *Organizational citizenship behaviour (OCB) in India: emerging trends and future directions* (pp. 1–208). Springer.

Pillai, R. H., Bi, A., Nagesh, N., Adarsh, R., & Sastri, A. (2024). Impact of AI-infused leadership on subordinate employee's job satisfaction: a study across select successful IT companies in Bengaluru City. In *Communications in Computer and Information Science* (Vol. 2050, pp. 156–166).

Pratt, M., Boudhane, M., Taskin, N., & Cakula, S. (2021). Use of AI for improving employee motivation and satisfaction. In *Advances in Intelligent Systems and Computing* (Vol. 1329, pp. 289–299).

Ragab, K. (2025). Empowering STEM education with AI and prompt engineering: personalized learning, adaptive instruction, and generative applications. In *Prompt engineering and Generative AI applications for teaching and learning* (pp. 175–187). IGI Global.

Rosak-Szyrocka J., Wolniak, R. (2025) *Smart universities in Smart Cities shaping the future of education and urban innovation*, Routledge.

Ruan, Y., & Mezei, J. (2022). When do AI chatbots lead to higher customer satisfaction than human frontline employees in online shopping assistance? Considering product attribute type. *Journal of Retailing and Consumer Services, 68*, 103059.

Rulandari, N., & Silalahi, A. D. K. (2025). Human-AI collaboration for efficiency and employee job satisfaction in public administration: insights from a resource-based perspective. *Transforming Government: People, Process and Policy, 19*(2), 264–287.

Shah, A., Ghugharawala, A., Patel, M., Rathore, N., & Naik, R. R. (2024). Impact of AI and ML on employee job satisfaction and performance. In *Proceedings of the 4th International Conference on Sustainable Expert Systems (ICSES 2024)* (pp. 1183–1188). IEEE.

Sharma, H., Maheshwari, S., Singla, S., Chopra, S., & Khandelwal, G. (2024). HeyMitra – a daily life assistant web application with todo list and time tracking ability. In *Proceedings of the 2024 International Conference on Knowledge Engineering and Communication Systems (ICKECS 2024)*. IEEE.

Shidaganti, G., Aditya Raj, V., Monish Raman, V. R., & Kumaran, S. (2025). Edge computing in educational technology: the power of edge AI for dynamic and personalized learning. In *Edge of intelligence: exploring the frontiers of AI at the edge* (pp. 121–152). Wiley.

Skubis, I., Wolniak, R., & Grebski, W. W. (2024). AI and human-centric approach in smart cities management: case studies from Silesian and Lesser Poland Voivodships. *Sustainability, 16*(18), Article 8279, 1–26.

Soman, G., Judy, M. V., & Abou, A. M. (2025). Human guided empathetic AI agent for mental health support leveraging reinforcement learning-enhanced retrieval-augmented generation. *Cognitive Systems Research, 90*, 101337.

Stecuła, K., & Wolniak, R. (2022a). Advantages and disadvantages of e-learning innovations during COVID-19 pandemic in higher education in Poland. *Journal of Open Innovation: Technology, Market, and Complexity, 8*(3), 159.

Stecuła, K., & Wolniak, R. (2022b). Influence of COVID-19 pandemic on dissemination of innovative e-learning tools in higher education in Poland. *Journal of Open Innovation: Technology, Market, and Complexity, 8*(2), 89.

Sweiss, M. I. K., & Yamin, M. A. Y. (2024). The role of AI-enabled human resource practices towards task satisfaction and employee creative willingness. *SAGE Open, 14*(3), 1–13.

Tanchuk, N. J., & Taylor, R. M. (2025). Personalized learning with AI tutors: assessing and advancing epistemic trustworthiness. *Educational Theory, 75*(2), 327–353.

Tao, G., & Pan, Y. (2025). AI-driven personalized learning in medical education: enhancing cognitive skills and addressing language proficiency challenges. *Forum for Linguistic Studies, 7*(4), 366–384.

Tummalapalli, H. K., Rao, A. N., Kamal, G., Kumari, N., & Swarup Kumar, J. N. V. R. (2025). Exploring AI-driven management: impact on organizational performance, decision making, efficiency, and employee engagement. *Journal of Advanced Research in Applied Sciences and Engineering Technology, 52*(2), 148–163.

Vashishth, T. K., Sharma, V., Tomer, T., Kaushik, S., & Singh, B. (2025). AI in HRM: transforming employee engagement and satisfaction amidst challenges and opportunities. In *Human Resource Management in the age of Generative AI* (pp. 157–187). IGI Global.

Vijayakanthan, S., Nesakumari, J. N., Uma, S., Sathish, A., & Avinash, S. (2024). Modernizing finance, HR: AI, IoT, and cloud solutions for enhancing efficiency and employee satisfaction. In *Proceedings of the 2024 International Conference on Intelligent Systems and Advanced Applications (ICISAA 2024)*. IEEE.

Vorobyeva, K. I., Belous, S., Savchenko, N. V., Nikitina, S. A., & Zhdanov, S. P. (2025). Personalized learning through AI: pedagogical approaches and critical insights. *Contemporary Educational Technology, 17*(2), ep574.

Waladi, C., Lamarti, M. S., & Khaldi, M. (2025). AI-driven personalized learning pathways: customizing education for every student. In *Supporting personalized learning and students' skill development with AI* (pp. 63–78). IGI Global.

Widyaswari, M., & Fakhrudin, A. (2025). Harnessing AI and mindfulness: a new wave of digital mental health solutions. *General Hospital Psychiatry, 94*, 108–109.

Widyaswari, M., Nikat, R. F., & Sari, D. P. (2025). The digital mental health revolution: how AI and big data are transforming modern therapy. *General Hospital Psychiatry, 94*, 118–119.

Wolniak, R., Gajdzik, B., Grebski, M., Danel, R., & Grebski, W.W. (2024). Business models used in Smart Cities—theoretical approach with examples of Smart Cities. *Smart Cities, 7*, 1626–1669.

Wolniak, R., & Jonek-Kowalska, I. (2022). The creative services sector in Polish cities. *J. Open Innov. Technol. Mark. Complex, 8*, 17.

Wolniak, R., & Stecuła, K. (2024). Artificial intelligence in Smart Cities—applications, barriers and future directions: a review. *Smart Cities, 7*, 1346–1389.

Zeghouani, O., Ali, Z., van Dijkhuizen, W. S., Hong, J. W., & Clos, J. (2024). AI in the classroom: examining the feasibility of AI-generated questions in educational settings. In *ACM International Conference Proceeding Series* (Vol. 36).

Zelenka, L. (2025). AI predicts risk of mental health disorders: psychiatric disorders. *Nature Neuroscience, 28*(4), 709.

Zhang, X., Li, Z., Zhang, M., Gao, D., & Li, H. (2025). Exploring artificial intelligence (AI) chatbot usage behaviors and their association with mental health outcomes in Chinese university students. *Journal of Affective Disorders, 380*, 394–400.

CHAPTER 5

AI for Sustainable Workforce Management

5.1 AI AND WORKFORCE ANALYTICS FOR SUSTAINABILITY

Organizations are no longer being measured in productivity rate and profit margin terms only; organizations are now being measured in terms of the sustainability of the environment, social responsiveness, and ability to cope with uncertainties in the future. For that, AI-powered workforce analytics is a future-focused and advanced frame through which organizations may be able to tackle sustainability—not only in the environmental sense but also from economic as well as human perspectives (Allil, 2023).

Sustainability has for many years been defined in terms of the "triple bottom line" of people, planet, and profit. Yet too often, the "people" component has itself been a byproduct—measured in diversity targets or regulatory tickboxes. Workforce analytics with AI can turn this worldview around. In casting light on human capital deployment, development, and retention, analytics can inform strategy that not only works but is ethically sustainable and socially regenerative (Krishna & Sidharth. 2023).

Consider the example of employee burnout in high-stress professions like healthcare, logistics, and manufacturing. Left unchecked, chronic stress appears as lower productivity, turnover, and rising health costs—classic indicators of an unsustainable workforce system. AI, through real-time sentiment analysis, schedule optimization, and fatigue detection, enables a more humane management approach. Rather than dealing with crises as a response, organizations are able to design working spaces that maintain mental and physical well-being in advance. This therefore re-shapes sustainability as an ever-present equilibrium between organizational output and human flourishing (Higgins & Wilson, 2025; Mobo, 2025).

DOI: 10.1201/9781003668282-7

One of the biggest advantages of AI workforce analytics is that it foretells. AI can foresee attrition risk, talent deficits, and even team cohesion failure by extracting prior labor history. This allows leaders to make informed recruiting, reskilling, or team rebalancing decisions. These forecasts are the cornerstone of sustainable workforce planning: the right people, with the right skills, in the right job—waste-free and with full engagement (Kumar et al., 2025).

But forecasting is just half the story. Proper use of AI entails that data-driven decisions not lock in existing disparities. If, for instance, algorithms learn from skewed historical data—such as minorities being underrepresented in executive positions—they will likely reinforce those disparities (Rosak-Szyrocka & Wolniak, 2025; Skubis, Wolniak, & Grebski, 2025). An ethics of sustainability consequently requires transparencies in algorithms, testing for bias, and representative datasets. Justice is not just an issue of legality or reputation, but a structural pillar of a sustainable workforce plan (Chandratreya, 2025).

To speak in concrete terms: a multinational retailer employed AI workforce analytics to conclude that there were patterns of shift scheduling underlying rising absenteeism among single parents. The answer proposed a flexible scheduling model, which was implemented across a number of stores. The result? Not only improved attendance, but also improved employee satisfaction and a dramatic reduction in attrition. Sustainability in this case was a byproduct of an ethical reawakening ignited by AI (Savelka et al., 2025; Gajdzik et al., 2024c, 2024d).

Labor market sustainability also relies on the ability of a society to upskill and reskill its labor force. In an era of rapidly evolving technologies, the half-life of skills is shrinking, yet new skills—particularly green and digital skills—are in growing demand. Again, here, AI is an accelerator. With skills mapping, learning path recommendation engines, and coaching bots, organizations can orchestrate learning strategies that are scalable as well as personalized (Hare et al., 2025).

This is not science fiction and is already a work in progress. IBM, SAP, and Amazon are just a few companies that have already put in place AI-powered learning analytics to trace out employee development trajectories. For instance, an AI system might recognize that a warehouse picker with high spatial reasoning and good pattern recognition skills can be upskilled into a data labeler for machine vision tasks. This redeployment not only avoids job substitution by automation but does so while preserving dignity and career progression. In addition, this approach supports environmental sustainability indirectly (Yoshida & Ince-Yenilmez, 2025; Gajdzik, Wolniak, & Grebski, 2023). By reducing the need for repeat external recruitment and the subsequent onboarding procedures—usually involving physical movement, documentation, and travel—companies minimize their carbon footprint. Retaining and reskilling internal talent is a sustainable strategy, not an HR strategy (Tenakwah & Watson, 2025).

Where pandemics, geopolitical uncertainty, and climate instability exist in chaotic environments, agile organizations have to be adaptable. Traditional organizational planning models are no longer appropriate. Workforce analytics based on AI provides real-time insights into decision-making to enable dynamic re-deployment of labor, project team rebalancing, and instant identification of skill gaps (Ianc, 2025).

Think, for example, of emergency response units in natural disasters. AI systems can sift through satellite image data, social media, and worker location sensors to figure out which workers are available, are present at the location, and possess the requisite skills to assist. These kinds of systems, when deployed along with human decision-makers, improve workforce deployment efficiency as well as make it ethical during crises. In this case, sustainability refers to resilience—a business firm's capacity for shock absorption without compromising its main mission or cheating its employees. The same things apply in business contexts (Gajdzik, Wolniak, & Grebski, 2025; Wolniak & Grebski, 2025). Others utilized AI dashboards amid the COVID-19 pandemic to identify who was suited to working remotely, who must be present on premises, and who was most vulnerable (Stecuła & Wolniak, 2022a, 2022b; Wolniak & Stecuła, 2024). Within hours, not weeks, the choices showcased how analytics can enable socially responsible agility—safeguarding health without halting operations (Omar & Weilbach, 2025; Pandita et al., 2025).

Perhaps the most extensively under-valued aspect of sustainable workforce management is trust. Without trust, even the best AI technology will be met with resistance, mistrust, or disengagement (Wolniak, Stecuła, & Aydın, 2024a, 2024b; Sieiwc et al., 2025). Workers have reason to be cynical: productivity tool Trojan horses of surveillance software, black-box algorithmic ratings, and automation anxiety have devastated trust in digital management (Lee, 2025; Chertow et al., 2024). The solution is radical transparency. Organizations need to not only be open about their use of AI systems, but also co-design them with employees. Engagement through participatory design processes, privacy assurances on data, and clear accountability mechanisms are a necessity. Meanwhile, AI, by being positioned as not a controller but a tool of shared good, can solidify rather than erode the social contract at work (Hole et al., 2025).

Transparency is sustainability. Trust-investing companies have reduced turnover, greater engagement, and increased resilience during times of disruption. And AI, paradoxically, can be a trust-enabler—if interacted with while displaying care, humility, and shared intention (Yamamoto et al., 2025; Jonek-Kowalska et al., 2022).

The AI role in workforce sustainability is not to automate what is but to help imagine what can be. AI must not be viewed as a tool to extract more from exhausted workers but as a partner in designing regenerative work systems—where meaning and productivity complement each other, and where the future of work is human and resilient (Wolniak & Stecuła, 2024). Such a vision demands a new kind of leadership (Shi, 2025). Leaders must be data literate yet ethically motivated, technologically proficient yet empathetically involved. They must ask not only "What can we measure?" but also "What should we value?" AI can tell a lot about efficiency, trends, and patterns. But it is the human leadership that must decide what makes a sustainable, equitable, and dignified work environment (Tona et al., 2025).

Table 5.1 presents aspects of AI implementation in the case of workforce analytics for sustainability, organized by thematic areas, types of technologies used, benefits, and challenges. The table is structured to provide a clear and comprehensive overview for academic, strategic, or practical use (Bonney et al., 2024; Carrara, 2024).

TABLE 5.1 AI implementation in the case of workforce analytics for sustainability

Thematic area	AI technologies and methods	Sustainability benefits	Challenges and risks
Human capital optimization	AI tools such as natural language processing and sentiment analysis can quantify employee communications, feedback, and degree of engagement. Predictive analytics identifies early warning signs of burnout, disengagement, or work-related stress.	By charting well-being trends and stress hotspots, organizations can implement targeted interventions to improve employees' mental health. This results in a healthier work environment, reduces absenteeism, and improves long-term workforce sustainability.	The collection and analysis of sensitive behavioral and emotional information may be problematic from a surveillance and data protection point of view. Additionally, without established ethical principles, the systems could be viewed as intrusive or manipulative.
Workforce planning	Machine learning algorithms and AI-driven simulations help in projecting workforce demands, turnover risk forecasting, and pointing out future skills gaps. They offer data-driven scenario-planning based on economic, seasonal, or organizational trends.	AI facilitates more adaptive and strategic deployment of human capital. Organizations can adjust staffing numbers and capacity based on demand, improving efficiency and long-term labor sustainability. It also reduces wastage of resources through overstaffing or bad forecasting.	AI models may learn to replicate historical biases if training data is imbalanced or biased. Algorithm-based decisions may disregard human factors such as motivation, informal leadership, or personal development goals.
Skills development and upskilling	AI tools can read job descriptions, performance data, and employee profiles to recommend personalized learning paths. They facilitate reskilling initiatives by matching future skills requirements to internal talent pools.	This approach facilitates internal mobility, allows workers to adapt to technological change, and facilitates transition to a knowledge-driven, environmentally sound economy. It reduces the economic and environmental cost of obtaining external talent and recruiting it.	Low digital literacy or limited access to learning environments for some workers may make them fall behind. Over-automation of learning paths may also be a danger that ignores individual learning styles, goals, or cultural factors.
Organizational agility and resilience	Real-time people analytics, which are now possible due to AI dashboards and scheduling automation tools, allow companies to act with agility in the face of changing conditions, whether they involve crises, supply chain disruptions, or policy changes.	Flexible reallocation of labor and assets enables firms to maintain continuity and reduce economic or operating shocks. Flexibility in workforce management increases organizational resilience, a key component of long-term survivability.	The tech challenge of integrating real-time AI tools into existing HR and operation frameworks may become a hindrance. High dependency on dynamic scheduling may reduce the predictability and stability of work for some workers.

TABLE 5.1 *(Continued)*

Thematic area	AI technologies and methods	Sustainability benefits	Challenges and risks
Equity, inclusion, and diversity	AI solutions also possess the capability to audit promotion, hiring, and salary figures to identify trends of underrepresentation or bias. Algorithmic systems also can be designed to support equitable recruitment processes through anonymized resumes or diversified shortlists.	These behaviors support more inclusive workplaces, eliminate opportunity gaps, and establish inclusion cultures. Equality in the treatment of people enhances staff retention and constructs the social pillar of sustainability.	Unless closely watched, AI systems have the potential to perpetuate systemic biases inadvertently, especially when training data reflects existing disparity. Moreover, equity efforts can fail without vigilant human oversight and organizational intention to transform.
Environmental sustainability	AI-driven workforce analytics also can be overlaid on patterns of facility usage, transportation, or energy consumption. Solutions can recommend sustainable practices such as remote working, green commuting incentives, or space optimization.	Telework and less unnecessary travel reduce carbon emissions and support environmental goals. Effective resource planning also assists in operating more leanly with reduced environmental impact.	Workforce value to the environment may be difficult to quantify or compare with short-term financial performance. Some sustainability decisions may also be counterproductive to traditional measures of productivity.
Ethical governance and trust	Explainable AI (XAI) frameworks and open decision protocols allow for explanations of how and why specific workforce decisions are made. Participatory design and ethical data collection norms form the basis of legitimacy.	Transparent and ethical application of AI fosters employee trust and psychological safety. As long as laborers understand that they are given a voice regarding the use of their data, AI stops being a tool for control but is utilized as a collaborative effort tool.	Mistrust in AI systems is possible when employees perceive that the decisions are unfair, arbitrary, or not transparent. Lack of transparency in terms of data use or lack of participative governance can lead to resistance and clashes.
Labor market transition	AI can model the effect of automation on work and design proactive reskilling programs. Predictive models can determine which jobs are most at risk and recommend transitional career paths based on proximal skills.	Such understanding empowers policymakers and organizations to more ethically respond to job displacement. By facilitating workers' transition, AI fosters social stability and fair economic adjustment during periods of technological disruption.	If the systems are abused, they will justify premature redundancy or lower investments in human capital. There exists a greater society risk of increased inequality between digitally skilled workers and those employed in precarious or decreasing sectors.

Source: Author's own work.

5.2 PREDICTIVE HR ANALYTICS FOR TALENT RETENTION

Predictive Human Resource (HR) Analytics is currently a major tool in this endeavor, allowing businesses not only to fulfill the causes of employee turnover but also to forecast and prevent it. This essay discusses the application of predictive HR analytics for talent retention, its mechanism, benefits, and weaknesses, and the overall implications for organizational sustainability and strategic human resource management (Pandita et al., 2025).

Turnover of staff, especially of high-performing or high-potential staff, is operationally and financially disastrous. It costs 30% to over 200% of the employee's annual salary to replace an employee, depending on the complexity of the job (Tariq, 2024; Kaditrov et al., 2024). But below these measurable expenses are less overt and more insidious effects: loss of institutional knowledge, teams falling apart, morale drained, and dilution of customer relationships (Hole et al., 2025; Lee, 2025). Keeping talent, therefore, especially priority talent, is not cost control—it is strategy. Retention of high performers is essential to innovation, continuity, and competitive resilience (Johnson et al., 2025; Ravesangar et al., 2025). Legacy HR practice has been reactive, not proactive. Exit interviews, questionnaires, and performance appraisal—helpful as they may be—are prone to being post hoc rationalizations. They tell us why an individual has left but rarely tell us who is ready to leave prior to the resignation arriving in the mailbox. Predictive HR analytics sets in (Yamamoto, 2025).

Predictive HR analytics employs statistical techniques, machine learning trends, and past employee data to predict future HR outcomes. Predictive analytics takes descriptive analytics that report nothing but history and prescriptive analytics recommending action one step further toward a domain of prediction where future behavior—like resignation likelihood—can be forecast with a reasonable level of certainty (Shi, 2025). One of the strongest features of talent retention predictive analytics is the development of models that identify patterns of employee turnover. Patterns can be established based on a wide range of variables: demographic data (age, tenure, education), performance level, promotion history, compensation history, absence levels, training completion, engagement survey scores, supervisor ratings, and even external labor market conditions (Tona et al., 2025). By combining such distinct sources of data, organizations are able to construct risk profiles and attribute attrition scores to specific employees. Such scores provide an educated estimate of the probability of an employee exiting the organization during a specified time period, enabling HR professionals to act early on with targeted retention efforts (Bonney et al., 2024).

Predictive HR analytics also has some use in real life where retention is an issue. It can be used for early detection of those employees who will likely become at risk. For example, a high-potential employee who has been skipped over for a promotion, or has gotten a negative performance review after an otherwise good past history, will begin to disengage. These conditions are recognizable through forecasting models, and the manager will be able to initiate positive dialogues or coaching or divert training paths (Carrara, 2024).

Predictive analytics enables segmentation and targeting. Not every worker is an equally risky flight risk, nor every flight equally undesirable. Organizations can invest in retention where it is most effective by stratifying low-risk employees from high-risk employees—and high-value occupations from lower-value occupations. This may involve tailored incentives, workload modification, internal mobility, or even job role redesign (Chertow et al., 2024). Predictive analytics can be used to inform policy and organizational design. Where analysis reveals that employees in a particular department or under a particular manager experience higher turnover than others, this may be a sign of expectation mismatch, leadership problems, or cultural disease. The company might then need to make more substantial structural changes than tactical retention efforts. Predictive HR analytics can also facilitate strategic workforce planning. With the prediction of attrition rates of different job families, geographies, or experience levels, the organizations can predict future talent gaps and pipeline requirements more precisely. Succession planning is easier and recruitment policies are improved (Pu et al., 2024; Xiao, Yan, & Bamber, 2025; Sharma, Bhattacharya, & Bhattacharya, 2025).

For getting the most out of predictive HR analytics with its advantage not diluted, organizations will have to transition to a people-first process. That is, they will have to integrate predictive tools within a broader culture of empathy, conversation, and transparency. HR professionals will have to be trained not just in technical competencies (e.g., data analysis, model validation) but also in transformational leadership and ethical decision-making. Predictive analytics must be positioned within a continuous learning process (Gupta et al., 2025; Bar-Gil, Ron, & Czerniak, 2024). The models will need to be re-tested, validated, and re-scaled continually against changing organizational conditions. There also needs to be feedback mechanisms—through which the staff are able to input issues or flag contextual nuances within the data—embedded within the analytics process. The optimal application of predictive HR analytics is therefore not in emotionless prediction but in getting the right balance of rational, empathetic, and contextual interventions. It is not just a case of knowing who is most likely to leave, but why, and acting sensibly, responsibly, and with empathy (Yadav, 2025; John & Pramila, 2025; Lenka & Chanda, 2025).

Table 5.2 summarizes key aspects of predictive HR analytics for talent retention. The structure highlights critical dimensions such as purpose, data sources, techniques, benefits, challenges, and ethical considerations.

IBM is no stranger to being an early adopter of advanced analytics and artificial intelligence applications within the HR space. Faced with the challenge of rising attrition rates among high-performing employees in key technical roles, IBM developed a bespoke AI-based predictive analytics tool that would forecast employee resignations with remarkable accuracy—up to 95%, according to internal reports. The platform ingested data from over 30 sources, including performance reviews, pay trends, internal movement, employee sentiment, and even management feedback patterns. Through the application of machine learning algorithms to the data, IBM was able to come up with individualized attrition risk scores. Alerts were sent to HR business partners with lists of the names of employees

TABLE 5.2 Predictive HR analytics for talent retention

Dimension	Description
Objective	The primary objective of predictive HR analytics for employee retention is to identify, in advance, those individuals most likely to leave the organization—even before they have consciously considered doing so. This proactive approach enables HR managers and executives to implement targeted, tailored retention strategies for at-risk employees, thereby reducing turnover without waiting for formal resignation notices.
Key questions addressed	Predictive analytics offers some of the most significant solutions to problems of staff stability. It aims to find out who from the staff are most likely to leave, what motivates them or are the most likely motivators that are propelling them in this direction, when to anticipate it will occur, and what targeted interventions are most likely to prevent it.
Primary data sources	The most common sources of data are demographic factors like age, tenure, and education level and internal HR data like performance appraisal, attendance records, promotion and pay history, employee attitudes, and exit interview data. These factors provide the lion's share of predictive modeling.
Advanced data sources	Even more sophisticated data feeds can be utilized to power model precision. These are some of the following: internal communication network analysis, collaboration behavior data from internal collaboration platforms, real-time sentiment via pulse surveys, and external labor market data. These data offer an even more complete and dynamic picture of worker behavior and risk.
Analytical techniques	Several statistical and machine learning techniques are employed for predictive HR analytics. They encompass logistic regression for categoric responses, decision trees, and ensemble methods such as random forests, survival analysis to determine time to leave, and natural language processing for unstructured text data collected through comments or surveys.
Outputs	Predictive model results are usually returned as individual attrition risk scores, interactive HR professional dashboards, risk segments by worker type, and scenario-based projections for planning targeted initiatives and resource allocation.
Strategic applications	Predictive data can be used in numerous strategic modes. They offer early warning of potential talent exits, action on specific jobs or stars to retain, clear HR policy and organizational form guidance more widely, and involvement in employee development programs and motivation initiatives at individual levels.
Benefits	The value of retention predictive analytics cannot be captured. They are real return on turnover investments, enhanced employee satisfaction and productivity, better and more data-driven human capital planning, and building an early warning system that would advise organizations of future retention challenges.
Challenges	Despite its benefits, there are some challenges in applying predictive HR analytics. These include low-quality or unstable data, analytically competent individuals being in short supply across all HR functions, model complexity whose results are hard to interpret, and manager and employee resistance to data-driven decision-making.
Ethical considerations	Ethical issues are center-stage in ethical uses of predictive HR analytics. First on their agenda are the privacy of employee data, informed consent, transparency of predictive tool use, lack of algorithmic bias for past prejudice, and human judgment as the fulcrum of interpretation and response to analytics.
Best practices	These best practices include updating and enshrining models in a consistent cycle, enabling data science and HR collaboration, establishment of ethical governing structures, and transparency of communications to employees of goals and safeguarding of employment of predictive analytics. These practices facilitate building trust and enhance the credibility of the analytics program.

Source: Author's own work.

who were most likely statistically to leave. Importantly, the model was not built in isolation. Human intervention was nevertheless essential; the managers were trained to read these signals contextually and initiate quality conversations with at-risk employees. In the majority of cases, interventions were in the form of customized development plans, mentoring, project rotation, or compensation structure modification.

The reward was tangible. IBM experienced substantial cost savings—some $300 million over several years—directly related to the reduction in turnover. More importantly, the project assisted in driving a cultural shift toward fact-based HR, in which retention efforts became more individualized, proactive, and business-focused.

Ascension Health, a premier United States not-for-profit healthcare system, was faced with an acute retention issue among its nurses. This level of turnover among this group not only incurred high training and recruitment costs but also negatively affected continuity of patient care and morale among the rest of the staff. The firm initiated a predictive HR analytics initiative for the analysis and reduction of nurse attrition. The analytics team in HR collected and analyzed data from a wide range of sources, including shift patterns, unit assignments, years of experience, engagement survey results, records of absenteeism, and responses to exit interviews. They discovered that nurses who had been rotated through more than two different units in a six-month period, or who permanently worked night shifts with no rotation, exhibited much higher turnover risk.

Based on these findings, Ascension built a predictive model that identified high-risk nurses and facilitated early intervention. Managers were provided with monthly dashboards that identified employees with high risk scores. Interventions consisted of balancing workload, flexible scheduling, access to wellness programs, and more communication from nursing leadership. Nurse turnover fell by more than 15% within a year. In addition, employee satisfaction scores improved in multiple dimensions, such as work-life balance and support from leadership. This case showed how even a less technology-intensive industry can derive benefit from predictive analytics if executed with sensitivity to human factors and operational constraints.

Credit Suisse, one of the world's leading financial services providers, turned to predictive HR analytics to understand and address early-career employee attrition—a challenge that was particularly acute in their investment banking division. The company created a composite data model from employee background information (education, prior experience), internal performance metrics, promotion trajectories, manager engagement levels, and pulse survey responses. Surprisingly, the analysis revealed that employees who had graduated from elite universities were more likely to leave within the first 18 months unless they were given early project ownership or global assignment opportunities.

From these insights, Credit Suisse created a "predictive engagement index" that identified high-potential employees who were at risk of disengaging unless they were given focused career acceleration. Talent management programs were redesigned to create accelerated pathways into leadership roles for selected cohorts. Managers were also coached to enhance feedback frequency and mentoring quality for employees who had been flagged as retention risks. The outcome was significant: early-career attrition dropped by over 20%, and the company saw improved internal mobility rates, an indicator of greater organizational commitment. The case underscored the importance of linking predictive analytics to overall talent strategy and the role of leadership in turning data insights into action.

5.3 AI IN GREEN HRM: REDUCING THE ENVIRONMENTAL IMPACT OF HR OPERATIONS

Human Resource Management (HRM) was a mere administrative function, but now it is a dynamic change agent—largely for environmental sustainability. Its metamorphosis could loosely be termed as Green HRM (GHRM), a practice incorporating environmental sensitivity into selection, training, appraisal, and general human resource management. During this green revolution process, artificial intelligence (AI) has also begun to play a role in founding capacities to reduce the environmental footprint of HR activities. The current essay lays particular emphasis on the way AI-based technologies are transforming Green HRM practices to make HR activities smarter, productive, and greener (John & Pramila, 2024; Tiwari et al., 2021; Garg, Srivastav, & Gupta, 2018).

Green HRM refers to such policies, practices, and systems that encourage sustainable usage of resources within business organizations and for the cause of overall environmental protection. It focuses not only on waste and emission reduction but also on raising environmental awareness among employees (Khan et al., 2025; Alafadel et al., 2025). Green HRM represents a collection of activities—a portfolio of e-paper recruitment, energy-saving office habits, green training measures, and encouraging telecommuting activities that reduce transport emissions (Vadithe, Rajput, & Kesari, 2025). While, previously, greening of HR practices was policy-prescription-driven and interventionist through manual processes (Nguyen & Nguyen , 2025), such measures, regardless of good intention, have been otherwise restricted in scope, specificity, as well as real-time feedback loops. With growing sustainability challenges, organizations are looking toward AI for introducing automation, intelligence, and responsiveness in sustainable HR practices (Chand et al., 2023; Sharif & Malik, 2025).

Artificial intelligence, as a part of HRM, is a range of technologies—ranging from machine learning and natural language processing to robotic process automation and intelligent chatbots. As a component of HR software, AI has the potential to lower significantly environmental costs that accompany traditional HR practices. Direct usage occurs in e-recruitment (John & Pramila, 2024). AI-based tools' screening of job candidates and video interviewing reduce organizations' paper work as well as interview-based travel over distances. CV parsing done by automated processes saves on the printing and storage cost of paper copies. Similarly, onboarding software based on AI can provide orientation and training modules through the internet, reducing carbon emissions and saving paper that would otherwise be wasted due to trips to centralized training (John & Pramila, 2025). Virtual collaboration software based on AI facilitates HR teams to facilitate and ensure hybrid or complete remote working setups.

This not only proves cheaper but also benefits the environment directly: less daily travel means less traffic on the road and a smaller overall emissions figure. AI can monitor productivity, interest, and satisfaction of workers in telework environments, so the environmental benefit is not achieved at the expense of employee productivity or disposition (Rashmi & Preeti, 2023). In managing employee performance, AI is used for automatically collecting and analyzing the employees' feedback, with reduced paper surveys and in-person interviews. Predictive employee satisfaction and risk of retention can be provided by the systems in such a manner that interventions can be individually focused without an environmental cost for travel or wasteful resource utilization.

The AI contribution to Green HRM is not just in operational effectiveness but also in enabling effective behavioral change, the secret to sustainability in the long term (Shahzad et al., 2025).

Workers' conduct—e.g., energy use, waste management, or even office material usage behavior—can be monitored by AI systems against which specific advice or nudge messages can be set off to facilitate more sustainable behavior (Chand et al., 2023; Din, Yang, & Zhang, 2025). For instance, the facilities management system, via artificial intelligence, is able to track the usage habits of intelligent office appliances (e.g., printers, HVAC, or lights) and compare this to the habits of the employees (Wolniak & Jonek-Kowalska, 2022; Jonek-Kowalska & Wolniak, 2023; Jonek-Kowalska & Wolniak, 2025). In turn, the system is then able to raise the alert, for example, that some departments keep the lights on after midnight. It becomes possible, respectively, to remotely trigger reminder messages or even shutdown procedures. These tiny efforts on a small scale can entail a phenomenal saving of energy and minimization of operation waste in the long run (Hossain et al., 2025; Abid et al., 2024). Even worker opinions on issues of green policy, green transportation behavior, or recycling behavior may be automated by AI chatbots so that availability of information and green practice enforcers in the company are assured (Gajdzik et al., 2024a, 2024b).

With more use of ESG metrics in business valuation and regulation, AI is a plus in the sense that data capture is automated and sustainability reporting may be merged with HR practices. AI-driven solutions are able to bring together environment data from multiple HR systems—tracking, for example, travel emissions, telework rates, and environmental training modules (John & Pramila, 2024). Such systems can then generate dynamic visualizations and dashboards in a way where real-time monitoring of progress can be facilitated by both HR leaders and sustainability officers. This integration allows for transparency, regulatory compliance, as well as strategic alignment of environmental goals with HR practice. Predictive analytics can be used for predicting the likely environmental effect of different HR-based policies in order to make informed decisions (Rashmi & Preti, 2023).

Artificial intelligence, properly used in the context of Green HRM practice, is one of the major pathways for the minimization of the environmental footprint of HR activity (Shahzad et al., 2025).

From enabling remote work and e-recruitment to influencing behavior and intelligent sustainability reporting, AI promises a new era of eco-efficiency and strategic

TABLE 5.3 AI implementation in Green HRM (Human Resource Management)

Dimension	Description
Strategic purpose	AI assists HR functions in moving away from their traditional administrative roles and becoming drivers of environmental sustainability through the streamlining and minimizing of green processes.
Recruitment and onboarding	AI-powered digital platforms enable paperless hiring, automated resume screening, and electronic interview and induction processes, cutting down on printing, commuting, and power consumption by a considerable amount.
Remote and hybrid work	Artificial intelligence technology enables off-site monitoring of productivity and management and hence enables flexible working hours that minimize daily transportation and the carbon footprint of office operations.
Digital training	AI-based virtual training simulations enable personalized, interactive, and completely digital training modules that eliminate paper-based documentation and extensive face-to-face interaction.
Behavioral nudging	AI solutions track the activities of employees and give them instant feedback or gentle reminder alerts to promote energy-saving habits, such as lights-off, waste reduction, or fewer prints.
Facilities and resource use	Integrated into intelligent buildings, AI can track and control office energy, water, lighting, and HVAC consumption according to employee activity and movement.
Performance management	AI substitutes feedback gathering and performance measurement with no paper or meetings, which renders processes leaner with fewer resources being utilized.
Sustainability reporting	AI interlaces environmental intelligence from HR solutions and generates real-time sustainability reports to enable organizations to track green KPIs and address ESG compliance requirements.
Employee engagement	Intelligent chatbots and AI assistants remind staff of green policies, promote sustainable commutes or recycling habits, and activate eco-friendly culture.
Challenges	While AI allows environmental success, it also takes digital energy; there has to be ethical utilization of the workers' data, explainability of the algorithm, and energy-saving infrastructure.
Long-term benefits	Use of AI in Green HRM saves the planet, improves the reputation of the organization, helps in attracting green employees, and meets global sustainability goals.

Source: Author's own work.

transparency. These benefits will not, however, occur automatically. They are the product of careful planning, ethical deployment, and strict adherence to the values of openness, accountability, and inclusiveness. As increasingly more businesses are put under pressure to go green, AI Green HRM will be an even greater game-changer—a differentiator, but most importantly—a long-term condition of survival for business and social legitimacy (Saini, Bhardwaj, & Gupta, 2023; Chand et al., 2023). Adoption of AI in Green HRM (Human Resource Management) is shown in Table 5.3. The table presents an orderly summary of how AI minimizes the environmental footprint of HR practices, segmented into pertinent dimensions with explanatory narrative points.

5.4 AUTOMATION AND ITS IMPLICATIONS FOR JOB SECURITY

Automation causing job loss is not new. Indeed, with every technological revolution in the past—the Industrial Revolution, the revolution in agriculture, etc.—there were fears of widescale job loss. What is new in the current wave, however, is how rapidly and on what a mass scale AI is developing and how much work it can do now. Unlike earlier innovations that were mostly displacing labor, AI is capable of emulating mental processes long thought to be uniquely human. Natural language processing, pattern recognition, decision-making, and even parts of creativity are at the machine's grasp (Mohaned Saad, 2025).

Manufacturing, transport, and customer service are particularly at risk. Autonomous vehicles put truck drivers out of work; chatbots are increasingly taking over customer service personnel; and high-tech robots can now assemble complex products with minimal human touch. Worse, white-collar work is no longer secure. Software is reviewing legal documents, preparing accounting reports, and even accurately diagnosing medical disease. According to research conducted by organizations like McKinsey Global Institute and World Economic Forum, millions of jobs can be automated over the next few decades. New professions will definitely emerge—most often as human-machine partnerships—yet the mismatch between emerging needs for work and existing labor force skills is a widespread concern (Malheiros, Lima, & Oran, 2024).

Consequences of mass job loss are multifaceted and long-lasting. Economically, the laid-off workers can face extended periods of unemployment or underemployment, which translate into lost income and purchasing power. This affects consumer demand and reduces the overall growth of the economy (Bhargava, Bester, & Bolton, 2021). Socially, the effect of job loss can be severe, with increased anxiety, depression, and isolation. For those societies that are more employment-based and thus more vulnerable to automation, whole societies will be economically impacted and even decline. Automation can increase inequality. More educated and technologically skilled individuals will succeed in the age of AI, while those in low-wage or routine jobs will be at greater risk of getting displaced. Such a trend might widen the gap between the poor and the rich, also further polarizing countries (Dowdeswell & Websdale, 2023; Mohamed Saad, 2024).

It requires a collective, proactive action on the part of of governments, businesses, education institutions, and workers themselves to meet these challenges. The basis of that action is reskilling—equipping workers with the skill and ability needed to transition to new, sustainable practices of work (Malik, 2024).

Reskilling is not just a technical issue; it is a social imperative. Successful reskilling programs must be inclusive, responsive, and forward-looking. They must be concerned not only with technical skills such as data analysis or coding, but also with soft skills—critical thinking, creativity, emotional intelligence—which are less prone to automation. Public-private partnerships (Budijono et al., 2024) is one of the most important strategies. Governments can also finance, create infrastructure, and provide policy incentives, with private businesses contributing industry expertise and in-work training. For instance, technology leaders IBM and Google have launched initiatives that focus on training employees in cloud computing, cyber security, and other emerging areas. Meanwhile, other governments are testing out lifelong learning accounts and tax benefits for businesses that invest in worker development (Budijono et al., 2024).

Education systems have to change as well. Old models of education are received upfront by youths and then get stuck there throughout a lifetime. They do not suit the dynamics of a rapidly changing job market very well. Instead, a more modular and lifelong learning model is needed. Micro-credentials, online courses, and competency-based certifications can enable workers to acquire new skills in a low-cost and flexible manner. Second, vocational training must be enhanced to incorporate AI literacy, data analysis, and online collaboration *(Al-Ansari & Al-Medfa, 2023). The second most important feature is career guidance and job matching. AI can be utilized autonomously to monitor labor market developments and recommend specific learning paths for an individual. Websites that provide matching of training courses with in-time available vacant jobs can reduce labor market frictions and encourage a smooth transition (Bhargava, Bester, & Bolton, 2021). Finally, there will have to be a shift in society's imagination of work and career advancement. In a world where a single lifetime of labor in one job is no longer the rule, flexibility and relentless self-redefinition must become recognized as fundamental values. Thereafter, employers ought to develop organizational culture so as to enable learning and internal mobility (Ghorbanzadeh et al., 2024).

Table 5.4 categorizes different sectors, types of tasks, levels of automation risk, and implications for job security, along with suggested mitigation strategies.

TABLE 5.4 Automation and its implications for job security

Sector	Types of tasks	Level of automation risk	Implications for job security	Suggested mitigation strategies
Manufacturing	Repetitive assembly, quality inspection, welding	High	Substantial job displacement in routine manual jobs. Human oversight still necessary for maintenance and safety.	Upskilling in robot maintenance, AI monitoring systems, and industrial design.
Transportation and logistics	Driving, scheduling, route optimization	High	AI planning tools and driverless vehicles threaten traditional driving jobs (e.g., taxis, trucks). New roles in fleet management emerging.	Training in logistics coordination, operation of AI systems, and vehicle maintenance.
Retail and customer service	Checkout operations, customer queries, inventory tracking	Medium to High	Kiosks and chatbots reduce need for human clerks. Human interaction and problem-solving jobs still needed.	Reskilling in customer experience, conflict handling, and digital sales platforms.
Financial services	Data entry, auditing, fraud detection	Medium to High	AI effectively performs risk analysis and document processing. Analytical and advisory roles still useful.	Training in financial analytics, regulation compliance, and advisory services.

TABLE 5.4 (*Continued*)

Sector	Types of tasks	Level of automation risk	Implications for job security	Suggested mitigation strategies
Healthcare	Diagnostics, administrative tasks, robotic surgery	Medium	AI assists with diagnosis and scheduling. Human empathy and clinical judgment remain unbeatable.	Reskilling in health informatics, AI-assisted diagnosis, and patient-centered care models.
Education	Grading, content delivery, tutoring	Medium	Online modules and AI tutors augment human teaching. Still, mentorship and social learning require human presence.	Training teachers in EdTech tools, digital pedagogy, and adaptive learning systems.
Legal compliance	Contract review, legal research, case analysis	Medium	AI reduces routine legal research time. Judgment-intensive tasks remain with humans.	Upskilling in ethical reasoning, case strategy, and technology-assisted law.
Creative industries	Content generation, video editing, music composition	Low to Medium	AI assists but rarely replaces creativity. Human imagination and emotional nuance remain one of a kind.	Building hybrid skills: using AI as a tool to enhance design, writing, and storytelling.
Agriculture	Harvesting, soil analysis, drone monitoring	Medium	Mechanization and precision agro tools reduce physical labor. Supervisory and tech support roles increase.	Learning agri-tech tools, drone operation, and sustainable agriculture techniques.
Construction	Bricklaying, site surveying, materials transport	Medium	Automation aids physical work but skilled trade and safety jobs are still human-oriented.	Cross-learning in digital blueprinting, safety inspection, and construction robotics.
Public sector	Records management, form processing, administrative tasks	Medium	AI can help bureaucratize, making clerical jobs fewer. Yet, citizen-facing services continue to need interpersonal interaction.	Reskilling in digital administration, policy analysis, and public communication.

Source: Author's own work.

REFERENCES

Abid, U. B., Faisal, M. N., Al-Esmael, B., Farooq, Z. H., & Nassour, S. (2024). Exploring the moderating role of technological competence and artificial intelligence in green HRM | Badanie moderującej roli kompetencji technologicznych i sztucznej inteligencji w zielonym HRM. *Polish Journal of Management Studies, 29*(2), 7–22.

Al-Ansari, A. M., & Al-Medfa, M. K. (2023). Psychiatrists' attitudes toward artificial intelligence: tasks, job security and benefits. *Bahrain Medical Bulletin, 45*(3), 1528–1531.

Alfadel, A., Al-Kahtani, S. M., Al-Mekhlafi, A.-W. A.-G. S., Alhebri, A., & Ahmed, A. (2025). Fostering sustainable development: the role of green HRM and green work engagement. *Discover Sustainability, 6*(1), 300.

Allil, K. (2023). *Synergizing AI and HRM: leveraging business analytics for a future-ready workforce.* In *Exploring the intersection of AI and human resources management* (pp. 182–201). Business Science Reference.

Bar-Gil, O., Ron, T., & Czerniak, O. (2024). AI for the people? Embedding AI ethics in HR and people analytics projects. *Technology in Society, 77*, 102527.

Bhargava, A., Bester, M., & Bolton, L. (2021). Employees' perceptions of the implementation of robotics, artificial intelligence, and automation (RAIA) on job satisfaction, job security, and employability. *Journal of Technology in Behavioral Science, 6*(1), 106–113.

Bonney, K., Breaux, C., Buffington, C., Kroff, Z., & Savage, K. (2024). The impact of AI on the workforce: tasks versus jobs? *Economics Letters, 244*, 111971.

Budijono, K., Hariyanto, M., Adnan, A. M., & Rosman, D. (2024). The impact of robotic, artificial intelligence, and service automation adoption on job security perception and work performance in hospitality sector. In *Proceedings of the 2024 9th International Conference on Business and Industrial Research (ICBIR 2024)* (pp. 691–695). IEEE.

Carrara, T. (2024). Generative-AI empowers workforce. *Manufacturing Engineering, 173*(3), 14–15.

Chand, R., Narula, G. S., Nijjer, S., & Jandwani, A. (2023). Utilizing AI in sustaining green HRM practices – a digital initiative towards socially responsible and environment sustainability. In *Proceedings of the IEEE 2023 5th International Conference on Advances in Computing, Communication Control and Networking (ICAC3N 2023)* (pp. 541–544). IEEE.

Chandratreya, A. (2025). The AI revolution implications for workforce dynamics and employment in supply chains. In *Ecological and human dimensions of AI-based supply chain* (pp. 433–460). Business Science Reference.

Chertow, M., Reck, B. K., Wrzesniewski, A., & Calli, B. (2024). Outlook on the future role of robots and AI in material recovery facilities: implications for U.S. recycling and the workforce. *Journal of Cleaner Production, 470*, 143234.

Din, A. U., Yang, Y., & Zhang, Y. (2025). The psychological benefits of green HRM: a study of employee well-being, engagement, and green behavior in the healthcare sector. *Acta Psychologica, 254*, 104823.

Dowdeswell, R., & Websdale, D. (2023). AI set to improve job security in the marine survey sector. *Hydro International, 27*(5), 61–63.

Gajdzik, B., Bartuś, K., Jaciow, M., Wolniak, R., Wolny, R., & Grebski, W. (2024a). Evolution of Polish e-consumers' environmental awareness and purchasing behavior over ten years. *Sustainability, 16*(11), 1–29.

Gajdzik, B., Jaciow, M., Hoffmann-Burdzińska, K., Wolny, R., Wolniak, R., & Grebski, W. (2024b). Impact of economic awareness on sustainable energy consumption: results of research in a segment of Polish households. *Energies, 17*(11), 1–31.

Gajdzik, B., Nagaj, R., Wolniak, R., Bałaga, D., Žuromskaitė, B., & Grebski, W. (2024c). Renewable energy share in European industry: analysis and extrapolation of trends in EU countries. *Energies, 17*(11), 1–38.

Gajdzik, B., Wolniak, R., & Grebski, W. (2023). Electricity and heat demand in steel industry technological processes in Industry 4.0 conditions. *Energies, 16*(2), 1–29.

Gajdzik, B., Wolniak, R., & Grebski, W. (2024d). Changes in the steel chain in Industry 4.0: some results of survey on the Polish steel market. *Production Engineering Archives, 30*(1), 1–16.

Gajdzik, B., Wolniak, R., Grebski, W., Szymszal, J., & Grebski, M. E. (2025). *Sustainability and smart manufacturing: the transformation of the steelwork industry*, Routledge.

Garg, V., Srivastav, S., & Gupta, A. (2018). Application of artificial intelligence for sustaining green human resource management. In *2018 International Conference on Automation and Computational Engineering (ICACE 2018)* (pp. 113–116). IEEE.

Ghorbanzadeh, D., Espinosa-Cristia, J. F., Abdelrasheed, N. S. G., Askar, S., & Almufti, S. M. (2024). Role of innovative behaviour as a missing linchpin in artificial intelligence adoption to enhancing job security and job performance. *Systems Research and Behavioral Science.* https://onlinelibrary.wiley.com/doi/epdf/10.1002/sres.3076

Gupta, R., Kumar, S., Karad, S., Lenka, R., & Nikam, P. (2025). Assessing the effect of AI-powered HR analytics on electronics m anufacturing decision-making. In *1st International Conference on Advances in Computer Science, Electrical, Electronics, and Communication Technologies (CE2CT 2025)* (pp. 862–867). IEEE.

Hare, B. K., Gladbach, J., Shah, S. J., & Xu, D. (2025). Building AI-powered responsible workforce by integrating large language models into computer science curriculum. In *Proceedings of the 56th ACM Technical Symposium on Computer Science Education* (Vol. 2, pp. 1709–1710).

Higgins, O., & Wilson, R. L. (2025). Integrating artificial intelligence (AI) with workforce solutions for sustainable care: a follow-up to artificial intelligence and machine learning (ML) based decision support systems in mental health. *International Journal of Mental Health Nursing, 34*(2), e70019.

Hole, S. R., Kolluru, V., Gangul, R., Chintakunta, A. N., & Mungara, S. (2025). AI-driven mobile healthcare: societal impact, workforce adaptation, and enhanced predictive modeling for diabetes risk assessment. In *Proceedings of the 2025 International Conference on Pervasive Computational Technologies (ICPCT 2025)* (pp. 557–564). IEEE.

Hossain, M. I., Islam, M. T., Kumar, J., & Jamadar, Y. (2025). Harnessing STARA for enhancing green performance of hospitality industry: Green HRM, employees' commitment as mediators and psychological climate as moderator. *Journal of Hospitality and Tourism Insights, 8*(6), 2117–2139.

Ianc, C. G., Dincă, L. G., & Ghinea, A. (2025). Future workforce and corporate accountability in AI-enhanced educational activities: addressing the impact on employment and ethical practice. In *Proceedings of the International Conference on Virtual Learning* (Vol. 20, pp. 243–253).

John, J. E., & Pramila, S. (2024). Integrating AI tools into HRM to promote green HRM practices. In *Lecture Notes in Networks and Systems* (Vol. 878, pp. 249–259).

John, J. E., & Pramila, S. (2025). Leveraging AI in HR analytics to foster green human resource management. In *Studies in Systems, Decision and Control* (Vol. 555, pp. 1067–1074).

Johnson, C. C., Harold, S., Chestnut, J., Glover, K., & Walton, J. B. (2025). Addressing the artificial intelligence (AI) talent gap: outcomes of the first U.S. nationally-registered AI apprenticeship program. *Education Sciences, 15*(3), 324.

Jonek-Kowalska, I., Wolniak, R., Marinina, O. A., & Ponomarenko, T. V. (2022). *Stakeholders, sustainable development policies and the coal mining industry: perspectives from Europe and the Commonwealth of Independent States*, Routledge.

Jonek-Kowalska, I., & Wolniak, R. (2023). *Towards sustainability and a better quality of life?*, Routledge.

Jonek-Kowalska, I., & Wolniak, R. (2025). *Exclusion in Smart Cities assessment and strategy for strengthening resilience*, Routledge.

Kadirov, A., Shakirova, Y., Ismoilova, G., & Makhmudova, N. (2024). AI in human resource management: reimagining talent acquisition, development, and retention. In *2024 International Conference on Knowledge Engineering and Communication Systems (ICKECS 2024)*. IEEE.

Khan, K., Gogia, E. H., Shao, Z., Rehman, M. Z., & Ullah, A. (2025). The impact of green HRM practices on green innovative work behaviour: empirical evidence from the hospitality sector of China and Pakistan. *BMC Psychology, 13*(1), 96.

Krishna, S., & Sidharth, S. (2023). AI-powered workforce analytics: maximizing business and employee success through predictive attrition modelling. *International Journal of Performability Engineering, 19*(3), 203–215.

Kumar, R., Singh, A., Kassar, A. S. A., Joshi, S., & Sharma, M. (2025). Unlocking the power of AI: healthcare workforce perception and its impact on their work performance in Saudi Arabia. *Pakistan Journal of Medical Sciences, 41*(3), 682–686.

Lee, H.-H. S. (2025). Rise of the agentic AI workforce. *IEEE Micro, 45*(1), 4–5.

Lenka, R., & Chanda, R. (2025). Generative AI for predicting employee engagement in HR analytics: a bibliometric analysis. In *Lecture Notes in Networks and Systems* (Vol. 1162, pp. 201–209).

Malheiros, P. S., Lima, R. R., & Oran, A. C. (2024). Impact of generative AI technologies on software development professionals' perceptions of job security. In *ACM International Conference Proceeding Series* (pp. 169–178). ACM International Conference Proceeding Series.

Malik, A. (2024). A study on the relationship of artificial intelligence applications in HR processes for assessing employee engagement, performance, and job security. *International Review of Management and Marketing, 14*(5), 216–221.

Mobo, F. D. (2025). AI in green HR practices: sustainable workforce management. In *Convergence of AI, education, and business for sustainability* (pp. 195–214). IGI Global.

Mohamed Saad, A. M. A. (2024). Adapting accountants to the AI revolution: university strategies for skill enhancement, job security and competence in accounting. *Higher Education, Skills and Work-based Learning, 15*(2), 290–305.

Nguyen, L. Q., & Nguyen, T. N. (2025). Exploring the relationship of green HRM practices with sustainable performance: the mediating effect of green innovation. *Journal of Hospitality and Tourism Insights, 8*(5), 1665–1687.

Omar, A., & Weilbach, L. (2025). AI integration in smart factories: a systematic review of success factors and challenges in operational efficiency and workforce development. In *Proceedings of the International Conferences IADIS Information Systems 2025 and e-Society 2025* (pp. 33–40). IADIS.

Pandita, S., Sharma, G., Sharma, N., & Sharma, N. (2025). AI in training and development: upskilling the workforce. In *Human resource management and artificial intelligence: automating and optimizing processes* (pp. 84–104). Routledge.

Pu, C., Liu, C., Wang, Y., & Du, L. (2024). Frontiers of emerging AI technologies: best practices and workforce development in transportation. *Journal of Transportation Engineering Part A: Systems, 150*(9), 02524002-1.

Rashmi, S., & Preeti, T. (2023). The effect of artificial intelligence-enabled work from the home culture in strengthening the green HRM. In *AIP Conference Proceedings, 2721*(1), 070025.

Ravesangar, K., Ng, W. C., Toh, G. G., & Singh, B. (2025). AI-powered talent acquisition: revolutionizing the hiring process. In *Artificial intelligence in peace, justice, and strong institutions* (pp. 1–21). IGI Global.

Rosak-Szyrocka J., & Wolniak, R. (2025) *Smart universities in Smart Cities shaping the future of education and urban innovation*, Routledge.

Saini, H. K., Bhardwaj, K., & Gupta, S. (2023). Technological advances in green human resource management using machine learning. In *2023 International Conference on Advances in Computation, Communication and Information Technology (ICAICCIT 2023)* (pp. 224–229). IEEE.

Savelka, J., Kultur, C., Agarwal, A., Zhang, A., & Sakr, M. (2025). AI technicians: developing rapid occupational training methods for a competitive AI workforce. In *Proceedings of the 56th ACM Technical Symposium on Computer Science Education* (Vol. 1, pp. 1029–1035).

Shahzad, M. A., Chen, S., Iqbal, T., & Li, Z. (2025). Sustainable futures: leveraging green intellectual capital, HRM, innovation and leadership. *Journal of Intellectual Capital, 26*(3), 807–838.

Sharif, S., & Malik, S. A. (2025). Does green HRM and intellectual capital strengthen psychological green climate, green behaviors and creativity? A step towards green textile manufacturing. *Journal of Intellectual Capital, 26*(3), 644–669.

Sharma, P., Bhattacharya, S., & Bhattacharya, S. (2025). HR analytics and AI adoption in IT sector: reflections from practitioners. *Journal of Work-Applied Management.* https://doi.org/10.1108/JWAM-12-2024-0179. www.emerald.com/jwam/article-pdf/doi/10.1108/JWAM-12-2024-0179/9774843/jwam-12-2024-0179.pdf

Shi, L. (2025). Global perspectives on AI competence development: analyzing national AI strategies in education and workforce policies. *Human Resource Development Review.* (Article in press).

Siwiec, D., Gajdzik, B., Gawlik, R., Wolniak, R., & Pacana, A. (2025). Open eco-innovations in sustainable product development: model framework of design thinking in quality life cycle assessment (DT-QLCA). *Journal of Open Innovation: Technology, Market, and Complexity, 11*(1), 1–24.

Skubis, I., Wolniak, R., & Grebski, W. W. (2024). AI and human-centric approach in smart cities management: case studies from Silesian and Lesser Poland Voivodships. *Sustainability, 16*(18), Article 8279, 1–26.

Stecuła, K., & Wolniak, R. (2022a). Advantages and disadvantages of e-learning innovations during COVID-19 pandemic in higher education in Poland. *Journal of Open Innovation: Technology, Market, and Complexity, 8*(3), 159.

Stecuła, K., & Wolniak, R. (2022b). Influence of COVID-19 pandemic on dissemination of innovative e-learning tools in higher education in Poland. *Journal of Open Innovation: Technology, Market, and Complexity, 8*(2), 89.

Tariq, M. U. (2024). AI and the future of talent management: transforming recruitment and retention with machine learning. In *Global practices on effective talent acquisition and retention* (pp. 1–16). IGI Global.

Tenakwah, E. S., & Watson, C. (2025). Embracing the AI/automation age: preparing your workforce for humans and machines working together. *Strategy and Leadership, 53*(1), 32–48.

Tiwari, P., Pandey, R., Garg, V., & Singhal, A. (2021). Application of artificial intelligence in human resource management practices. In *Proceedings of the Confluence*

2021: 11th International Conference on Cloud Computing, Data Science and Engineering (pp. 159–163). IEEE.

Tona, O., Leidner, D. E., van der Meulen, N., Nunes, J., & Shagam, D. (2025). The deployment of AI to infer employee skills: insights from Johnson & Johnson's digital-first workforce initiative. *Information Systems Journal.* (Article in press).

Vadithe, R. N., Rajput, R. C., & Kesari, B. (2025). Impact of green HRM implementation on organizational sustainability in IT sector: a mediation analysis. *Sustainable Futures, 9*, 100507.

Wolniak, R., & Grebski, W. (2025). Sustainable trends and determinants of wheat cultivation in Poland (2004–2023): a spatiotemporal analysis of productivity, resilience, and climate adaptation. *Sustainability, 17*(5), 1–35.

Wolniak, R., & Stecuła, K. (2024). Evaluation of quality of innovative e-learning in higher education: an insight from Poland. *Applied System Innovation, 7*(6), 109. https://doi.org/10.3390/asi7060109.

Wolniak, R., Stecuła, K., & Aydın, B. (2024a). Digital transformation of grocery in-store shopping - scanners, artificial intelligence, augmented reality and beyond: a review. *Foods, 13*(18), Article 2948, 1–34.

Wolniak, R., Gajdzik, B., Grebski, M., Danel, R., & Grebski, W.W. (2024b). Business models used in Smart Cities—theoretical approach with examples of Smart Cities. *Smart Cities, 7*, 1626–1669.

Wolniak, R., & Jonek-Kowalska, I. (2022). The creative services sector in Polish cities. *J. Open Innov. Technol. Mark. Complex, 8*, 17.

Xiao, Q., Yan, J., & Bamber, G. J. (2025). How does AI-enabled HR analytics influence employee resilience: job crafting as a mediator and HRM system strength as a moderator. *Personnel Review, 54*(3), 824–843.

Yadav, G. (2025). AI and analytics conundrum: unpacking the barriers in modern HR with ISM and MICMAC analysis. *International Journal of Organizational Analysis*. Emerald Publishing Limited. https://doi.org/10.1108/IJOA-08-2024-4782. www.emerald.com/ijoa/article-abstract/doi/10.1108/IJOA-08-2024-4782/1259066/AI-and-analytics-conundrum-unpacking-the-barriers?redirectedFrom=fulltext

Yamamoto, M., Xu, S., Kee, K. F., & Li, W. (2025). Testing a dynamic model of trust in AI: how trust develops and affects critical thinking in the American workforce. *Journal of Trust Research, 15*(1), 12–31.

Yoshida, H., & İnce-Yenilmez, M. (2025). AI and workforce dynamics: unravelling productivity | Yapay zekâ ve işgücü dinamikleri: Üretkenliğin çözülmesi. *Sosyoekonomi, 33*(63), 143–159.

III

Ethical and Governance Frameworks for AI in HRM

CHAPTER 6

Ethical Considerations and AI Governance in HRM

6.1 THE ETHICAL CHALLENGES OF AI IN HR

AI holds out the prospect of more efficiency, consistency, and data-driven decision-making. With these technical advances, however, come tremendous ethical hurdles. AI in HR foreshadows significant issues of fairness, accountability, transparency, privacy, and the future of work. They are not simply technical issues—they are human-centered, at the heart of how organizations manage their people (Rao & Zhao, 2025).

Among the serious ethical concerns with AI in HR is perpetuating—or even intensifying—bias and discrimination. AI technology is only as objective as the data that have been used to train it. If the historical data used to train recruitment algorithms reflect existing biases, then such systems learn and magnify them. For instance, if a firm's previous hires were skewed toward male candidates, then an AI system trained on this data will automatically prefer the same type of profiles and systematically disadvantage women or nonbinary candidates (Groß, 2021).

The case of Amazon's AI recruitment tool from 2018 is one that is widely cited in this regard. The algorithm, which was trained on résumés received over ten years, picked up a gender bias against female candidates because past data reflected men holding technical roles previously (Beccalli, Elliot, & Virili, 2020). The example raises the ethical issue of deploying machine learning systems for sensitive domains without vigorous auditing and protection-against-bias policies. Recruitment unfairness is not just a legal or reputational issue—it is an ethical imperative on the basis of equal opportunity (Singh et al., 2025).

Another ethical concern is that so many AI systems are not transparent. Deep learning algorithms, for instance, are "black boxes" that make decisions by undertaking complex, nonobvious calculations that their own creators frequently cannot fully explain. This is

DOI: 10.1201/9781003668282-9

particularly an issue in HR, where people have decision results foisted upon them that affect their career and happiness (Bar-Gil, Ron, & Czerniak, 2024).

If a candidate is rejected by an AI system, he or she has both an ethical and, in most situations, a legal right to understand why. Several AI models are not able to produce explanations in natural language though. Such unexplainability is damaging to trust and can negate the legitimacy of organizational processes. AI in HR must be auditable and interpretable. Individuals must have a right to appeal and challenge decisions, particularly where decisions are taken or at least influenced by algorithms (Muralidharan et al., 2024; Wolniak et al., 2024b).

HR AI is being applied not only in recruitment but throughout the employee lifecycle. It varies between monitoring productivity, communication patterns, and even emotional states and predicting turnover. These applications can enhance organizational effectiveness at the cost of employees' privacy (Pandey et al., 2024).

There are not many workers who are aware of the extent to which their data are being collected and analyzed. Even where transparency is present regarding data collection, the doctrine of informed consent is being breached in situations where workers are being pressured to enroll due to workplace power relationships. Additionally, the use of AI for the inference of sensitive attributes—such as personality type or stress level—invites invasive profiling and undermines workplace autonomy and dignity (Dugyala et al., 2024; Skubis, Wolniak, & Grebski, 2024; Wolniak, Stecuła, & Aydın, 2024a).

Organizations must tread a delicate balance between optimizing performance and protecting individual workers' rights. Ethical use of AI demands open data practice transparency, limits on data collection, and robust safeguards for the assurance that employee monitoring can never mean digital surveillance. Accountability diffusion is a hallmark ethical issue of AI. When a human takes a biased or unfair decision, accountability, relatively speaking, is simple. Yet if an AI system makes an incorrect decision, then who is to blame? The software developer? The HR manager who installed it? The vendor who sold the system?

Such diffusion of accountability can create moral blind spots. Organizations are inclined to hide behind the algorithm, blaming unpleasant consequences on the system and declining to take ownership of the processes that it automates. Ethical leadership, however, demands that organizations take ownership of decisions regardless of whether they are taken by humans or machines. This includes proactively auditing the AI tools, rectifying their biases, and ensuring that human intuition is always included in the decision-making loop (Bhatt et al., 2024).

Looking beyond immediate issues, the use of AI in HR also presents questions about the broader ethical implications for the future of work. As automation is increasingly inserting itself into work that has always been the domain of HR professionals, one questions the role of the human in people management. Will HR operations become data centers and no longer a space for empathy, dialogue, and compassion? Will employees be reduced to data points rather than human beings with aspirations, fears, and personal narratives?

There is a risk of AI reliance eroding the human touch in HR—the same thing that makes it so valuable. Ethical AI must augment, not replace, human judgment. It must make HR practitioners smarter, more empathetic, and more equitable in their decisions, not impose moral accountability on the machines. The challenge here is not just to create ethical algorithms but to create organizational cultures that prioritize humanity as well as efficiency (Paul Dhinakaran et al., 2023; Uunona & Goosen, 2024).Table 6.1 summarizes the ethical challenges of AI implementation in human resources, organized to include the ethical issue, a brief description, and potential consequences or risks.

While businesses are increasingly dependent on AI to power auto-hiring, there is a serious problem that needs to be highlighted: such sites can unwittingly reinforce current workplace bias if taught on historical hiring data. This is no hypothetical future scenario but a real and present moral concern that needs to be dealt with by HR managers, policy-makers, and engineers here and now (Muralidharan et al., 2024).

TABLE 6.1 The ethical challenges of AI in human resources

Ethical Challenge	Description	Potential consequences / Risks
Bias and discrimination	AI systems can inherit and perpetuate historical biases in training data.	Unfair treatment of candidates or employees; legal challenge; reduction in diversity and inclusion.
Lack of transparency	The majority of AI systems (especially deep learning systems) are "black boxes" with low interpretability.	Inability to explain decisions; loss of trust; inability to appeal outcomes.
Privacy invasion	Continuous monitoring and data collection on employee behavior, communication, or emotions.	Dissolution of personal boundaries; rise in anxiety and stress; misuse of sensitive personal information.
Informed consent issues	Employees might not be aware of or feel obligated to consent to AI-driven data collection.	Ethical breaches; legal breach of data protection law; reputational harm to the organization.
Diffuse accountability	Accountability for AI-driven decisions is unclear and often shared among developers, vendors, and HR staff.	Absence of moral accountability; difficult to undo harm; loss of trust in organizational ethics.
Overreliance on automation	Over-delegation of human judgment to AI systems in decision-making.	Loss of empathy and contextual understanding; risk of dehumanization of HR processes.
Data quality and integrity	Decisions by AI rely heavily on information that can be potentially outdated, incomplete, or inaccurate.	Contaminated appraisals; biased recruitment or disciplinary procedures; bureaucratic inefficiencies.
Job displacement in HR	Automation of AI can displace traditional HR jobs, thus reducing the chance of human professionals being involved.	Loss of employment; undermining of relational aspects of HR; moral concerns about employment equity.
Legal and regulatory gaps	Existing labor and data protection laws can be unable to counter AI's powers.	Legal uncertainty; organizational exposure to litigation; compliance complexity.
Cultural sensitivity	AI might not be capable of taking into account differences in cultural values and norms in global workforces.	Misinterpretation of behavior; exclusion of minority viewpoints; inconsistencies in international HR policies.

Source: Author's own work.

The origin of the scandal is in a very simple yet commonly overlooked fact: AI algorithms are trained on datasets. Where these datasets mirror past decisions—i.e., human-created decisions—they necessarily carry with them the baggage of past prejudice. If, for instance, the hiring trends of a company in the past have been to choose from male applicants, graduates of leading universities, or members of a specific race, then an AI model trained on such data will reproduce the biases. It doesn't "know" they are biased; it thinks that these patterns are predictive of success simply because they existed in the first place (Rao & Zhao, 2025).

A case in point is the highly publicized Amazon AI hiring test from the late 2010s. The project was designed to screen résumés automatically and select the top performers. But because it was trained on a decade's worth of corporate recruitment information—when men were the standard in technical positions—it started marking down women's applications, especially those with mentions of women's colleges or gendered terms such as "women's chess club." This was not poor design but a lack of awareness about the biases present in previous data. The project was abandoned in the end, but the point remains central: algorithms can empower and amplify human biases with horrific potency.

This amplification of bias has repercussions that have far-reaching consequences. Racist or sexist AI programs can generally screen out qualified candidates based on gender, race, age, or financial status. Not only does this remove diversity and inclusion, but it damages organizational performance by eliminating possibilities due to collateral or unscrupulous motives. Reliance on flawed AI models exposes organizations to legal liability under anti-discrimination law and erodes the trust of employees and job applicants. Fairness in this case is not only a moral obligation—it is a business necessity for any organization that wants to ensure long-term sustainability and social legitimacy (Gajdzik et al., 2024a, 2024b; Gajdzik et al., 2025; Wolniak & Grebski, 2025).

This is where HR leadership's initiative begins. No longer can HR experts remain passive while utilizing AI systems (Rosak-Szyrocka & Wolniak, 2025; Jonek-Kowalska & Wolniak, 2025). They must be proactively engaged in deciding on the employment of ethics. It is only through being better informed about the development, training, and deployment of these kinds of systems that fairness in AI-based decision-making can be ensured. HR leaders need to require AI suppliers to be transparent, require frequent algorithm audits, and work with data scientists to catch and turn off potential biases before they affect real individuals.

HR staff can contribute to the choice of training data, defining open standards for what constitutes "success" or "fit" in making the hiring choice. Such definitions must be subjected to careful scrutiny to avoid having them encode stagnant or exclusionary assumptions. If, for example, past success at hiring is defined as tenure or promotion in a homogeneous workforce, then the model will skew toward conformity over innovation or diversity of culture.

Equity must also be adhered to in the sense of putting in place accountability and redress mechanisms. Workers and employment applicants should understand and challenge AI-based decisions, especially those regarding employment, promotion, or dismissal. Explainability—the capacity of a system to provide understandable explanations for its outputs—is important in this case. Black-box models churning out unexplainable outputs can't be morally justified in making decisions impacting people's livelihoods profoundly.

Education and cultural transformation in HR departments are just as necessary. HR professionals need to be educated both on the technical aspects of AI and its ethical considerations. A culture of critical thinking, willingness to listen to critique, and challenging the existing order is imperative. Fairness cannot be ensured through algorithms but needs a human-centric ethos within the organization.

6.2 DATA PRIVACY, SECURITY, AND HR COMPLIANCE

Data privacy is the proper utilization, processing, and protection of personally identifiable information (PII). To organizations, it implies not just protecting data from unauthorized access, but also disclosure concerning the collection, processing, and storage of the same. Regulatory structures such as the European Union's General Data Protection Regulation (GDPR), the California Consumer Privacy Act (CCPA), and other legislations globally have elevated data privacy from a secondary IT concern to a top concern of corporate governance (Olorunfemi & Ogwu, 2025).

From an ethical standpoint, data privacy considers the dignity and autonomy of individuals. It entrenches people's right to have control over their own information and not be subjected to intrusive surveillance or profiling without their permission. The rule is especially relevant in HR settings, where employers manage confidential information about health, family, background screening, and even psychometric testing. Violations of privacy promises can result in reputation loss, regulatory penalties, and erosion of employee morale. Privacy-by-design is increasingly a necessary system design concept. It involves the integration of privacy concerns in every step of the technology lifecycle—from ideation and prototyping, all the way to implementation and scaling. Incorporating privacy into digital tool architecture allows organizations to proactively counter threats rather than merely reacting to a breach (Shams, 2025).

Whereas data privacy is all about using it properly, data security is concerned with protecting information against threats—internal and external alike. At a time when increasingly complex cyber attacks, ransomware attacks, and social engineering threats are prevalent, organizations have no choice but to implement multi-layered security practices that deal with the entire spectrum of threats. Some of the most critical parts of an effective data security posture are encryption, access controls, network segmentation, and incident response planning. But technology alone is insufficient. Human error remains a potent vector for breaches; phishing attacks, poor password behavior, and unauthorized disclosures emphasize the need for constant security awareness training (Lu et al., 2025).

In the HR context, the implications of a data breach can be particularly disastrous. When employee personal data are hacked—social security numbers, financial information, or medical records—the impact is both legal and personal. HR departments need to therefore cooperate with IT security departments closely to ensure that databases, cloud platforms, and third-party service providers are fully in sync with best practices in cybersecurity. Organizations increasingly use artificial intelligence (AI) and machine learning algorithms in HR functions such as recruitment, performance evaluation, and workforce analysis (Mwaisengela et al., 2025; Wolniak & Stecuła, 2024). While they bring efficiency, they also create issues of algorithmic bias, data misuse, and transparency. A secure system is not merely about protecting information from input but about ensuring its processing is ethical, legal, and aligned with an organization's values (Vemula, 2025).

Compliance with human resources is following labor regulations, occupational health and safety practices, diversity and inclusion laws, and record-keeping regulations (Singh et al., 2025). But in the digital economy era, compliance entails ferocious management of employee data—where, for how long, and by whom? Regulatory landscapes are getting increasingly knotty. To mention just one example from the United States, employers must deal with a patchwork of federal, state, and industry-specific legislation, ranging from the Fair Labor Standards Act (FLSA) to the Health Insurance Portability and Accountability Act (HIPAA). In Europe, HR compliance cannot be separated from GDPR requirements, which extend to employee consent, data minimization, and the right to be forgotten (Nadella et al., 2025; Pean-Assounga & Bindel Sibassaha, 2024).

A best-in-class HR compliance program must be end-to-end and holistic in nature. This means combining legal expertise with process automation, training, and auditing (Hussein, Mohammed, & Kumar, 2023). It also requires creating a culture of accountability, where HR practitioners are aware not only of the letter of the law but of its spirit. Technologies such as compliance dashboards, secure document management systems, and digital consent-tracking mechanisms are increasingly important for staying abreast of evolving standards (Li et al., 2025; Mussa, Kabonda, & Ulomi, 2022). HR compliance also overlaps with organizational ethics beyond regulation. Consider, for example, the matter of handling whistleblower grievances. If mishandled, such exposures lead to complaints of retaliation, loss of reputation, and regulatory focus. On the other hand, when handled authentically and securely, they enhance institutional integrity and demonstrate belief in transparency (Kshetri, 2025).

The convergence of data privacy, security, and HR compliance is not a question of technical convenience—it is a requirement of strategy. These industries are mutually supportive, an ecosystem of strength, transparency, and ethics. A breach in one area can cascade into failures in the others. For example, a cyber threat can lead to privacy invasions and make an entity susceptible to HR noncompliance if employee records are breached (Ojha & Thakur, 2025).

Accordingly, high-performing organizations are transitioning to integrated governance models. These break down silos around legal, IT, and HR activities and build cross-functional strategies. They enable the implementation of shared policies, shared risk management, and unified incident response procedures. Organizations increasingly have Chief Privacy Officers (CPOs) or Data Protection Officers (DPOs) to oversee integration, ensuring that compliance and security become part of the organization's culture. Transparency to stakeholders—including workers—has also become an integral aspect of

TABLE 6.2 Data privacy

Area	Description	Practical examples	Consequences of non-compliance
Data collection	Collecting personal data with specified purpose and limited scope	Job applications, onboarding forms, employee surveys	Legal sanctions, reputational harm, loss of staff trust
Data processing	Processing data for specified, legitimate purposes only	Processing payroll, tracking attendance	Misuse allegations, data protection agency investigation
Consent management	Having informed, explicit, and revocable consent of data subjects	Opt-in checkboxes, privacy notices	Illegal processing, GDPR breaches
Data access control	Restricting access to personal data to authorized personnel only	Role-based access in HR systems	Data privacy breaches, abuse of internal access rights
Retention and deletion	Retaining data only for the required time, with secure disposal thereafter	Employee record archiving, deletion after contract termination	Regulatory fines, unjustified release of data
Data subject rights	Allowing access, rectification, erasure, and objection to data processing	Right to be forgotten, data portability requests	Legal complaints, costly compliance processes

Source: Author's own work.

this comprehensive approach. Regular communication about data practices, rights, and security measures not only fosters trust but also enhances organizational reputation in a world where responsible data stewardship is a mark of distinction (Alsudais, 2025; Wang et al., 2025).

Table 6.2 gives an outline of the guiding principles and organizational requirements of data privacy in today's organizations. It emphasizes ethical data collection, meaningful processing, and secure access control, in addition to data subjects' rights under existing legislations such as the GDPR. Each element—whether it is one of gaining valid consent or of carrying out appropriate data retention practices—is an indicator of a broader organizational obligation to act openly and responsibly in handling personal data. This is particularly pertinent within the human resources domain, as depicted in Table 6.3, which supplements the privacy framework by presenting principal areas of HR compliance. From complying with labor laws and anti-discrimination statutes to protecting whistleblowers and secure keeping of records, HR compliance as a statutory prescription and ethical precept of the well-being of workers performs as a legal requisition and ethic of doing well. Together, these tables render data privacy and HR compliance as supplementary rather than individualistic domains to each other with each playing vital roles in ensuring legal compliance, worker trustworthiness, and organizational integrity.

TABLE 6.3 HR compliance

Compliance domain	Description	Examples	Consequences of non-compliance
Labor law compliance	Adherence to national and local employment laws	Overtime pay regulations, maximum working hours regulations	Legal penalties, employee lawsuits
Anti-discrimination and D&I	Treating individuals equally in spite of protected characteristics	Inclusive hiring practices, equal pay audits	Discrimination claims, brand damage
Employee data protection	Managing personal data in accordance with privacy laws	HRIS security, handling of sensitive medical information	GDPR fines, loss of employee confidence
Health and safety	Ensuring a safe working environment and appropriate procedures	COVID-19 workplace health and safety policy, ergonomic assessment	OSHA penalties, increased workplace accidents
Whistleblower protection	Safeguarding employees who whistleblow on misconduct	Anonymous reporting procedures, no retaliation policies	Retaliation claims, compliance failures
Record-keeping	Keeping employment records as required by law	Disciplinary actions, contracts, payroll records	Regulatory scrutiny, lack of audit trail

Source: Author's own work.

6.3 AI BIAS AND THE RISK OF DISCRIMINATION

In order to comprehend the gravity of the issue, one needs to understand, first, how AI bias gets created. Unlike the common belief that algorithms remain objective, algorithms learn from previously available data. If such data bears existing organization or society prejudice, the algorithm will have iterated the pattern. For example, if hiring information gathered in the past by a company that disproportionately employed white men in senior positions is applied to train a recruitment AI, the algorithm may learn to favor similar candidates—implicitly punishing women or minority candidates (Modanlo & Jafferany, 2025).

The bias can be inherent in many stages: from data choice and tagging to features weighted by the model and the user engagement that generates the feedback loops. Interestingly, such biases tend to be transparent to the end-user. While a human recruiter can be held accountable for discriminatory judgments, AI judgments will appear neutral, shielded by the complexity of their design and the ambiguity of their recommendations. This opacity is further added to when vendors offer proprietary "black box" systems where HR professionals cannot interrogate or audit the rationale employed by algorithmic choices (Goh et al., 2025; Gu et al., 2025).

The notion of "fairness" in AI is also highly contentious. Should AI systems be aimed at statistical parity, equal opportunity, or individual fairness? These mathematical and philosophical constructs do tend to conflict with each other, and the choice of one approach over another will in itself introduce a form of bias. AI in HR is thus not operating in a moral vacuum—it is embedding human judgment at every stage of development, often in imperceptible fashion until the damage has already been inflicted (Saumure, De Freitas, & Puntoni, 2025).

AI bias in HR can manifest in a variety of concrete ways throughout the employment process. Recruitment and selection processes are most clearly affected. Automated résumé-screening programs, chatbots, and AI-powered video interviews are the new standard. These tools can inadvertently filter out qualified candidates based on irrelevant traits, such as speech patterns, regional dialects, facial expressions, or schools attended—all of which may be linked to racial or socio-economic backgrounds (Kasek, Sepsi, & Lázár, 2025; Moon & Kahlor, 2025).

An eye-opening example comes from the highly publicized case of a giant technology company junking an AI recruitment tool after it was discovered that the system routinely ranked lower applications that used the word "women's," e.g., "women's chess club captain." It was not the result of explicit programming, but a consequence of training data containing disproportionately fewer female candidates for high-level vacancies (Carter & Liu, 2025).

Bias does not end at recruitment. AI performance management tools can also reinforce inequalities. For instance, productivity metrics that reward extroversion or time on task at the expense of actual output quality will unfairly penalize neurodivergent employees or staff with caregiving responsibilities. Once more, employee monitoring software that records keystrokes, email behavior, or webcam content can introduce risk based on ability, language ability, or cultural practices (Kekez, Lauwaert, & Begičević Ređep, 2025).

The threat is not in discrete choices but in the combined effect of such systems. AI will never undertake a discrete overt act of discrimination, but it can collectively bias the game—excluding particular profiles, losing promotion scores, or increasing the danger of attrition for already weak groups. Such a process of "digital redlining" could remain unknown for decades unless companies implement strong auditing and moral watchdog mechanisms (Chang et al., 2025).

With the risks in mind, the regulatory landscape of AI in HR is evolving rapidly. In the European Union, the proposed AI Act would establish a risk-based categorization regime that would put most HR applications—such as AI in hiring—under the "high risk" umbrella, with transparency, human oversight, and bias mitigation controls mandated. Similarly, some U.S. states, such as Illinois and New York, have already enacted legislation mandating that employers disclose their use of automated job-screening software and conduct periodic bias audits on an annual basis. Compliance is only part of the solution (van Bekkum, 2025; Kim et al., 2025). The ethical component demands something more proactive. Organizations must move beyond technical solutions and develop a more robust framework for AI governance. This includes ensuring diversity in the teams that develop and implement AI systems, engaging affected stakeholders, and integrating practices such as impact assessments, explainability testing, and human-in-the-loop review models (Van Busum & Fang, 2025; Wei, Kumar, & Zhang, 2025).

In the HR environment, this means that algorithmic results should not be considered absolute determinations, but as inputs to be contextualized by human experts who have been trained to recognize both the potential and the limitations of such tools. In addition, transparency needs to be applied to employees and candidates themselves, who have the right to know how decisions concerning them are being made—and to contest those decisions when they must (Goel, Yadav, & Verma, 2025; Marsico & Amigo, 2025).

Ethical application of AI in HR also intersects with the broader cultural and strategic values of the organization. It is an articulation of a company's stance on equity, inclusion, and accountability. Just as bias training and diversity programs are perceived as markers of good corporate citizenship, so must good use of AI become a part of the modern employer's ethical identity (Table 6.4).

Arguably, the most widely publicized example of AI bias in hiring was Amazon's, which created an internal AI system to screen resumes for technical jobs. The AI system was trained on a decade's worth of hiring data that revealed a predominantly male workforce, especially in technical roles. As a result, the algorithm began penalizing resumes containing the word "women's" (e.g., "women's chess club captain") and ranked graduates of all-women colleges low. The company attempted to rebalance the model, but the bias was systemic and embedded. Amazon eventually canceled the tool in 2017. This was an example of how biased training data was able to learn and exacerbate institutional bias via unconscious programming or deliberate intent.

HireVue, an AI-driven video interviewing software provider, was slammed for judging candidates based on facial expressions, tone of voice, and speech habits. Critics argue that those variables have little scientific grounding for assessing performance in the workplace and would discriminate unfairly against neurodiverse candidates, non-native English speakers, or those from specific cultures. Despite the fact that HireVue claimed its technology was tested for bias and streamlined hiring, advocacy group pressure from organizations like the Electronic Privacy Information Center (EPIC) compelled the company to eliminate facial analysis features in 2021. This is a testament to the risks of using unexplainable behavioral markers in AI testing and the strength of public discussion and independent critique.

Workday, a major HR software provider, was sued in court in 2023 by an applicant who charged the company's AI recruitment platform with discriminating against him on the grounds of age, race, and disability. While the case is pending, it is part of a growing number of legal lines where companies that use third-party AI software can be held liable for biased outcomes even when the bias resides in the vendor's algorithms. The lawsuit is a sign of growing concern over algorithmic accountability and legal liability for employers if they implement AI tools without proper testing and fairness monitoring.

LinkedIn, the world's largest professional network, uses AI-powered algorithms that suggest job recommendations to users based on profile, behavior, and history. It was in 2021 when LinkedIn's own research indicated that women were being presented with fewer senior or well-paying job positions than comparably qualified men. What lay behind it was that the algorithm was designed for engagement—i.e., clicks—rather than equity. Women were less likely on average to click through to roles requiring more experience (potentially because of overall social conditioning), so the model "learned" that the roles weren't as applicable to women.

TABLE 6.4 Strategies to address AI bias and the risk of discrimination in HR

Challenge	Strategy	Implementation example	Expected outcome
Biased training data	Conduct data audits and sanitize training sets	Remove historical biases from recruitment data that favor a specific group	More inclusive and fair AI decisions
Opaque "black-box" algorithms	Provide algorithmic transparency and explainability	Use models that provide explanations for their choices (e.g., SHAP values)	More responsibility and trust in AI systems
Lack of diverse development teams	Build diverse, cross-disciplinary AI project teams	Involve DEI specialists, ethicists, and HR professionals in AI system creation	Fewer blind spots and more equitable system outputs
Discriminatory impact in candidate selection	Use fairness-aware algorithms and bias mitigation techniques	Apply re-weighting methods to offset underrepresented groups	More hiring equity and lower adverse effect
Automated systems replacing human judgment	Provide human-in-the-loop decision-making	Require HR managers to sign off on AI suggestions before final decisions are made	Equitable, contextualized decisions that bring together data and human judgment
Lack of employee awareness and recourse	Provide transparency and appeal processes	Inform candidates about use of AI; allow them to challenge or request review	Empowered candidates and higher procedural fairness
Unmonitored performance evaluation metrics	Regularly audit performance algorithms for bias	Monitor promotion or attrition predictions by gender and ethnicity	Systemic inequalities found and fixed sooner
Non-compliance with emerging AI laws	Provide alignment of AI use with local and global regulatory frameworks	Compliant with the EU AI Act and local bias audit legislations (e.g., NYC Local Law 144)	Legal compliance and lower risk of litigation
Vendor accountability gaps	Impose external bias audits and ethical standards from vendors	Contractually require bias testing and transparency from third-party software	Greater reliability and ethical integrity of outsourced services
Feedback loops reinforcing bias	Use periodic system retraining on new, inclusive data	Refresh hiring algorithms every 6–12 months based on updated datasets	Adaptive systems that adapt as organizational diversity goals shift

Source: Author's own work.

This feedback mechanism inadvertently reinforced pre-existing gender gaps in the pool of talent. LinkedIn reacted by altering its model to prioritize more balanced visibility rather than raw engagement. The firm also highlighted this problem and took efforts to apply fairness-aware modeling in its recommendation engine. This is just one instance of how even user utility-driven algorithms can become biased if optimizing for superficiality is profit-generating. It is also a testament to the power of active monitoring and intentional design choices in order to make AI act toward inclusivity and not toward perpetuating inequality.

Singaporean recruitment automation firm X0PA AI partnered with government departments and multinational corporations to offer AI-driven candidate ranking and scoring solutions. They were customized to introduce more efficiency and objectivity in hiring by analyzing resumes, academic records, and the answers of candidates. Early applications in mission-critical contexts such as government hiring showed that there were biases surrounding school, origin country, and language spoken, which were against foreign-background or minority-background candidates.

There was bias from training datasets that significantly overlapped with top-performing local colleges' data and exacting demographic portraits of previous recruits. Even if the algorithm never actively preferred one group, it simply reflected the data histories upon which it was modeled. To flip this around, X0PA comprehensively updated and broadened the training datasets. Secondly, the business required algorithmic fairness testing on deployment. The photograph is used to demonstrate the dangers of assuming future success based on past achievement, especially in multicultural and diverse workplaces where fairness needs to be a byword.

6.4 FRAMEWORKS FOR ETHICAL AI GOVERNANCE IN HRM

Human resources have traditionally been regarded as an area necessarily engaged with relational, affective, and ethical considerations. Recruitment, performance appraisals, promotions, and terminations have important personal and professional implications for individuals. Applying AI in such areas is likely to amplify ingrained biases, cloak accountability, and drain away the people-oriented nature of HR unless strictly regulated. For example, algorithms based on past records of employment can reproduce discrimination based on race or gender and thus reinforce systemic inequality further behind the veil of objectivity (Chakrabarti et al., 2025).

Lack of transparency in the majority of AI systems, particularly deep learning models, poses risks to explainability and accountability. The employees whose jobs are impacted by AI-supported decisions need to be informed as to why exactly these decisions were made. This points to the significance of stringent ethical standards that can enable organizations' embracement of accountable use of AI mechanisms in HRM activities (Chang et al., 2025).

Several global organizations and research institutions have promoted high-level ethical standards to govern the development and application of AI, if not HRM itself. But they provide general advice. They are the OECD AI Principles, the EU Ethics Guidelines for Trustworthy AI, and the IEEE Ethically Aligned Design framework. Despite differences in definition and scope, all these models have a common set of values (Archana & Kamakshi Prasad, 2025; Chakrabarti et al., 2025; Mehra et al., 2025; Jha et al., 2025):

- Explainability and Transparency – The behavior and decision-making of AI systems need to be explainable and transparent to the stakeholders, particularly those affected by their impact.

- Justice and Non-Discrimination – AI systems must be designed and tested so that they do not produce discriminatory results based on race, sex, age, or other protected bases.
- Responsibility – Human control must bear effective responsibility for the outcomes of AI, the latter being the foundation.
- Data Stewardship and Privacy – Personal data of employees has to be handled with extreme care, with the right to privacy maintained and safe data handling.
- Human Agency and Control – AI should support and never substitute human decision-making, maintaining the agency of employees and HR professionals.

These form the ethical basis of AI governance, but it requires context-specific strategies with technical, organizational, and cultural dimensions to convert them into operational components to HRM situations.

Table 6.5 sets the primary requirements of ethical AI governance backed by transparent comprehensions, attuned to the Human Resource Management (HRM) context.

TABLE 6.5 The principles of ethical AI governance

Principle	Description
Transparency and explainability	Transparency, in the context of HR, is both the explainability of AI systems and the information upon which they are trained being comprehensible to all involved. Explainability is the ability to explain in simple terms how and why an AI system has made a particular decision—whether in hiring, measurement of performance, or promotion. This needs to be achieved in order to create trust and enable employees to question decisions they believe are unfair. Untransparency would make AI decisions appear capricious or biased, even justifying HR practices. Explainability that can be used involves simple-to-use interfaces and transparent disclosure.
Fairness and non-discrimination	The AI systems need to be implemented with intent in such a way that they do not perpetuate present social biases and structural inequities. In HRM, it is used specifically for hiring algorithms that may have the effect of discriminating against particular demographic groups on behalf of others because of unbalanced historical data. Fairness requires that the systems be regularly audited for disparate impact and training data which is fair and diverse. Ethical governance must also address intersectionality—how various social categories (e.g., race and gender) intersect to create outcomes. Fairness is made inherent through algorithmic tweaking, adding debiasing techniques, and adding human oversight where necessary.
Accountability	AI used in HR should never blur lines of responsibility. Whether or not a decision is actually made by an algorithm, there needs to be a strict process defining who's accountable for its creation, deployment, and results. This involves creating audit trails, setting up control committees, and providing employees with a way to appeal decisions. In reality, this would imply that compliance officers, AI developers, and HR professionals are collectively held accountable for AI-driven consequences. Ethical governance of AI requires that accountability procedures be institutional, transparent, and exercisable.

(Continued)

TABLE 6.5 (*Continued*)

Principle	Description
Privacy and data governance	AI applications in HRM are generally based on massive databases of personal and sensitive data, including performance records, behavioral records, and even biometric records. There needs to be appropriate data governance so that such data is collected ethically, kept securely, and utilized for appropriate, simply defined purposes only. Employees need to know what data is collected, for what, and who can see it. Organizations need to comply with data protection laws like GDPR and have data minimization, encryption, and anonymization procedures. Ethical governance would also include providing employees with the right to opt out wherever it is suitable.
Human agency and oversight	Ethical AI must augment and not supplant human decision-making. In HRM, it would provide the guarantee that final decisions—particularly those concerning one's career or home—ought to involve human judgment and discretion. AI must be a decision-support system rather than an independent decision-maker. Procedures for supervision must always position human beings "in the loop," in a position to comprehend AI recommendations and override them as necessary. It also involves expanding human agency by training HR personnel to critically engage with AI tools rather than blindly accepting algorithmic outcomes.
Safety and reliability	AI tools must be able to operate reliably and accurately over the long term and in a variety of contexts. In the HR context, AI decision-making or prediction errors—i.e., incorrect candidate matching or performance forecasting errors—can result in harm to persons and damage to organizational reputation. Dependability entails rigorous testing, scenario simulation, monitoring, and insensitivity to adversarial attacks or system crash. Ethical governance models should necessitate periodic refresh and re-validation of AI models, especially with changing organizational environments and workforce data.
Inclusiveness and stakeholder participation	HR AI regulation needs to be participatory. This involves engaging a broad cross-section of both internal and external stakeholders—employees, HR managers, ethicists, lawyers, and even union officials—in envisioning, experimenting with, and operating AI systems. Participation ensures the system incorporates diversity of values, requirements, and perspectives. Participation enhances legitimacy, reduces resistance to use, and enhances the system's ability to discover unanticipated ethical concerns. Co-design and feedback procedures, such as in the guise of ethics committees or focus groups, are essential to bringing inclusiveness to life as a lived organizational practice.

Source: Author's own work.

As more abstract ethical concerns provide the philosophical underpinning, these need to be presented as operational tools of policy application pertinent to the nature of HRM. Several agencies and researchers have proposed operational frameworks purporting to fulfill such a function. Just like environmental or data protection effects assessments, AI-EIAs ensure a methodical way of balancing possible ethical harms before introducing AI tools into HR (Al-Omari et al., 2025; Pretorius & de Caux, 2025; Agrawal, 2025). The evaluation will typically cover:

- Purpose and context of the AI system.
- Potential social and ethical risks.

- Stakeholder examination.
- Mitigation strategies.
- Monitoring and assessing plans.

Through integrating ethical thinking as a focal point in AI application, AI-EIAs ensure a proactive and responsible practice. This is most helpful in the recruitment process, wherein algorithmic processes by their design favor some individuals over others (Lan et al., 2025). Third-party analyses of AI programs can detect and remove discriminatory bias in algorithmic metrics that are used to quantify performance or determine promotions. Such audits can utilize statistical tests for disparate impact, simulations, or counterfactual analysis. Most importantly, audits must be iterative and ongoing rather than singular processes because data environments are changing and there may be biases developing over time (Yu, Fang, & Wang, 2025; Donvir & Sharma, 2025.

Internal AI ethics boards are being established in some companies to oversee such audits, comprising data scientists, ethicists, HR professionals, and lawyers. Multidisciplinary boards of this kind guarantee technical examination as well as ethical examination (Akila et al., 2024; Bani Ahmad, 2024).

More engaged again is embedding ethicality into the lifecycle of software development itself. This involves:

- Requirements for design established during the requirements phase.
- Demographically representative training data that is inclusive.
- Interpretability features built into user interfaces.
- Feedback loops that allow users to complain about or dispute AI responses.

By incorporating ethics as a design criterion rather than an afterthought, organizations can make AI tools complementary by default to HR values. In addition, engaging multiple voices—especially those that are marginalized—through the design process of these systems makes them stronger and legitimate (Zafeirakopoulos & Stefanas, 2024; Ammah et al., 2024).

Ethical management of AI in HRM is not compliance or tick-boxing—it is a cultural imperative. It requires organizations to build ethical reflexivity among HR workers, challenging assumptions within AI technologies and safeguarding the human values at stake. It can be done through training workshops, stakeholder models of governance, or incentive schemes that enable ethical action (Kaur, 2024; Minz, 2024).

Leadership needs to lead the way. By discussing openly the need for ethical AI, investing dollars in open systems, and making employees integral to empowering them to be vocal, leaders will create a culture of integrity that will echo throughout the company.

Table 6.6 outlines how HR professionals can integrate responsible AI deployment strategies into their organizations. Each strategy is paired with practical actions and its ethical or organizational benefit.

TABLE 6.6 Integration of responsible AI deployment strategies into organizations

Strategy	Description	Ethical/Organizational benefit
Conduct AI impact assessments	Before deploying any AI system to all HR processes, organizations need to perform comprehensive impact assessments that account for ethical, legal, and social considerations. These enable future risks associated with bias, privacy invasion, or the automation of sensitive decisions to be recognized upfront and stimulate planning in advance to mitigate them.	This practice guarantees ethical values to be employed from the beginning, preventing harm and guaranteeing maximum foresight.
Establish cross-functional AI ethics committees	HR professionals must advocate for or join cross-functional committees addressing AI ethics governance. The committees should have HR, legal, IT, compliance, and diversity and inclusion functions as members to guarantee that all the issues are brought up when designing, deploying, and tracking AI technology.	These committees promote collective responsibility and internalize ethical thinking, providing strong leadership.
Implement algorithmic fairness audits	There should be ongoing audits of AI systems to identify the presence of algorithmic bias or disparate treatment by demographic group. Audits are statistical analysis and scenario-testing, such that the systems used in hiring, promotion, or evaluation are no longer continuing past discrimination.	Guaranteeing fair audits guarantees lawfulness compliance and organizational justice as well as reputational integrity.
Ensure explainability and transparency	HR departments should ensure that any used AI system would be explainable to the experts involved and on the receiving end of its judgments. That is to say, adequate explanations will be provided to rationalize decisions made, keeping on record system logic, as well as provide avenues for questioning by employees or objecting to judgments they have realized to be unjust.	Improves procedure justice and psychological safety, improves trust in HR technologies, and improves employee dignity.
Embed ethics in procurement and vendor selection	In selecting AI suppliers, HR practitioners must look beyond performance indicators and scrutinize a supplier's commitment to ethics in AI. This must include ensuring that suppliers respect data privacy, finding out whether the models are explainable, and finding out whether third-party audits are permitted. Ethical clauses must be included in procurement agreements and service-level agreements.	Aligning with values protects the firm from buying latent or irresponsible technologies.
Train HR staff in AI literacy and ethics	One of the critical facilitators of ethical AI usage is making certain that HR practitioners possess a rudimentary knowledge base of how AI functions, its limitations, and its ethical connotations. This includes offering structured training in the principles of AI, detection of bias, ethics of data, and best practices for interpreting outputs from algorithms to allow employees to engage critically and responsibly with AI systems.	Improves organizational capacity to utilize AI for moral purposes so that it will not abuse but expand knowledge-based, moral decision-making.

TABLE 6.6 (*Continued*)

Strategy	Description	Ethical/Organizational benefit
Adopt "human-in-the-loop" decision frameworks	Rather than having AI decide independently, HR activities must be designed in a manner such that human beings are not left behind at the center of decision-making. AI can construct ideas, but final decisions—most specifically related to employment, termination, or compensation—must be brought forward for human judgment, reflection, and accountability.	Protects human values and situational discernment as the foundation of decisions for work.
Monitor and iterate post-deployment	Once AI systems are in place, their impact must be tracked on an ongoing basis to make sure they are working and to determine unforeseen effects. Businesses must establish benchmarks for fairness, accuracy, and customer satisfaction and build structures where employees can offer feedback or comment on areas of concern.	Improves learning and system development agility and protects functional AI design based on company value and interest.
Ensure data privacy and consent	Responsible AI for HR demands close care of data collection, processing, and storage for employees. Businesses must ensure that the usage of data is compliant with legal standards such as the GDPR and obtain explicit consent when consent is required. Practices such as anonymization, minimization of data, and safe storage are key to ethical data management.	Ensures compliance with laws and articulation of organizations' privacy concerns and people's sovereignty.
Foster an ethical AI culture	Along with practices and policies, the HR practitioner has to work toward the development of a culture of ethical thinking and critical discourse on AI. This entails beginning open dialogue on the consequences of automation, public expression of ethical leadership, and ethics-driven use of AI as an organizational core value and learning imperative.	Creates legitimacy from within, solidifies moral alignment, and promotes social license to innovate through the use of AI in HRM.

Source: Author's own work.

REFERENCES

Agarwal, B. (2025). Ethical framework for AI in education. In *CEUR Workshop Proceedings, 3927* (pp. 40–44). CEUR-WS.org (University of Cologne).

Akila, S., Mohanbabu, B., Balraj, B., & Sivakumar, C. (2024). Traversing the ethical terrain of AI: a conceptual framework for practicing research and publication in the AI era. *Asian Journal of Interdisciplinary Research, 7*(4), 19–54.

Al-Omari, O., Alyousef, A., Fati, S., Shannaq, F., & Omari, A. (2025). Governance and ethical frameworks for AI integration in higher education: enhancing personalized learning and legal compliance. *Journal of Ecohumanism, 4*(2), 80–86.

Alsudais, A. (2025). Training vision AI models with public data: privacy and availability concerns. *Communications of the Association for Information Systems, 56*.

Ammah, L. N. A., Lütge, C., Kriebitz, A., & Ramkissoon, L. (2024). AI4people – an ethical framework for a good AI society: the Ghana (Ga) perspective. *Journal of Information, Communication and Ethics in Society, 22*(4), 453–465.

Archana, K., & Kamakshi Prasad, V. (2025). Public sector leadership in the age of AI: a framework for ethical governance. In *Public Governance Practices in the Age of AI* (pp. 223–232). IGI Global.

Bani Ahmad, A. Y. A. (2024). Ethical implications of artificial intelligence in accounting: a framework for responsible AI adoption in multinational corporations in Jordan. *International Journal of Data and Network Science, 8*(1), 401–414.

Bar-Gil, O., Ron, T., & Czerniak, O. (2024). AI for the people? Embedding AI ethics in HR and people analytics projects. *Technology in Society, 77*, 102527.

Beccalli, E., Elliot, V., & Virili, F. (2020). Artificial intelligence and ethics in portfolio management. In *Lecture Notes in Information Systems and Organisation* (Vol. 38, pp. 19–30).

Bhatt, A., Singh, T., Pandey, S., Kumar, R., & Sunil, G. (2024). Monitoring of smart human resource (HR) using artificial intelligence and Internet of Things. In *Proceedings – 2024 3rd International Conference on Sentiment Analysis and Deep Learning, ICSADL 2024* (pp. 613–617). IEEE.

Carter, L., & Liu, D. (2025). How was my performance? Exploring the role of anchoring bias in AI-assisted decision making. *International Journal of Information Management, 82*, 102875.

Chakrabarti, M., Fabozzi, F. J., Narain, A., & Sood, A. (2025). Ethical AI in asset management: frameworks for transparency, compliance, and trust. *Journal of Financial Data Science, 7*(1), 18–35.

Chang, M. A., Tissenbaum, M., Philip, T. M., & D'Mello, S. K. (2025). Co-designing AI with youth partners: enabling ideal classroom relationships through a novel AI relational privacy ethical framework. *Computers and Education: Artificial Intelligence, 8*, 100364.

Donvir, A., & Sharma, G. (2025). Ethical challenges and frameworks in AI-driven software development and testing. In *2025 IEEE 15th Annual Computing and Communication Workshop and Conference, CCWC 2025* (pp. 569–576). IEEE.

Dugyala, R., Gaddam, V. K., Eroju, H., Dantuluri, M. V., & Madhubabu, C. H. (2024). Smart recruitment system. In *2024 15th International Conference on Computing Communication and Networking Technologies, ICCCNT 2024*. IEEE.

Gajdzik, B., Jaciow, M., Hoffmann-Burdzińska, K., Wolny, R., Wolniak, R., & Grebski, W. (2024a). Impact of economic awareness on sustainable energy consumption: results of research in a segment of Polish households. *Energies, 17*(11), 1–31.

Gajdzik, B., Nagaj, R., Wolniak, R., Bałaga, D., Žuromskaitė, B., & Grebski, W. (2024b). Renewable energy share in European industry: analysis and extrapolation of trends in EU countries. *Energies, 17*(11), 1–38.

Gajdzik, B., Wolniak, R., Grebski, W., Szymszal, J., & Grebski, M. E. (2025). *Sustainability and smart manufacturing: the transformation of the steelwork industry*, Routledge.

Goel, P. K., Yadav, S. P., & Verma, S. (2025). Building trust in AI-driven mental health tools: addressing bias and fairness in NLP models. In *Demystifying the role of natural language processing (NLP) in mental health* (pp. 51–69). IGI Global.

Goh, E., Bunning, B., Khoong, E. C., Centola, D., & Chen, J. H. (2025). Physician clinical decision modification and bias assessment in a randomized controlled trial of AI assistance. *Communications Medicine, 5*(1), 59.

Groß, M. (2021). Yes, AI can: the artificial intelligence gold rush between optimistic HR software providers, skeptical HR managers, and corporate ethical virtues. In *Management for professionals* (Part F454, pp. 191–225).

Gu, T., Pan, W., Yu, J., Wang, Y., & Li, M. (2025). Mitigating bias in AI mortality predictions for minority populations: a transfer learning approach. *BMC Medical Informatics and Decision Making, 25*(1), 30.

Hussein, H. W., Mohammed, A. A., & Kumar, S. (2023). Reducing the negative effects of non-compliance and unethical behaviour by adopting the risk approach to human resources management. *International Journal of Work Innovation, 4*(3), 211–226.

Jha, D., Durak, G., Sharma, V., Håkegård, J. E., & Bagci, U. (2025). A conceptual framework for applying ethical principles of AI to medical practice. *Bioengineering, 12*(2), 180.

Jonek-Kowalska, I., & Wolniak, R. (2025). *Exclusion in Smart Cities assessment and strategy for strengthening resilience*, Routledge.

Kasek, R., Sepsi, E., & Lázár, I. (2025). Overconfident, but angry at least. AI-based investigation of facial emotional expressions and self-assessment bias in human adults. *BMC Psychology, 13*(1), 223.

Kaur, J. (2024). Responsible artificial intelligence (AI) governance: ethical frameworks for business decision-making. In *Ethical quandaries in business practices: exploring morality and social responsibility* (pp. 339–370). IGI Global.

Kekez, I., Lauwaert, L., & Begičević Ređep, N. (2025). Is artificial intelligence (AI) research biased and conceptually vague? A systematic review of research on bias and discrimination in the context of using AI in human resource management. *Technology in Society, 81*, 102818.

Kim, S. H., Schramm, S., Riedel, E. O., Wiestler, B., & Hedderich, D. M. (2025). Automation bias in AI-assisted detection of cerebral aneurysms on time-of-flight MR angiography. *Radiologia Medica, 130*(4), 555–566.

Kshetri, N. (2025). Building trust in AI: how blockchain enhances data integrity, security, and privacy. *Computer, 58*(2), 63–70.

Lan, G., Feng, X., Du, S., Song, F., & Xiao, Q. (2025). Integrating ethical knowledge in generative AI education: constructing the GenAI-TPACK framework for university teachers' professional development. *Education and Information Technologies, 30*, 15621–15644.

Li, N., Lewin, A., Ning, S., Tinmouth, A., & Shih, A. W. (2025). Privacy-preserving federated data access and federated learning: improved data sharing and AI model development in transfusion medicine. *Transfusion, 65*(1), 22–28.

Lu, Y., Yang, M., Guo, K., Lu, X., & Li, B. (2025). Fusion of differential privacy algorithm and advanced AI: innovating customer information protection in transaction data. In *CSAI 2024 – Proceedings of 2024 8th International Conference on Computer Science and Artificial Intelligence* (pp. 474–481). Association for Computing Machinery (ACM).

Marsico, F., & Amigo, M. (2025). Ethical and security challenges in AI for forensic genetics: from bias to adversarial attacks. *Forensic Science International: Genetics, 76*, 103225.

Mehra, S., Das, T., Meher, S. M., & Khan, S. (2025). Ethical AI: a framework for building responsible artificial intelligence systems. In *Convergence of AI, education, and business for sustainability* (pp. 1–23). IGI Global.

Minz, N. K. (2024). Ethical considerations in AI applications in finance: frameworks, transparency, accountability, and case studies. In *Risks and challenges of AI-driven finance: bias, ethics, and security* (pp. 277–290). IGI Global.

Modanlo, N., & Jafferany, M. (2025). Integration of AI into psychodermatology: concern for racial bias. *Archives of Dermatological Research, 317*(1), 536.

Moon, W.-K., & Kahlor, L. A. (2025). Fact-checking in the age of AI: reducing biases with non-human information sources. *Technology in Society, 80*, 102760.

Muralidharan, V., Ravi, B., Pachar, S., Chakraborty, N., & Sahaya Lenin, D. (2024). Ethical considerations in applying machine learning to HR practices: balancing efficiency with fairness. In *Proceedings of International Conference on Contemporary Computing and Informatics, IC3I 2024* (pp. 1392–1398). IEEE.

Mussa, T. A., Kabonda, V. J., & Ulomi, J. J. (2022). Human resources compliance in selected large tour companies in Arusha, Tanzania. *African Journal of Hospitality, Tourism and Leisure, 11*(4), 1459–1473.

Mwaisengela, S. M., Materu, P. A., German, C. J., Yahya, T. A., & Eliakimu, E. S. (2025). Contribution of human resources for health competence and skill mix on compliance with healthcare quality standards among primary healthcare facilities in Tanzania: evidence from dispensaries. *Discover Public Health, 22*(1), 132.

Nadella, G. S., Addula, S. R., Yadulla, A. R., Meduri, K., & Gonaygunta, H. (2025). Generative AI-enhanced cybersecurity framework for enterprise data privacy management. *Computers, 14*(2), 55.

Ojha, N. K., & Thakur, S. (2025). Privacy laws and leak of financial data in the era of generative AI. In *Generative artificial intelligence in finance: large language models, interfaces, and industry use cases to transform accounting and finance processes* (pp. 265–281). John Wiley & Sons.

Olorunfemi, O., & Ogwu, P. C. (2025). Harnessing AI in nursing care: strategies to improve patient outcomes and overcome data privacy challenges. *Digital Medicine, 11*(1).

Pandey, P., Pandey, A., Srivastava, A., Bisht, S., & Mahajan, N. (2024). Intelligent HR systems in global organizations: embracing Industry 4.0 for a smart future. In *IEEE International Conference on Signal Processing and Advance Research in Computing, SPARC 2024*. IEEE.

Paul Dhinakaran, D., Bhat, V. A., Vijayakumar, N., Bhuvaneswari, L., & Namadevan, R. (2023). Artificial intelligence impacts on human resource digitalization Industry 4.0. In *Proceedings of the 2023 International Conference on Innovative Computing, Intelligent Communication and Smart Electrical Systems, ICSES 2023*. IEEE.

Pea-Assounga, J. B. B., & Bindel Sibassaha, J. L. (2024). Impact of technological change, employee competency, and law compliance on digital human resource practices: evidence from Congo Telecom. *Sustainable Futures, 7*, 100195.

Pretorius, L., & de Caux, B. C. (2025). The AI literacy framework for higher education: a grounded theory exploration of the foundational, social, conceptual, ethical, and affective domains of AI literacy. In *Reimagining literacy in the age of AI: theory and practice* (pp. 11–32). CRC Press.

Rao, S., & Zhao, T. (2025). Ethical AI in HR: a case study of tech hiring. *Journal of Computer Information Systems*, 1–38. https://doi.org/10.1080/08874417.2024.2446954. www.tandfonline.com/doi/citedby/10.1080/08874417.2024.2446954?scroll=top&needAccess=true

Rosak-Szyrocka J., & Wolniak, R. (2025) *Smart universities in Smart Cities shaping the future of education and urban innovation*, Routledge.

Saumure, R., De Freitas, J., & Puntoni, S. (2025). Humor as a window into generative AI bias. *Scientific Reports, 15*(1), 1326.

Shams, A. (2025). Data protection and privacy laws and regulations: lessons for AI in democratic processes. In *Democracy and democratization in the age of AI* (pp. 235–258). IGI Global.

Singh, L., Randhelia, A., Jain, A., & Choudhary, A. K. (2025). Ethical and regulatory compliance challenges of generative AI in human resources. In *Generative artificial intelligence in finance: large language models, interfaces, and industry use cases to transform accounting and finance processes* (pp. 201–214). John Wiley & Sons.

Skubis, I., Wolniak, R., & Grebski, W. W. (2024). AI and human-centric approach in smart cities management: case studies from Silesian and Lesser Poland Voivodships. *Sustainability, 16*(18), Article 8279, 1–26.

Uunona, G. N., & Goosen, L. (2024). Leveraging ethics in artificial intelligence technologies and applications: e-learning management systems in Namibia. In *Semantic web technologies and applications in artificial intelligence of things* (pp. 173–185). IGI Global.

van Bekkum, M. (2025). Using sensitive data to de-bias AI systems: Article 10(5) of the EU AI Act. *Computer Law and Security Review, 56*, 106115.

Van Busum, K., & Fang, S. (2025). Bias analysis of AI models for undergraduate student admissions. *Neural Computing and Applications, 37*(12), 7785–7795.

Vemula, V. R. (2025). AI-enhanced self-healing cloud architectures for data integrity, privacy, and sustainable learning. In *Smart education and sustainable learning environments in smart cities* (pp. 93–105). IGI Global.

Wang, C., Wang, C., Zheng, W., & Gu, W. (2025). AI-enhanced secure data aggregation for smart grids with privacy preservation. *Computers, Materials and Continua, 82*(1), 799–816.

Wei, X., Kumar, N., & Zhang, H. (2025). Addressing bias in generative AI: challenges and research opportunities in information management. *Information and Management, 62*(2), 104103.

Wolniak, R., & Grebski, W. (2025). Sustainable trends and determinants of wheat cultivation in Poland (2004–2023): a spatiotemporal analysis of productivity, resilience, and climate adaptation. *Sustainability, 17*(5), 1–35.

Wolniak, R., Stecuła, K., & Aydın, B. (2024a). Digital transformation of grocery in-store shopping – scanners, artificial intelligence, augmented reality and beyond: a review. *Foods, 13*(18), Article 2948, 1–34.

Wolniak, R., Gajdzik, B., Grebski, M., Danel, R., & Grebski, W.W. (2024b). Business models used in Smart Cities—theoretical approach with examples of Smart Cities. *Smart Cities, 7*, 1626–1669.

Wolniak, R., & Stecuła, K. (2024). Artificial intelligence in Smart Cities—applications, barriers and future directions: a review. *Smart Cities, 7*, 1346–1389.

Yu, M., Fang, M., & Wang, B. (2025). Ethical frameworks for data-driven environmental health studies in the AI era. *Environment and Health, 3*, 443–445.

Zafeirakopoulos, D., & Stefaneas, P. (2024). Toward responsible AI: a framework for ethical design utilizing deontic logic. *International Journal on Artificial Intelligence Tools, 33*(8), 2550003.

CHAPTER 7

AI and Corporate Social Responsibility (CSR) in HRM

7.1 AI'S ROLE IN ADVANCING ESG (ENVIRONMENTAL, SOCIAL, GOVERNANCE) GOALS

The way businesses address environmental, social, and economic issues has fundamentally changed as a result of the intentional incorporation of AI technology into sustainability initiatives. Many nations have chosen to approach AI development strategically, and so far, over 30 nations have done so, with the United States and Western Europe setting the standard (Jankovic & Curovic, 2023). According to one piece of research from a Finances online article, AI and machine learning are to be game changers in 2023 (Gilbert, 2019). According to the same report, 90% of corporate leaders questioned anticipate that AI would be completely implemented by 2027 (Gilbert, 2019).

ESG measures how well businesses perform in environmental management, social responsibility, and corporate governance, and it is a good indicator of the potential for sustainable corporate growth. The influence of businesses on the environment and the steps taken to preserve it throughout operations and production are referred to as environmental indicators. This covers programs for managing waste, wastewater, and gas emissions; it also covers energy and resource management and use; and it covers environmental protection measures. Social indicators relate to the social responsibility that businesses have when interacting with communities, governments, suppliers, workers, and consumers. Concerns and safeguards pertaining to worker rights and working conditions, consumer rights, community service, social welfare, safety, and health are all included in this. Governance indicators, which include corporate governance, information disclosure, internal controls, and risk management, concentrate on the soundness,

DOI: 10.1201/9781003668282-10

transparency, and compliance of internal management and governance systems (Chen & Zhang, 2025a; Mohamed Riyath & Inun Jariya, 2024).

AI serves as a lighthouse, showing the way to a future where companies not only achieve their financial goals but also perform exceptionally well in terms of ethics, the environment, and society as the whole community becomes more dedicated to sustainable practices (Sklavos et al., 2025).

A revolutionary way to improve the efficacy and efficiency of sustainability activities is by incorporating AI into ESG frameworks (Dumitrescu & Buzatu, 2020; Isensee, Griese, & Teuteberg, 2021; Jankovic & Curovic, 2023; Saxena et al., 2023; Toniolo et al., 2020). Because of its strengths in data processing, pattern recognition, and predictive analytics, artificial intelligence has emerged as a crucial instrument for achieving ESG goals (Agrawal et al., 2022; Govindan, 2024; Khan et al., 2022b). AI tools like computer vision, natural language processing, and machine learning (ML) are used to evaluate large datasets, spot sustainability possibilities and threats, and maximize resource use. Businesses' sustainability performance is enhanced by these skills, which empower them to make well-informed choices that support ESG objectives (Rane, Choudhary, & Rane, 2024).

AI technologies greatly enhance the environmental component of ESG (Bickley, Macintyre, & Torgler, 2025; Djalic et al., 2021; Musleh Al-Sartawi, Hussainey, & Razzaque, 2022). AI-driven analytics are able to optimize energy use, forecast climate-related hazards, and track environmental footprints (Musleh Al-Sartawi, Hussainey, & Razzaque, 2022; Rane et al., 2024; Senadjki et al., 2023). To measure carbon emissions, monitor deforestation, and evaluate biodiversity loss, for instance, machine learning systems may examine satellite photos. By using predictive models to predict how climate change may affect business operations, organizations can take early steps to reduce risks. Furthermore, AI-powered optimization methods may lower waste and increase energy efficiency, which helps to promote more sustainable resource management (Kitsios & Kamariotou, 2021; Sjödin, Parida, & Kohtamäki, 2023; Larbi-Siaw et al., 2022).

Making strategic decisions is made easier by artificial intelligence, which provides data-driven insights on ESG problems. Companies may use machine learning algorithms to assess the impact of various ESG operations and determine the best ways to achieve sustainability goals. AI also helps in the creation of ESG policies by evaluating past performance information and forecasting the possible effects of different policy approaches. By ensuring that companies adopt ESG policies that are both successful and well-founded in knowledge, this promotes favorable social and environmental outcomes. Table 7.1 presents AI's role in advancing ESG goals.

AI HRM applications grounded in ESG demonstrate a larger interest in corporate social responsibility (Kvasničková Stanislavská et al., 2023; Rosak-Szyrocka et al., 2022b). AI ensures that strategic aspirations for sustainability are consistent with the ethical demands of CSR by facilitating transparent reporting, advancing equity, and nurturing environmental care (Gagliardi & Tomaselli, 2025).

TABLE 7.1 AI's role in advancing ESG goals

ESG	AI application/HRM area	Description	Results
Environmental	Employee Carbon Footprint Analysis/ Mobility and Benefits Management	AI processes information from HR and travel-management tools (such as SAP Concur). AI tracks carbon footprints down to the place, frequency, and how we travel. It also suggests alternative remote or green travel alternatives.	CO_2 emission reduction and adoption of Green HRM policy.
Environmental	Sustainable Office and Remote Work Planning/Hybrid Work Strategy	AI processes office energy usage, team size, and the geographical location of employees to suggest the ideal remote or hybrid working model. It can predict resource (e.g., HVAC, building systems) utilization in accordance with the building occupation.	Lowering the cost of energy, improving the work environment, making less of an environmental impact.
Environmental	Environmental Education for Employees/Training and Development	AI-driven e-learning systems tailor ESG-related learning paths to employee roles. These systems analyze the environmental knowledge and attitude in order to customize the delivery of content.	Better ecological consciousness and staff engagement.
Social	DEI Analysis in Recruitment and Promotions/Equal Opportunity and Inclusion	AI scans job postings, resumes, and promotion information to look for biased language and a lack of diversity in job change paths and recommends ways to fix these problems.	Equal recruitment and promotion, better employer branding.
Social	Emotion and Sentiment Analysis of Employees/Employee Experience/HR Analytics	AI evaluates data from surveys, Slack, or MS Teams as well as the tone of messages, engagement rates, and keywords themselves to identify burnout, or drops in morale, or likelihood of flight.	HR early intervention and the retention of talent.
Social	Preventing Workplace Bullying and Discrimination/ Compliance & HR Ethics	AI reviews internal messages (emails, chats) and HR reports to uncover patterns of aggression, exclusion, or sexism.	Increased psychological safety, decreased legal risk.
Social	Occupational Safety Monitoring/ Workplace Safety	AI-enabled wearable sensors track health indicators (such as heart rate and fatigue) of physical workers to signal alerts under unsafe situations.	Less accidents, better risk management.
Social	Leadership Communication Analysis/Leadership and Organizational Culture	AI scans manager communications (emails, townhalls) for ESG values, to flag whether leaders are promoting inclusion and transparency or not.	Reliable and honest leadership, integrity-based company culture.

(*Continued*)

TABLE 7.1 (*Continued*)

ESG	AI application/HRM area	Description	Results
Governance	Automated HR-ESG Reporting/Reporting & HR Analytics	AI connects HR data (e.g., turnover, ESG-specific training and other workforce data) and provides ESG-compliant reporting.	Transparency, time-saving, regulatory certainty (CSRD).
Governance	HR Policy Compliance with ESG/HR Compliance	AI algorithms screen internal documents (codes of ethics, procedures) and compare them with ESG regulations and GRI standards.	Risk mitigation for legal contexts and image.
Governance	Employment Ethics Audits/HR Audits	Artificial intelligence assesses employment, dismissals, promotions, and training to spot discrepancies compared to stated ESG commitments.	Trust between organizations and between policy and practice.
Governance	Evaluating ESG Policy Effectiveness in HR/ HR and ESG Strategy	Use AI to extract intelligence on links between HR policies (e.g., flexible work, ESG training) and ESG outcomes via predictive modeling.	Smarter strategic and investment choices.
Governance	Board Composition Analytics/Corporate Governance & HR	AI analyzes company boards for diversity, ESG literacy, and experience to help companies comply with investor expectations.	More trust from stakeholders, leading to more ESG compliance.

Source: Own study, based on: Chang & Ke (2024); Chen & Zhang (2025b); Khan et al. (2022a); Saxena et al. (2023).

7.2 AI AND FAIR COMPENSATION POLICIES

A crucial organizational function, payroll and compensation administration has a direct bearing on financial success, employee happiness, and compliance. However, issues like human error, slowness, and the difficulty of handling various compensation schemes are common problems with conventional payroll systems. By combining AI with Finance Information Systems (FIS) and HRM technologies, payroll and compensation procedures may become much more accurate, efficient, and successful. In order to ensure that businesses satisfy both employee expectations and legal obligations, AI-driven solutions may automate computations, optimize pay plans, improve compliance, and provide real-time insights into financial data (Ashrafuzzaman, Prince, & Rahman, 2024; Bandara et al., 2025; Sklavos et al., 2024).

AI additionally helps with pay equity audits by examining historical payroll records to identify any unexplained pay discrepancies between different demographic segments (e.g., men versus women or between specific ethnicities) so that the organization is in compliance with regulatory requirements like the EU's Pay Transparency Directive (Cowgill et al., 2020; Tambe, Cappelli, & Yakubovich, 2019; Wachter, Mittelstadt, & Russell,

TABLE 7.2 AI and fair compensation policies

AI application/HRM area	Description	Results
Automation of Payroll Processing/Payroll Administration	AI systems determine salaries, bonuses, and taxes from data in time-tracking systems and employee databases, reducing errors and delays.	Improved payment accuracy and timely payments, reduced payroll errors.
Data-Driven Designs of Compensation Structures/ Compensation Policy	Pay levels will be compared to market benchmarks, employee performance, and internal structures, enabling the development of equitable and competitive pay structures.	Fair salary, increased talent retention, and enhanced employer brand.
HR Budgeting and Forecasting/ Controlling the Human Resources Budget	Algorithims project future payroll costs through employment trends and historical data to assist in long-term HR financial plans.	Optimization of resource and financial planning.
Compliance, Regulations/ Legal Compliance, & Risk Management	AI keeps an ongoing eye on labor and tax legislation changes and dynamically recalculates pay slips for compliance purposes.	Reduction of legal and compliance risk.
Reporting and Payroll Data Analysis/HR Analytics	AI reporting provides real-time updates on compensation costs, bonuses, ESG compliance, and salary trends.	Evidenced-based HR decision-making, ESG reporting mandate.
Providing Employees with a Transparent and Personalized Compensation Experience/ Employee Experience/HR Comunication	AI gives employees open visibility into what goes into their pay and individualized paths for compensation growth.	Higher employee engagement and employee satisfaction, less turnover.

Source: Own study, based on: "Optimizing payroll and compensation with AI: Integrating HRM and Finance Information Systems for improved efficiency" (2021).

2021; Northern Ireland Human Rights Commission, 2024). When well-designed and audited, machine learning algorithms can remove biases from compensation decisions through standardizing salary evaluations—taking subjective human judgments out of the decision-making process (Agrawal et al., 2022; Cowgill et al., 2020). Table 7.2 presents AI and fair compensation policies.

7.3 SUSTAINABLE LEADERSHIP DEVELOPMENT WITH AI

In order to promote long-term social, economic, and environmental growth, sustainable leadership is essential. Businesses are incorporating sustainability into their fundamental goals more and more, so executives need to take measures that balance ethical obligation with profitability (Rosário & Boechat, 2025).

Businesses that are both financially stable and socially and ecologically conscious must have sustainable leadership. This kind of leadership is defined by Liao (Liao, 2022) as one that seeks to balance the relationship between people, profits, and the earth and promote the sustainability of the enterprise through corresponding management practices. Leaders who practice sustainability understand that companies function in a broader socio-environmental framework and that their choices affect communities, shareholders, workers, consumers, and the environment.

Accordingly, Tideman et al. (Tideman, Arts, & Zandee, 2013) clarified that they support corporate sustainability programs, encourage eco-friendly solution creation, and foster a corporate culture that harmonizes company aims with more general sustainability objectives. Incorporating sustainability into business strategy and decision-making enables sustainable leaders to assist organizations in reducing risks, improving brand recognition, and generating a long-lasting societal effect (Rosário & Boechat, 2025).

Businesses are changing as a result of the introduction of AI technologies like generative AI, which require employees to upskill in order to stay relevant in the digital age (Behki, 2023). Generative AI tools are enabling us to create fresh leadership and management models, a development that is driving the need for new leadership and management methods at organizations around the world ("McKinsey, 2023). 33% of organizations have adopted GenAI in one or more business areas already, with 40% intending to invest more heavily in AI because of the strategic value it brings. In such a scenario, the idea of future-ready leadership is starting to gain recognition (Afolabi, 2025; Ng Foo Seong, 2019).

Future-ready leadership isn't simply the ability to bring in new technologies, either, but to integrate them with the pillars of long-term success: a commitment to social responsibility, the steel of organizational resilience, and the ethical governance of data and talent. As Afolabi (2025) has highlighted, the next generation of leaders will need to know how to spot the potential of AI and manage the risk and facilitate inclusive work environments where technology increases organizational resilience rather than excluding a section of the workforce.

In the realm of sustainability-oriented development, the future-ready leader is one who ushers in reskilling and skill transformation programs rather than making humans redundant with automation. McKinsey (2023) found that 39% of companies expect to reskill more than 20% of their workforce over the next three years from the introduction of AI compared to just 8% that expect substantial reductions in the workforce. This is a significant departure from "automate and eliminate" toward "automate and elevate."

With the increasing use of GenAI, policy on its use is lacking in 79% of organizations and only 32% are managing the most commonly cited threat—inaccurate data (McKinsey, 2023) This shows that technology evolution in itself is not all-powerful—it is leadership that has to usher in the innovation that has to be tamed.

This makes future-ready leadership strategic, ethical, and always ready leadership. These are the leaders who don't wait for change; they build organizations that are nimble, include and work for others, and prepare for the next crisis because it could be around the corner—the players in building a sustainable, technologically advanced future.

A recent survey of 179 HR leaders conducted by Gartner in 2024 found that 38% of organizations are already piloting or in further phases of implementing generative AI (GenAI) in HR, up from 19% in the middle of 2023 (Gartner, 2025a). Despite the increased momentum, 67% are not planning on creating any dedicated GenAI roles over the next 12 months, indicating that accountability for adopting AI is becoming woven into existing leadership roles (Gartner, 2025b). The most common use cases for GenAI are employee-facing chatbots (43%), automating administrative tasks (42%), and creating recruitment content like job descriptions and skill profiles (41%). Yet only 34% of HR departments are updating development plans to reskill employees to work with AI. However 41% of HR leaders have not yet started any training programs related to GenAI. These results continue to highlight the value of self-directed learning and leadership development. While recent digitalization and developing workforce dynamics might be forging a new landscape, for now at least, the organizations that support HR leaders to retrain employees, cautiously implement AI, and instil adaptive learning cultures will probably be the ones to see the best long-term ROI and develop resilience among their leadership.

Self-upskilling is a proactive approach to professional progression and skill development for leaders. Among its numerous benefits are agility, flexibility, bridging skill gaps, promoting creativity, and cultivating a mindset of lifelong learning. Prominent corporate leaders who have embraced self-directed learning include Sheryl Sandberg, Elon Musk, Angela Ahrendts, and Satya Nadella. In order to foster an inventive and creative culture, these leaders emphasized the need for continual education and personal growth (Vroman & Danko, 2022). By practicing self-upskilling, leaders may stay successful and relevant in changing circumstances. Leaders need to control risks, make wise choices, and prepare their companies for unforeseen challenges. Adopting new technologies like generative AI, being informed about upcoming trends, and taking a proactive approach to self-development are all necessary to overcome these challenges. Technological advancements, geopolitical unpredictability, and changing workforce dynamics all contribute to the ongoing development of leadership. By offering individualized, effective, and data-driven learning experiences, GAI can help leaders maintain their competitiveness in the job (Rukadikar & Khandelwal, 2024).

Leadership development platforms powered by AI enable personalized learning curricula, ability assessment capabilities for leads-in-waiting, and decision-making simulations that are reflective of actual business issues (Chen & Zhang, 2025a; Sposato & Dittmar, 2025). This is because these platforms foster the growth of the strategic mind as well as emotional intelligence—the two most fundamental qualities of VUCA leadership (Rosak-Szyrocka, Gupta, & Boccia, 2024; Rosak-Szyrocka et al., 2025; Rosak-Szyrocka, Żywiołek, & Mrowiec, 2022a). Table 7.3 introduces the opportunities and risks of AI in sustainable leadership development.

7.4 HR'S ROLE IN PROMOTING ETHICAL AI ADOPTION

The increasingly accelerated digitalization of HR processes will produce a paradigm shift in the expectations and tasks of HR personnel (Madanchian & Taherdoost, 2025; Pan et al., 2023; Rosak-Szyrocka, 2024). Artificial intelligence is not only changing how we recruit, assess, and manage talent; it also creates a series of ethical considerations which cannot be ignored (Alzeiby et al., 2025).

TABLE 7.3 Opportunities and risks of AI in sustainable leadership development

Opportunities	Challenges
Individual leadership development with data and machine learning	Algorithmic bias in leader election/ performance appraisals
Hidden leadership talent unlocked through behavioral data	Algorithmic opacity could decrease trust of employees
Support for moral leadership through decision simulations with ESG value embedment	Over-dependence on AI advice resulting in loss of leader autonomy
Scalable and inclusive leadership trainings for all segments of the community	Data privacy and security concerns for board members and staff
Automation of learning pathways—lower cost and time investment for training	Danger in supplanting the human element with technocratic rationality
Enhancing organizational resilience with AI-enabled leadership agility	Possible further widening of skills gaps across firms and sectors
Rapidly identify future-ready leaders' critically needed competencies through predictive analytics	Reliance on tech providers reduces internal leadership development
Sharper insights into team dynamics and leadership through analysis of digital interactions	Threat of AI being employed to surveil, resulting in trust and autonomy erosion

Source: Own study, based on: Afolabi (2025); "The state of AI in 2023: Generative AI's breakout year | McKinsey" (2025b); Forbes (2024); Gartner (2025b).

55% percent of the companies it surveyed now use AI in at least one business function, but only 21% have established clear rules for employees when it comes to using generative AI tools in the workplace, according to the "State of AI in 2023" report released by the consulting firm McKinsey & Company (McKinsey, 2023). That will be a clear mark that HR is not a passive technology recipient but a guarantor for its ethical implementation (Alzeiby et al., 2025; Madanchian & Taherdoost, 2025).

At a time when people management processes are increasingly mechanized and algorithmized, the HR department plays a new and crucial part: not only as a user of AI-driven technology, but primarily as the guardian of ethical values in the company (Senadjki et al., 2023). Emphasizing the need for responsible AI adoption more than knowledge, it requires a profound understanding of the social, cultural, and organizational implications of technology implementation. In this sense, then, HR will emerge as a broker between business goals and employee interests and as a defender of the position that technology will augment the human side of work, not destroy it (Stein, 2025).

It's HR's job to play an active role in designing and deploying AI solutions not simply from a technical point of view but from a human one. It requires working with IT, compliance, and leadership to create ethical AI guidelines in categories from hiring and performance appraisals to promotion, training, and more. HR must take the lead in the development of internal ethical codes for the use of AI as well as systems that can monitor the transparency and fairness of algorithmic decision-making. It is particularly critical to make sure AI-enabled processes do not mirror existing biases or deepen workplace inequalities (Imam & Schaffer, 2024; Raghavan et al., 01272020).

Just as important is HR's responsibility to educate companies' leadership and ranks with respect to their digital and ethical competencies in the AI domain. HR should be the department responsible for fostering AI literacy across the business: ensuring that everyone knows how algorithms work, what dangers they represent, how to challenge their decision, and what their rights are when it comes to human-in-the-loop automation (Kumar et al., 2024; Islami & Mulolli, 2024). Only when all stakeholders are informed can an organization utilize AI in a fair and responsible way (Tripathi & Rosak-Szyrocka, 2024).

Another important factor is to create a working culture based on trust, responsibility, and openness to new technology. HR must function as a champion of values which protect the human side of work in the algorithms era—values like empathy, fairness, autonomy, and responsibility (Ainsworth & Pekarek, 2025; Stein, 2025). This is where HR is most powerful in deciding how technology is experienced by the employee—either as a means of support and growth or one of control and oppression (Tripathi & Rosak-Szyrocka, 2024).

Lastly, HR needs to act as a strategic partner in AI systems ethics oversight (Andreas, 2024). That means contributing to building early-warning instruments on unethical algorithmic outcomes, contributing to reporting channels for violations, and contributing to internal governance bodies responsible for technological ethics (e.g., AI ethics committees or ethical digital transformation working groups.) HR can also introduce ethical audits of AI tools used in employee management and making use of participatory design practices, where the voices of employees will be taken into account from the onset when developing systems (Bar-Gil, Ron, & Czerniak, 2024).

REFERENCES

Afolabi, J. A. (2025). Harnessing predictive analytics and machine learning for minority business resilience, crisis management, and competitive advantage. *International Journal of Research Publication and Reviews, 6*(4), 1810–1827.

Agrawal, R., Wankhede, V. A., Kumar, A., Upadhyay, A., & Garza-Reyes, J. A. (2022). Nexus of circular economy and sustainable business performance in the era of digitalization. *International Journal of Productivity and Performance Management, 71*(3), 748–774, from www.emerald.com/insight/content/doi/10.1108/ijppm-12-2020-0676/full/pdf?casa_token=pm64bkndm8caaaaa:jtyjhqlrj1htkytz-drwulal93cs9hjskb-zi2wdni1dq_5xrrpn8imo5sko8jpz5vema4ckbqcbunkzappxzoqo9hbozs30hxlaqnrhrplmduhn.

Ainsworth, S., & Pekarek, A. (2025). *Between a rock and a hard place: ethics in Human Resource Management,* SAGE Publications: SAGE Business Cases Originals.

Alzeiby, E. A., Islam, N., Shaik, A. S., & Yaqub, M. Z. (2025). AI adoption in enterprises for enhanced strategic human resource management practices: benefiting the employee engagement and experience. *Journal of Enterprise Information Management, ahead-of-print*(ahead-of-print), from www.emerald.com/insight/content/doi/10.1108/jeim-05-2024-0249/full/pdf?casa_token=emryw6shsqmaaaaa:xdjmgnlp2m_-spmln5lrcvraadgtpui8dbtnew8_rt3rjh0vgu0hc3u23kfaaknloulekfxzugpvgjozm0majtkrg9ys0-_o_xdnap4mph9k6tq2.

Andreas, N. B. (2024). Ethics in international HRD: examining conversational AI and HR chatbots. *Strategic HR Review, 23*(3), 121–125, from www.emerald.com/insight/content/doi/10.1108/shr-03-2024-0018/full/pdf.

Ashrafuzzaman, M. D., Prince, K. B., & Rahman, A. (2024). Integrating artificial intelligence in HRM: The role of management information systems in enhancing decision-making processes. *International Journal of Management Information Systems and Data Science, 1*(4), 1–16. Available at SSRN: https://ssrn.com/abstract=5031919 or http://dx.doi.org/10.2139/ssrn.5031919

Bandara, R. J., Biswas, K., Akter, S., Shafique, S., & Rahman, M. (2025). Addressing algorithmic bias in AI-Driven HRM systems: implications for strategic HRM effectiveness. *Human Resource Management Journal,* 1–17. https://doi.org/10.1111/1748-8583.12609

Bar-Gil, O., Ron, T., & Czerniak, O. (2024). AI for the people? Embedding AI ethics in HR and people analytics projects. *Technology in Society, 77,* 102527.

Behki, N. (2023). *The future of work: the urgency of reskilling and upskilling in the age of generative AI.* Retrieved June 05, 2025, from www.linkedin.com/pulse/future-work-urgency-reskilling-upskilling-age-generative-nitin-behki

Bickley, S. J., Macintyre, A., & Torgler, B. (2025). Artificial intelligence and big data in sustainable entrepreneurship. *Journal of Economic Surveys, 39*(1), 103–145.

Chang, Y.-L., & Ke, J. (2024). Socially responsible artificial intelligence empowered people analytics: a novel framework towards sustainability. *Human Resource Development Review, 23*(1), 88–120.

Chen, R., & Zhang, T. (2025a). Artificial intelligence applications implication for ESG performance: can digital transformation of enterprises promote sustainable development? *Chinese Management Studies, 19*(3), 676–701.

Chen, R., & Zhang, T. (2025b). Artificial intelligence applications implication for ESG performance: can digital transformation of enterprises promote sustainable development? *Chinese Management Studies, 19*(3), 676–701.

Cowgill, B., Dell'Acqua, F., Deng, S., Hsu, D., Verma, N., & Chaintreau, A. (2020). Biased programmers? Or biased data? A field experiment in operationalizing ai ethics. In *Proceedings of the 21st ACM Conference on Economics and Computation* (pp. 679–681). ACM.

Djalic, N., Nikolic, M., Bakator, M., & Erceg, Z. (2021). Modeling the influence of information systems on sustainable business performance and competitiveness. *Sustainability, 13*(17), 9619, from www.mdpi.com/2071-1050/13/17/9619.

Dumitrescu, B. I., & Buzatu, A. I. (2020). Sustainable businesses enhanced through digital transformation and artificial intelligence in the context of Industry 4.0. *New Trends in Sustainable Business and Consumption,* 910-917.

Forbes. (2024). *AI and leadership: how to thrive in the digital transformation age.* Retrieved June 05, 2025, from www.forbes.com/councils/forbestechcouncil/2024/09/18/ai-and-leadership-how-to-thrive-in-the-digital-transformation-age/.

Gagliardi, A. R., & Tomaselli, G. (2025). Aligning corporate social responsibility with artificial intelligence in healthcare in the context of the post-COVID-19 recovery: a viewpoint. *Journal of Health Organization and Management, ahead-of-print*(ahead-of-print), from www.emerald.com/insight/content/doi/10.1108/jhom-06-2024-0244/full/pdf?casa_token=ywtu5imrenkaaaaa:adrqnovnbucc3xsnz53h_tlrfvkodnzuym6h_matndwqz4p0ynczqqksacsamz-dpp01ujddn-1phts0o6xcdmwdpfljx7cnzixt9eyoayrinuk5.

Gartner. (2025a). *Gartner survey finds 38% HR leaders reported they are piloting, planning implementation, or have already implemented Generative AI.* Retrieved June 05, 2025, from www.gartner.com/en/newsroom/press-releases/2024-02-27-gartner-finds-38-percent-hr-leaders-piloting-generative-ai.

Gartner. (2025b). *Gartner survey finds 38% HR leaders reported they are piloting, planning implementation, or have already implemented Generative AI.* Retrieved June 05, 2025, from www.

gartner.com/en/newsroom/press-releases/2024-02-27-gartner-finds-38-percent-hr-leaders-piloting-generative-ai.

Gilbert, N. (2019). *70 vital artificial intelligence statistics: 2024 Data Analysis & Market Share – Financesonline.com.* Retrieved June 04, 2025, from https://financesonline.com/artificial-intelligence-statistics/.

Govindan, K. (2024). How artificial intelligence drives sustainable frugal innovation: a multitheoretical perspective. *IEEE Transactions on Engineering Management, 71*, 638–655.

Imam, H. & Schaffer, A. (2024). *Ethical Implications of Artificial Intelligence Implementation in Human Resources Job Performance Evaluation.* http://dx.doi.org/10.13140/RG.2.2.22782.40001

Isensee, C., Griese, K.-M., & Teuteberg, F. (2021). Sustainable artificial intelligence: a corporate culture perspective. *Sustainability Management Forum | NachhaltigkeitsManagementForum, 29*(3-4), 217–230, from https://link.springer.com/article/10.1007/s00550-021-00524-6.

Islami, X., & Mulolli, E. (2024). Human-artificial intelligence in management functions: a synergistic symbiosis relationship. *Applied Artificial Intelligence, 38*(1).

Jankovic, S. D., & Curovic, D. M. (2023). Strategic integration of artificial intelligence for sustainable businesses: implications for data management and human user engagement in the digital era. *Sustainability, 15*(21), 15208, from www.mdpi.com/2071-1050/15/21/15208.

Khan, M. A., Abbas, K., Su'ud, M. M., Salameh, A. A., Alam, M. M., Aman, N., et al. (2022). Application of machine learning algorithms for sustainable business management based on macro-economic data: supervised learning techniques approach. *Sustainability, 14*(16), 9964, from www.mdpi.com/2071-1050/14/16/9964.

Kitsios, F., & Kamariotou, M. (2021). Artificial intelligence and business strategy towards digital transformation: a research agenda. *Sustainability, 13*(4), 2025, from www.mdpi.com/2071-1050/13/4/2025.

Kumar, N., Pal, S. K., Agarwal, P., Rosak-Szyrocka, J., & Jain, V. (Eds.). (2024). *Human-Machine Collaboration and Emotional Intelligence in Industry 5.0*, IGI Global.

Kvasničková Stanislavská, L., Pilař, L., Vogli, X., Hlavsa, T., Kuralová, K., Feenstra, A., et al. (2023). Global analysis of Twitter communication in corporate social responsibility area: sustainability, climate change, and waste management. *PeerJ Computer Science, 9*, e1390.

Larbi-Siaw, O., Xuhua, H., Owusu, E., Owusu-Agyeman, A., Fulgence, B. E., & Frimpong, S. A. (2022). Eco-innovation, sustainable business performance and market turbulence moderation in emerging economies. *Technology in Society, 68*, 101899.

Liao, Y. (2022). Sustainable leadership: a literature review and prospects for future research. *Frontiers in Psychology, 13*, 1045570, from www.frontiersin.org/articles/10.3389/fpsyg.2022.1045570/full.

Madanchian, M., & Taherdoost, H. (2025). Criteria for AI adoption in HR: efficiency vs. ethics. *Procedia Computer Science, 258*, 233–241.

McKinsey & Company. (2023, August 1). *The state of AI in 2023: Generative AI's breakout year* [McKinsey Global Survey on AI]. McKinsey & Company. www.mckinsey.com/capabilities/quantumblack/our-insights/the-state-of-ai-in-2023-generative-ais-breakout-year

Mohamed Riyath, M. I., & Inun Jariya, A. M. (2024). The role of ESG reporting, artificial intelligence, stakeholders and innovation performance in fostering sustainability culture and climate resilience. *Journal of Financial Reporting and Accounting.* https://doi.org/10.1108/JFRA-10-2023-0621

Musleh Al-Sartawi, A. M. A., Hussainey, K., & Razzaque, A. (2022). The role of artificial intelligence in sustainable finance. *Journal of Sustainable Finance & Investment*, 1–6. https://doi.org/10.1080/20430795.2022.2057405

Northern Ireland Human Rights Commission. (2024). The EU Pay Transparency Directive.

Ng Foo Seong, D. (2019). Future-ready leadership development. In Townsend, T. (Ed.), *Instructional Leadership and Leadership for Learning in Schools* (pp. 165–192). Palgrave Studies on Leadership and Learning in Teacher Education. Palgrave Macmillan. https://doi.org/10.1007/978-3-030-23736-3_7.

Pan, M., Zhao, X., lv, K., Rosak-Szyrocka, J., Mentel, G., & Truskolaski, T. (2023). Internet development and carbon emission-reduction in the era of digitalization: where will resource-based cities go? *Resources Policy, 81*, 103345.

Raghavan, M., Barocas, S., Kleinberg, J., & Levy, K. (01272020). Mitigating bias in algorithmic hiring. In M. Hildebrandt, C. Castillo, E. Celis, S. Ruggieri, L. Taylor, & G. Zanfir-Fortuna (Eds.), *Proceedings of the 2020 Conference on Fairness, Accountability, and Transparency* (pp. 469–481). ACM.

Rane, N., Choudhary, S., & Rane, J. (2024). Artificial intelligence driven approaches to strengthening Environmental, Social, and Governance (ESG) criteria in sustainable business practices: a review. *SSRN Electronic Journal.* https://ssrn.com/abstract=4843215 or http://dx.doi.org/10.2139/ssrn.4843215

Rane, N., Paramesha, M., Choudhary, S., & Rane, J. (2024). Business intelligence and artificial intelligence for sustainable development: Integrating internet of things, machine learning, and big data analytics for enhanced sustainability. *Machine Learning, and Big Data Analytics for Enhanced Sustainability (May 20, 2024).*

Rosak-Szyrocka, J. (2024). The era of digitalization in education where do Universities 4.0 go? *Management Systems in Production Engineering, 32*(1), 54–66.

Rosak-Szyrocka, J., Gupta, S. K., & Boccia, F. (2024). New role of value for customer 5.0 in augmented era. In *Aspects of quality management in value creating in the Industry 5.0 way* (pp. 1–20). CRC Press.

Rosak-Szyrocka, J., Gupta, S. K., Shahbaz, M., & Launer, M. (Eds.). (2025). *Enhancing smart universities with emotional intelligence: competences for digital age learning,* Routledge.

Rosak-Szyrocka, J., Żywiołek, J., & Mrowiec, M. (2022a). Analysis of customer satisfaction with the quality of energy market services in Poland. *Energies, 15*(10), 3622, from www.mdpi.com/1996-1073/15/10/3622.

Rosak-Szyrocka, J., Żywiołek, J., Shengelia, N., Stverkova, H., Santo, P. E., & Pilař, L. (2022b). Employee perception of CSR and its effects on the company's image. *Production Engineering Archives, 28*(3), 210–216.

Rosário, A. T., & Boechat, A. C. (2025). How sustainable leadership can leverage sustainable development. *Sustainability, 17*(8), 3499.

Rukadikar, A., & Khandelwal, K. (2024). Leadership development through self-upskilling: role of generative artificial intelligence. *Development and Learning in Organizations: An International Journal, 38*(4), 27–30.

Saxena, A., Singh, R., Gehlot, A., Akram, S. V., Twala, B., Singh, A., et al. (2023). technologies empowered Environmental, Social, and Governance (ESG): an Industry 4.0 landscape. *Sustainability, 15*(1), 309.

Senadjki, A., Ogbeibu, S., Mohd, S., Hui Nee, A. Y., & Awal, I. M. (2023). harnessing artificial intelligence for business competitiveness in achieving Sustainable Development Goals. *Journal of Asia-Pacific Business, 24*(3), 149–169.

Sjödin, D., Parida, V., & Kohtamäki, M. (2023). Artificial intelligence enabling circular business model innovation in digital servitization: Conceptualizing dynamic capabilities, AI capacities, business models and effects. *Technological Forecasting and Social Change, 197*, 122903.

Sklavos, G., Theodossiou, G., Papanikolaou, Z., Karelakis, C., & Lazarides, T. (2025). A new direction in Human Resources Management and ESG: transforming business models. In *Sustainability through Green HRM and performance integration* (pp. 329–352). IGI Global Scientific Publishing; IGI Global.

Sklavos, G., Theodossiou, G., Papanikolaou, Z., Karelakis, C., & Ragazou, K. (2024). Environmental, Social, and Governance-based artificial intelligence governance: digitalizing firms' leadership and human resources management. *Sustainability, 16*(16), 7154, from www.mdpi.com/2071-1050/16/16/7154.

Sposato, M., & Dittmar, E. C. (2025). The AI-powered future of digital transformation: enhancing organizations and leadership development. *Journal of Work-Applied Management, ahead-of-print*(ahead-of-print), from www.emerald.com/insight/content/doi/10.1108/jwam-02-2025-0039/full/pdf.

Stein, E. (2025). *Human resource development competencies for HR business partners,* Kohlhammer Verlag.

Tambe, P., Cappelli, P., & Yakubovich, V. (2019). Artificial intelligence in human resources management: challenges and a path forward. *California Management Review, 61*(4), 15–42.

Tideman, S. G., Arts, M. C., & Zandee, D. P. (2013). Sustainable leadership: towards a workable definition. *Journal of Corporate Citizenship, 2013*(49), 17–33.

Toniolo, K., Masiero, E., Massaro, M., & Bagnoli, C. (2020). Sustainable business models and artificial intelligence: opportunities and challenges. In: Matos, F., Vairinhos, V., Salavisa, I., Edvinsson, L., & Massaro, M. (Eds.), *Knowledge, People, and Digital Transformation. Contributions to Management Science* (pp. 103–117). Springer. https://doi.org/10.1007/978-3-030-40390-4_8

Tripathi, S., & Rosak-Szyrocka, J. (2024). *Impact of artificial intelligence on society,* CRC Press.

Vroman, S. R., & Danko, T. (2022). How to build a successful upskilling program. *Harvard Business Review.* https://hbr. org/2022/01/how-to-build-a-successful upskilling-program.

Wachter, S., Mittelstadt, B., & Russell, C. (2021). Why fairness cannot be automated: bridging the gap between EU non-discrimination law and AI. *Computer Law & Security Review, 41*, 105567.

IV

Case Studies and Future Directions

CHAPTER 8

Case Studies

AI in Sustainable HRM Practices

8.1 CASE STUDY 1: AI-DRIVEN DEI (DIVERSITY, EQUITY, AND INCLUSION) INITIATIVES

Today's organizations are learning that sustainability objectives are impossible to achieve without taking human capital management responsibilities seriously. One of the clearest examples of how to accomplish that has been the role that AI has played in the field of HRM, specifically with regard to efforts like diversity, equity, and inclusion (DEI) (Tripathi & Rosak-Szyrocka, 2024).

Fair AI technologies, as detailed in Microsoft's Global Diversity & Inclusion Report 2024, not only help create fairer hiring processes but help build a fairer work environment, one in which every employee, regardless of background, identity, or ability, has the opportunity to thrive and fully participate in the life of the organization. Table 8.1 presents Case study Microsoft – AI for bias-free hiring and inclusive workplaces.

Case Study 2: Accenture – AI for Inclusive Hiring and DEI Analytics

The global consulting giant Accenture has been at the forefront of using AI to advance diversity, equity, and inclusion (DEI). The company uses natural language processing (NLP) and machine learning (ML) to find biases in its recruitment that can be improved to support more inclusive hiring pools. Inclusive teams are 80% better on team-based assessments (Accenture, 2024). Accenture also uses DEI dashboards that allow real-time tracking of representation, pay equity, and recruitment flows. These systems engender transparency and accountability and yield measurable improvements in workforce diversity and engagement.

DOI: 10.1201/9781003668282-12

TABLE 8.1 Case study Microsoft – AI for bias-free hiring and inclusive workplaces

Focus Area	AI Solutions Employed	Strategic Goal	Results
Inclusive Hiring & Fair Access for Talent	Microsoft Copilot (inclusive language in job postings), candidate matching powered by AI (Mentra), accessible recruitment platforms	Mitigate hiring bias and broaden opportunities for neurodivergent and underrepresented candidates	In Microsoft's own studies, 91% of people who self-identified as neurodivergent (meaning they had autism, ADHD, dyslexia, or something similar) found that Copilot was a useful assistive technology. These results imply that AI interventions such as Copilot are successful at increasing clarity, breaking down communication barriers, and increasing job readiness for a variety of cognitive profiles. In addition, Microsoft's collaboration with Mentra allows for the creation of custom neuroinclusive hiring pipelines—interviews not just brought to meet candidates where they are, but seeking and leveraging the unique strengths of neurodivergent applicants. It also creates a more diverse recruiting pool, positioning Microsoft as an example of inclusive tech recruitment.
Collaboration and Productivity with Accessibility Built in	Copilot integrated into Microsoft Outlook, Teams, and Word—providing summarization, auto scheduling, and inclusive writer support	Empower more inclusive communication and lessen the cognitive burden of overseeing information and meetings	Feedback from customers indicate that 87% indicated great overall productivity through the automation of tasks and simplification enabled by Copilot. 80% said their ability to communicate had improved, in terms of being more coherent with messages or feeling more at ease during virtual meetings. Only 83% would feel confident using Copilot in their daily work. These findings suggest that not only does Copilot increase efficiency, but it also reduces accessibility barriers, particularly for individuals with learning differences or attentional impairments.
Organizational Culture & Sentiment Monitoring	Daily Signals (sentiment analytics), AI-augmented pulse surveys, allyship behavior tracking	Work out how to make the company "work better" by gauging sentiment in the workplace and pivoting as necessary.	With the help of Microsoft AI offerings, 83.5% of employees said they have observed active allyship in the workplace, such as the use of inclusive language, speaking out in support of others, and actively listening to diverse perspectives. Collecting data on employee experiences regularly and at scale allows the organization to respond more quickly to inclusion problems, formulating policies and culture in accordance proactively. And that's basing DEI management on a "pull" system. It's very different from a "push," where we react to things.

Inclusive Leadership & Development	Copilot for building tailored leadership training, AI-enhanced DEI learning journeys	Inclusive leadership capabilities are enhanced and there is increased representation in leadership positions of authority.	For 2024, the percentage of women holding executive positions at Microsoft totals 24.9%, demonstrating continued growth toward more gender parity at the most senior levels of leadership. Additionally, more than 20,000 employees have gone through immersive DEI training simulations, suggesting how Microsoft is investing in scaling inclusive behavior at the various leadership levels. AI allows personalized content as well as in-the-moment learning cues that can be far more inclusive and effective in leadership development.
Employee Empowerment & Belonging	Copilot inspiration, design for confidence, inclusive task management tools, recognition-prompting interfaces	Embracing strategy: Make your employees feel valued, competent, and psychologically safe in their job	76% of employees said Copilot enables them to succeed in their role, helping them better prioritize tasks, communicate more clearly, and take the lead. Users wrote back that they felt an increased sense of autonomy and self-efficacy, they have more of a sense of control over their work, and they felt better when recognized by their teams.
Flexible Work & Digital Inclusion	Copilot meeting summaries, workload management, intelligent prioritization for hybrid work scenarios	Empower remote and hybrid workers to achieve digital equity and fairness while minimizing stress and distraction.	As per the Future of Work 2024: - 84% reported that Copilot allowed them to concentrate on high-priority tasks – 79% were more prepared for meetings – they were 72% better at prioritizing their daily tasks – 78% had reduced mental fatigue, and – 80 % experienced a decrease in information overload

Source: Own study, based on: Microsoft (2025); McIntyre (2024).

Case Study 3: JPMorgan Chase – AI for Unbiased Promotions and Pay Equity

JPMorgan Chase, the world's leading financial services company, has programmatically implemented artificial intelligence (AI) with its human resources management systems to drive fairness in promotions and pay equality. The company uses machine learning (ML) algorithms and natural language processing (NLP) to help uncover and counter unconscious bias in its internal hiring systems (JPMorgan Chase & Co., n.d.; Raji & Buolamwini, 01272019).

JPMorgan Chase also leans on NLP tools to parse the language in employee performance reviews to spot biased or stereotypical wording that might affect decisions around advancement, according to the firm's 2022 ESG Report. Simultaneously, ML models study promotion by demographic groups (e.g., gender, race, ethnicity), identifying systemic inequities and recommending specific interventions (JPMorgan Chase & Co., n.d.). All of that work is also done with the help of AI to perform pay equity audits. This involves measuring pay among similar roles that a person can hold with similar experience and qualifications. At differences, if not justified by legitimate reasons, the system produces salary adjustment recommendations to eliminate the undesired gaps (JPMorgan Chase & Co., n.d.).

To encourage corporate accountability, the company also offers leadership executives access to real-time dashboard insights that show the composition of the workforce, the hiring and promotion rates, and equal pay indicators. This evidence-based approach is based on best practices in algorithmic auditing (Raji & Buolamwini, 01272019) and is consistent with the company's overall approach to promoting diversity, equity, and inclusion (DEI) through empirical research.

Case Study 4: (Meta) Facebook – AI for Inclusive Hiring and Culture in the Workplace

Meta has used AI to promote diverse hiring and work culture. Meta in its 2021 Diversity Report employed AI tools to eliminate bias from hiring and to foster a more inclusive employee experience (Mann, 2025). AI models review interview data and resume-filtering processes looking for discrepancies and flag patterns of exclusion. Feedback obtained in interviews is evaluated using NLP to uncover the slant in biased phrases, which is an extension of recommendations by the WEF (World Economic Forum, 2025a) for inclusive hiring.

Within itself, Meta relies on sentiment analysis to keep tabs on employee feedback on subjects ranging from microaggressions and belonging to team dynamics. The ensuing lessons have resulted in policy adjustments on everything, from remote work to onboarding to inclusive leadership training measures (Isolomons, 2021a; Mann, 2025). Meta's AI in DEI is all about hiring, real-time sentiment analysis, and creating an inclusive company culture. Table 8.2 presents Case study (Meta) Facebook - AI for inclusive hiring and culture in the workplace.

Case 5: Deloitte Innovation – AI for DEI Training and Unbiased Performance Reviews

The consultancy has introduced AI-based tools to improve diversity, equity, and inclusion (DEI) within both the employee development and performance measurement systems.

TABLE 8.2 Case study (Meta) Facebook – AI for inclusive hiring and culture in the workplace

Focus Area	AI Solutions Employed	Strategic Goal	Results
Inclusive Hiring & Equal Access to Opportunity	Meta itself relies on AI tools in candidate screening and to reduce hiring bias. That includes AI coding tests, job-candidate matching, automatically transcribed interview notes, the detection of overlapping job postings, and prompts for question generation for the interviewer.	To make the hiring process fairer and more effective by eliminating repetitive tasks and alerting hiring teams to exclusory patterns at an early stage in the candidate journey	Better candidate-interviewer matching, reduced time to hire, diverse talent pools, and early detection of non-inclusive hiring practices
Interviewer Quality & Inclusivity Monitoring	An AI assistant that is built in gives ratings for your interviewers based on non-inclusive language, the quality of their feedback, and the candidate progress rate. It also tracks interviewer workloads and language abilities.	To increase fairness and quality in interviewing by providing interviewers with helpful feedback, bias detection, and schedule optimization	Increased interviewer accountability, improved interview consistency, more representative interactions, and better utilization of internal HR capacity
Recruitment Operations & Administrative Optimization	Automating HR admin tasks, including scheduling interviews, sending automated reminders, analyzing interviewers' availability, de-duping job ads, and matching candidates by role/skill fit	To simplify the hiring process while eliminating manual coordination and to efficiently deal with high-volume hiring requirements	Dramatically decreased operational burden, more synchronized, shorter cycle times, and more positive candidate experience
Inclusive Workplace Culture & Sentiment Analytics	The sentiment analysis of employee feedback, NLP software for internal comms, and AI tools for real-time tracking of issues such as microaggressions, belonging, and team cohesion	To create a data-driven, inclusive work environment by uncovering and actioning internal equity gaps and cultural friction points	Policy that adjusts with the real-time feedback, onboarding that gets better every time, and leadership and decision-making that are more transparent
Representation & DEI Results	Dashboards and analytics to monitor workforce and leadership cross-cultural diversity across demographic segments; resources for ERGs and programs promoting equity	To ensure that such goals are met through direct action and efforts to integrate data and promote the practice of asking for, and not just capturing, business value	38.2% year-over-year growth in Black leadership roles; women, people with disabilities, and veterans together accounted for 45.6% of the workforce in 2023, up from 45.3% in 2020; improved global DEI accountability and ERG growth.
Ethical Innovation & Product Inclusion	Internal Responsible Innovation Dimensions system and Inclusive Product Councils leading product teams with DEI values	Toward the goal of AI products and platforms being designed and used in inclusive, accessible, and equitable ways	Goods closer to the needs of the global user and higher ethical standards around AI deployment, with inclusive design principles integrated into building tech

Source: Own study, based on: Isolomons (2021b); Mann (2025); Workplaces (2024).

In its recent Equity Imperative and Human Capital Trends reports, the company's philosophy illustrates the ways in which responsible AI can further fairness and inclusivity within the workforce (Deloitte Insights, 2025a).

In the classroom, in order to cultivate inclusive learning, Deloitte offers adaptive learning platforms and other resources that tailor DEI training content to an employee's role, prior experiences, and personal learning needs. Such platforms dynamically adapt to engagement levels and feedback to enable scalable DEI training experiences that are far more personalized and effective (Deloitte Insights, 2025b).

When it comes to performance management, Deloitte is leveraging (NLP) technology to review employee feedback and determine whether biased language is being used, and also to check for scoring discrepancies with respect to attributes such as age, gender, and ethnicity. This allows the organization to identify patterns that could indicate unconscious bias and take data-driven action to support fairness in appraisal outcomes (Deloitte Insights, 2025a). In addition, instant feedback systems help managers get insights that can be acted upon on the spot. These instruments serve to not only allow transparency, but also strengthen accountability in performance conversations. Managers are invited to consider their appraisal practices, enhance the integrity of talent judgments, and develop a culture of ongoing learning (Deloitte Insights, 2025a).

Deloitte makes a point of stating that AI tools should be used in ways that are ethical, with a human in the loop. Artificial intelligence complements human judgment, but it doesn't replace it. Collaborating with organizations such as Dalhousie, Deloitte aims to ensure that the direction of AI is consistent with inclusivity goals and reflects its larger Corporate Plan. Together, they work on the appraisal and learning systems that encourage fairness and equity at all levels of the organization (Deloitte Insights, 2025b).

Case Study 6: LinkedIn – AI for DEI-Driven Talent Acquisition

As a key player in talent acquisition, LinkedIn leverages AI to support its own internal and customer-facing DEI practices. LinkedIn uses its own internal AI systems to boost real-world DEI hiring efforts and to help customers build more inclusive recruiting pipelines. AI tools for hiring and recruiting as well as for job-seeking and resume-building are being used by LinkedIn at various points of transaction. Key tools include LinkedIn Recruiter, which features bias alerts, and AI-powered demographic fairness optimizations in search results rankings. It's the eyes for monitoring progress on diversity across all industries and regions (Weisi & Hajizadeh, 2025; LinkedIn Corporation, 2025).

LinkedIn further utilizes algorithmic auditing to monitor its AI systems for fairness and equity, also in accordance with best practices (LinkedIn Corporation, 2021). In addition, recruiters enjoy AI-integrating messaging tools, which allow them to engage better with candidates from different backgrounds via more targeted and inclusive messages (LinkedIn Corporation, 2025). With these AI-powered tools, LinkedIn hopes to help reduce the effects of bias, increase access for underrepresented groups, and develop evidence-based diversity strategies for itself and its customers (LinkedIn Corporation, 2025).

Case Study 7: PwC – AI for Inclusive Leadership Development

PwC leverages AI-supported platforms to uncover and cultivate leaders from every corner of the talent pool. In its Inclusion and Diversity Strategy 2025b (PricewaterhouseCoopers, 2025), the firm has introduced AI-driven career-tracking systems designed to reduce bias in leadership succession planning.

Such systems take into account several performance-related aspects, like project roles, peer feedback, and development activities. NLP tools are applied to 360-degree feedback to measure tones and inclusivity, provide personalized coaching recommendations for managers, and deploy employees (PricewaterhouseCoopers, 2025).

PwC UK's Annual Report 2023 also states that ethnic minorities currently represent 32% of its staff, compared to 29% last year. Although that number also represents workforce diversity overall, it is an indication of progress that helps underpin the firm's leadership-level inclusion goals (PricewaterhouseCoopers, 2025).

PwC has shared that AI in talent development led to helping build a more diverse leadership pipeline and driving innovation and increased inclusivity at the company (PricewaterhouseCoopers, 2025).

8.2 CASE STUDY 2: AI FOR EMPLOYEE WELL-BEING AND PRODUCTIVITY

Artificial intelligence is proving to be an invaluable resource in aiding employee well-being, particularly at a time when the world is experiencing a shortage of mental health services which means that even in high-income countries, only one third of people with a condition such as depression receive appropriate care (Casu et al., 2024; Tripathi & Rosak-Szyrocka, 2024). The market for AI-powered mental health apps was at $6.2 billion by 2023, with the market expected to grow by 15.2% a year until 2030 (Mental Health Innovations, 2025). AI chatbots, even GPT-4-based ones, have been found to be effective in alleviating stress, lifting the mood, and increasing productivity, especially in hybrid and remote work environments (Chakraborty, et al., 2023). Table 8.3 presents Case study: Google – AI-powered well-being and mental health support.

TABLE 8.3 Case study: Google – AI-powered well-being and mental health support

Area	AI technology	Partners	Description
Chatbots for mental health support	Conversational AI	DeepMind, Google.org	AI chatbots conduct stress-related chats and move things to HR as needed.
Burnout and stress analysis	ML, NLP	Google People Analytics, Workspace AI	Calendrical data mining and looking at the tea leaves of email to identify overwork and burnout
Well-being recommendations	Context-aware AI	Google Health team, Pixel/Nest team	Customized different prompts for micro-recovery and daily rhythm fit.
CSR tools	AI-driven simulations	ReflexAI, NGOs, Google.org	Artificial intelligence training for veterans in supportive messaging during mental health crises.

Source: Own study, based on: Kingson (2023); Mental Health Innovations (2025).

Case Study 2: Walmart – AI for Workforce Well-Being in Retail

Walmart, the world's largest private employer, has the daunting task of looking after more than two million employees, a high concentration of whom are men and women toiling in ever-changing, often high-pressure retail workplaces. The company has endeavored to address the same, through its integrated AI ecosystem that advocates for mental wellness and efficient working (Walmart Inc., 2025).

At the heart of all this is an AI-driven tool for organizing shifts and checking in on how workers are feeling. Communicative agents, e.g., as in the case of Woebot Health products, can be used for brief emotional check-ins, with the opportunity to indicate a more serious need for mental health resources. Predictive scheduling algorithms optimize rosters by looking at shifts in the past, the distributions of workloads, and employees' preferences and, as such, help reduce overtime and scheduling conflicts—the common cause of burnout.

Walmart uses sentiment analysis, enabled by natural language processors, to search internal communications and feedback for early signs of frustration or disengagement. That allows HR and store leaders to intervene early. The company also offers context-aware chimes for wellness with Thrive Global audible reminders secured by users, prompting hydration, stretching, and micro-meditation based on the intensity and length of each shift.

Already, 69% of consumers are using chatbots or voice assistants during the shopping process, with 47% relying on AI to make purchasing decisions for them, according to the Retail Rewired 2025 report (Walmart Inc., 2025). Walmart employs a similar strategy inside the company, where it has launched smart digital assistants through its Me@Walmart app to help frontline workers navigate shift changes, work assignments, and real-time information flow (Alam & Akter, 2025). This minimizes cognitive overload, particularly during busy periods, and streamlines the workflow (Alam & Akter, 2025; Li & Wang, 2023).

These systems are built around a principle of a "human-in-the-loop"—that the AI will empower, not replace, human judgment. Indeed, 24% of employees surveyed say they are more secure using AI tools when they have the power to approve or reject automatic recommendations (Walmart Inc., 2025). Walmart pragmatically acknowledges this feedback by utilizing explainable AI systems that can explain why a particular schedule or suggestion was created, in order to inspire trust and autonomy (Xiong et al., 2018).

Walmart's AI initiatives are not only about automation, but about creating a healthier, more sustainable company. Through the integration of predictive analytics, conversational AI, and human-centered design, Walmart is breaking new ground in what workforce well-being looks like in retail, blending operational speed with empathy and trust (Walmart Inc., 2025).

Case Study 3: Salesforce – AI for Workplace Productivity and Well-Being

Salesforce has fully integrated AI into its "human-first workplace" vision by unifying well-being and productivity using a single data intelligence model. At the heart of this methodology lies Einstein AI (Shrivastava, 2017), a technology that constantly monitors the workflows, communication flows, and meeting frequency of employees for early signs of stress, overload, procrastination, or even potential burnout. This analysis informs tailored prompts in Slack that support employees in creating attainable goals, minimizing digital disruptions, and scheduling wellness breaks—transforming AI into an always-on, but unobtrusive, wellness assistant (George, 2005).

Salesforce is integrating clinical-grade mental health services directly into the work environment, working with Lyra Health and Modern Health, among others. Employees are able to get therapy, coaching, or self-guided programs whenever they want, without disrupting the flow of work. And managers get live feeds of team sentiments and performance resiliency, and they know when to intercede on a human level.

Leveraging lessons from across its diverse technology ecosystem, Salesforce has also adopted a composable architecture model, as discussed in the Salesforce Commerce Cloud 2024 Report. This modular process also allows companies to choose and incorporate the best AI solutions, such as those that help in managing employee mental health, into their stack. And internally, this versatility empowers Salesforce to trial and tailor well-being solutions for different teams, locations, and roles—maximizing their relevance and adoption (Alokai, 2025).

Additionally, user interface (UI) is front and center in Salesforce's AI design philosophy, with 64% of users saying that improving UI is their top priority, as revealed in the report. They also have to ensure that their internal AI tools are user-friendly and enable access to non-intrusive AI assistance with which associates can work side-by-side in their existing tasks. Rather than adding yet another cognitive burden to our already overtaxed human brains, AI is becoming a digital teammate—enriching the rhythm of work rather than disrupting it (Alokai, 2025).

Salesforce has made an AI strategy for the new world of work that is scalable and human-first—combining performance data, emotional cues, and real-time support within a unified, responsive framework. In so doing, the company is an example of how smart technology, machine learning, and AI can serve not only business metrics, but the higher purpose of human flourishing on the job (Alokai, 2025).

Case Study 4: IBM – AI-Powered Mental Health and Wellness Programs

IBM has built an AI-powered mental healthcare strategy that is global in scale and designed to benefit a workforce with widespread diversity. Key to its innovation is its Watson AI ecosystem, which utilizes machine learning, NLP, and biometric data analytics to help promote psychological well-being in a proactive manner. Leveraging data from wearables, communication platforms, and workplace systems, IBM uses predictive models to identify the early signs of chronic stress, cognitive overload, or burnout. This data is analyzed as it happens and supports "just-in-time" interventions and personalized encouragement. It's a shift away from reactive employee assistance and toward proactive mental health stewardship (IBM ASEAN Newsroom, 2025).

IBM also has a strategic partnership with BetterUp, providing IBMers with on-demand access to personalized resilience coaching, psychological support, and behavioral nudges, based on AI. The coaching programs are designed around the person's psychological composition as well as their work environment and stress dynamics, ensuring everyone receives scalable yet highly personalized support in multiple departments and locations (Hayes & Downie, 2025; IBM ASEAN Newsroom, 2025; myHRfuture, 2025).

IBM also uses generative AI to create culturally relevant, multilingual content on mental health and spiritual care education. These materials work toward destigmatization, inclusion, and emotional intelligence among teams. Through solutions like Watsonx Orchestrate, IBM also provides methods for HR leaders to automate wellness-related workflows, including managing time-off requests, promoting mindfulness events, and routing wellness alerts—all while adhering to privacy and ethical AI standards (Anuradha & Sailaxmi, 2024; AI HR Institute, 2025; Olawade et al., 2024).

Further, IBM espouses a "human-centered design" approach to workplace wellness, derived from its AI Ethics Guidelines. Employees maintain control over how AI is applied, with clear visibility into how their data is being used and privacy consent. This fits into a broader aim: not just higher productivity, but a sustainable, healthy organizational culture (Anuradha & Sailaxmi, 2024).

What makes IBM's strategy unique is that it embraces its multifaceted approach—including predictive analytics, digital coaching, educational inclusivity, and ethical automation—to increase workplace wellness at large. It's a shining example of how AI can be leveraged to not only improve human performance but also elevate human dignity, empathy, and resilience in a high-tech workplace (AI HR institute, 2025; myHRfuture, 2025; IBM ASEAN Newsroom, 2025).

Case Study 5: Microsoft – AI for Remote Work Productivity and Well-Being

Microsoft is leading the charge to reimagine remote and hybrid work culture by thoughtfully leveraging AI in daily workflow. At the center of this turn is Viva Insights, which draws on Microsoft 365 data to measure workers' digital tempo—how often they meet, how often they communicate after hours, and how broken up their tasks are. According to this, the system serves up ideas ranging from focus time blocks to virtual commutes to recovery breaks—all tailor-made as an antithesis to digital overload. Telemetry indicates that the average knowledge worker is interrupted 275 times per day, highlighting the need for measures like this (Microsoft 2025 annual Work Trend Index, 2025).

Continuing to build upon productivity tools, Microsoft is leading in creating the "human-agent team" model that banks on AI agents functioning as digital teammates—taking on tasks that are repeatable (or cognitively demanding) for the human-agent team under human supervision (Xiong et al., 2018). That puts employees in a new role, the "agent boss," who is no longer the end-user of AI, but is also someone who has to manage agents across workflows (Daly, 2025). Microsoft believes that within just five years, most of the workforce will manage AI agents on a daily basis in their roles, making them more empowered and more valuable and helping them to grow in their careers, faster than ever before, and transforming a workplace so that people can focus on doing their life's best work (Microsoft 2025 annual Work Trend Index, 2025).

To facilitate this transition, it has invented the notion of "human-agent ratio," a new operational KPI to strike a balance between automated agents and human supervision. And Microsoft has been shifting from traditional hierarchical organizational charts to something it calls the "Work Chart," a more fluid, outcome-oriented model in which teams assemble around certain goals and then disband when they are met, often aided by AI agents that help the company scale expertise on demand.

This goal aligns with a larger organizational aspiration: it's not enough to simply augment human work with AI; knowledge work itself has to be redefined. Microsoft is also doubling down on upskilling—employees will continue to mirror their companies in their ability to ask, iterate, and collaborate with AI. Through initiatives including Copilot Journey and AI Career Essentials, the company is prepping its workforce to live in a future where digital colleagues are not so much assistants as companions in innovation and wellness (Microsoft 2025 annual Work Trend Index, 2025).

Case Study 6: Amazon – AI for Warehouse Worker Well-Being

Amazon uses artificial intelligence in its warehouses to maintain the health of its employees, both physical and mental. Computer vision systems monitor posture and movement in real time, identifying ergonomically risky behavior and then nudging users to correct it or to take a break to prevent injuries (Fairwork Amazon Report, 2024).

Meanwhile, Amazon is installing 750,000 mobile robots into its fulfillment centers, which are acting in unison to redistribute physical labor from humans to bots. Tasking is optimized by dealing with AI-based algorithms which assess individual work rates, fatigue, and historic behavior. Path-planning algorithms are used to minimize travel distance for workers, thus minimizing fatigue and improving workflow. These systems coordinate in an effort to meet productivity objectives while keeping employees comfortable/safe (Fairwork, 2024).

Amazon also uses digital mood check-ins and AI-driven sentiment analysis to monitor emotional health. Workers are able to rate how they feel throughout shifts, which then enables the system to identify stress patterns and alert managers to respond promptly. And, custom VR training modules are created using generative AI, based on the employee's experience, role, and language, which reduces anxiety and builds confidence around their ability to complete tasks (Fairwork Amazon Report, 2024). All of these applications in AI are part of a holistic approach not only to improve operations, but also to create a safer, more responsive, and human-centric workplace.

8.3 CASE STUDY 3: GREEN HRM INITIATIVES USING AI

The green transition is a significant force of transformation, together with digitalization and automation, certain to impact the labor market in the years to come (World Economic Forum, 2025b). Companies expect demand for the so-called green skills, and the rise of jobs supporting sustainability goals and objectives. Here, HR activities have not only an operational but a strategic implication as a core driver of the ESG transformation overall (Napathorn, 2022; Rosak-Szyrocka et al., 2025). AI is a key tool that facilitates green skills and HR process management. AI is applied to analyze employee behavior data, suggest greener work options (like hybrid models), automate e-learning on eco-literacy, and even evaluate the environmental footprint of the HR programs on the company's sustainability goals (Rosak-Szyrocka et al., 2022b; Rosak-Szyrocka & Knop, 2024; Rosak-Szyrocka et al., 2023). Table 8.4 presents case studies of Green HRM initiatives using AI.

TABLE 8.4 Case studies of Green HRM initiatives using AI

Case study	AI area	Description
Siemens	**AI for Sustainable Workforce Management**	Siemens embeds AI into its "Digital Enterprise," a holistic approach that connects the physical and digital worlds to squeeze greater efficiency out of everything from production to workforce performance. AI is not an overlay, it is an engine that accelerates sustainable change. As per Reuters Events & Siemens report 2024, 69% of industry leaders consider AI to be a critical aspect of resolving environmental complexity, while 91% expect it to be a major force behind energy transition (Reuters Events & Siemens, 2024). However, 26% now identify skill shortages as a primary obstacle, the implication being that integrating AI into the workforce is essential (Coursera, 2025; Kishorre Annanth, Abinash, & Rao, 2021). Siemens uses machine learning to predict staffing requirements, fill skill gaps, and support reskilling. Solutions like Building X Comfort AI work to optimize working conditions in real time, leading to both reduced energy consumption and better health and well-being for employees. Microservices and edge computing-inspired AI lifecycle management allow for scalable resilient deployment. Magazine-printed components quality control In PCBs, Siemens reduced the false rejection rate by 60%, ensuring that costs were kept down and process consistency was improved (Kishorre Annanth, Abinash, & Rao, 2021). The company is also taking advantage of digital twins to simulate workforce changes and plan training investments. These initiatives correspond to SDGs 8, 9, and 12, respectively, and represent ways in which AI can be leveraged to boost productivity or to develop sustainable human capital (Coursera, 2025).
Unilever	**AI for Sustainable Talent Mobility and Carbon Footprint Reduction**	Unilever Industry Leaders in Sustainable Transformation:Unilever uses AI as a major springboard for sustainability and workforce transformation. The company is now using an AI-enabled Flex Experiences platform that helps connect employees to short-term projects throughout the organization in order to promote internal talent mobility. This system is designed to improve skill development, engagement, and workforce mobility, all at a distance—thus limiting the need to travel, relocate, or hire new employees, with the resulting reduced carbon footprint (Unilever, 2025). At the same time, Unilever uses predictive analytics to streamline production lines. thanks to better predicting demand, cutting the amount of waste it produces on its production line by 40%. AI also enables cuts in energy and water usage and fosters hybrid work models by processing office space and employee behavior data (Aly, 2025). The developments are in line with Unilever's commitment toward achieving net zero emissions by 2039. The machine learning company represents a thought leadership in the space of AI as a strategic bridge between sustainability and human capital development, minimizing both the operational wastage and climate waste (Aly, 2025; Unilever, 2025).
Nike	**AI-Powered Green HRM for Sustainable Workforce**	Nike is embedding AI into how it tackles sustainability and human resources challenges, using it as a tool to drive operational efficiency and environmentally responsible practices. Artificial intelligence-based applications help in skilling as well as reskilling, workforce planning and internal mobility, and talent development and cut down on carbon footprints (Nike report, 2023). Take Nike Fit, a computer vision- and machine learning-based 3D foot-scanning solution, for example, which has reduced return rates and emissions associated with logistics and waste. Internal analogy technologies are also used to predict staffing needs, reduce non-essential travel, and match talent to emerging business demands (Nike report, 2023; Mathews, 2024). Nike also invests in digital capabilities through acquisitions such as Datalogue and Zodiac, creating new careers in data, AI, and innovation. Initiatives like Nike By You and the Athlete Imagined Revolution (AIR) are examples of how generative AI

		supercharges co-creation and product design, minimizing prototyping and material waste (Mathews, 2024). That's in line with Nike's climate targets, like all of its owned facilities running on 100% renewable energy by 2025 and, more generally, moving to tech-enabled human capital management that's sustainable (Mathews, 2024).
Coca-Cola	**AI-Powered Green HRM for Sustainable Workforce and Operations**	AI in sustainability and the workforce: Coca-Cola uses AI in its programs to help it to become more efficient, more sustainable, and more resilient in the face of long-term challenges. In HR, AI enables predictive workforce planning, reskilling programs, and employee retention—avoiding the needless turnover of employees and the emissions caused by recruitment and relocation. In operational terms, AI allows for real-time logistics planning, predictive maintenance, and waste reduction. These technologies are helping to advance Coca-Cola's broader climate goals to reduce Scope 1, 2, and 3 emissions aligned with a 1.5°C pathway by 2035 (The Coca-Cola Company, 2025). AI also powers progress-oriented goals for the planet, like returning 100% of water used in finished products by 2035 in 200+ high-risk water stress-affected areas and improving packaging circularity with better material forecasting. Moreover, AI-enabled supply chain assessments help achieve more sustainable agriculture by recognizing ESG risks and increasing the efficiency of resources. Combined, these efforts demonstrate the ways in which Coca-Cola is leveraging AI not just for digital transformation, but for responsible, sustainable management of people and the planet (Coca-Cola report, 2023; "Sustainability", 2025o).
Amazon	**AI for Eco-Friendly Supply Chain and Green HRM**	AI at Amazon powers sustainability in operations and personnel management. One piece of AI logistics was route optimization during the Coronavirus pandemic, electric fleet planning, and the Package Decision Engine, which has, through multidimensional data algorithms since 2015, helped to remove more than 2 million tons of packaging material by predicting best box sizes (Amazon Sustainability Report, 2023). AI is also showing the way in powering Amazon's clean energy ambitions by monitoring solar and wind operations, weather predictions, and storage facilities—bringing the company that much closer to reaching 100% renewable energy by 2025 (Amazon Sustainability Report, 2023). Other inventions include self-driving delivery robots (Scout) and drone systems (Prime Air) [these eliminate last-mile emissions] ("Amazon's AI-driven approach to sustainable packaging and efficient delivery | LinkedIn", 2025c). With AI, HR will be able to fine-tune shift planning, mitigate risk of injury through wearables, and staff in line with real-time demand. Amazon also looks to sprinkle some magic on AI's own environmental impact through its work on the Sustainability Data Initiative and the low-carbon infrastructure at Amazon Web Services (AWS) (Milanesi, 2024). Combined, these efforts demonstrate how AI is enabling Amazon to strike a balance between innovation, operational efficiency, and environmental responsibility—creating a model for green digital transformation across industries.
Nestlé	**AI for Sustainable Workforce Training and Eco-Friendly HRM**	Nestlé is using AI to achieve sustainability and HR targets. In South Africa, the company trialed WhiteBox machine learning technology to convert Scope 1 CO_2 emissions into green products and recycle as much as 100 million liters of industrial water annually (USA, 2025b). At the same time, in the context of its digital HR transformation, Nestlé rolled out NesGPT, a generative AI model now used by more than 7,000 employees in North America. From content creation and EI data analysis to ideation and beyond, the platform saves team members 45 minutes per week on average. And it can mitigate "shadow AI" risks through internal governance and training. Nestlé is taking digital upskilling seriously to ensure there is fair adoption, particularly with staff members who are non-digital-native. These initiatives are part of a broader AI endeavor for emission abatement, productivity improvement, and human resources development and represent the values of Green HRM and ESG-driven transformation (Consumer Goods Technology, 2025; Forbes, 2022; USA, 2025a).

Source: Own study.

TABLE 8.5 Case studies of AI-powered workforce planning in sustainable companies

Case study	AI use area	Description
Intel	**AI for Sustainable Workforce Optimization**	Intel's efforts for responsible workforce optimization combines the responsible development of AI with inclusive global education initiatives. Started in 2020 with Maricopa County Community College District (MCCCD), the AI for the Workforce program provided more than 200 hours of AI curricula, initially meant for educators to support the development of the nation's first associate degrees and certificates in AI (Intel, 2021). It has since grown to 19 schools in 12 U.S. states, all of them serving more than 800,000 students, including eight that are Minority-Serving Institutions (MSIs). In 2024, Intel expanded the program to a global scale as part of its "Digital Readiness" initiative and has been working with 100-plus public and private partners in 28 countries. In the U.S., over 500 hours of free AI education have been delivered and 40% of participating schools were MSIs — further highlighting Intel's commitment to equity and access (AP News, 2024). By jointly emphasizing skills, ethics, and sustainability, Intel isn't just redefining job readiness but making certain that diverse communities are positioned to lead in an AI-fueled, environmentally responsible economy (Staff, NaN).
DHL	**AI-Powered Workforce Planning for Sustainable Logistics**	DHL leverages artificial intelligence as a strategic lever for connecting sustainable logistics with a best-fit workforce. In the framework of its Strategy 2030, DHL applies predictive analytics and machine learning to predict parcel volumes with high precision, to adjust staff in a flexible manner, and to optimize parcel delivery routes in order to save fuel and decrease emissions (DHL, 2025). These AI models also optimize driver scheduling and container utilization to ensure service levels while minimizing labor hours and CO_2 emissions (Emerj Artificial Intelligence Research, 2025b; Rosak-Szyrocka & Wolniak, 2025). AI planning tools are closely related to DHL's GoGreen Plus program where it also considers the reduction of emissions and greener transportation modes when assigning workers (Emerj Artificial Intelligence Research, 2025a). In addition, AI-driven scheduling increases efficiency and takes employee well-being into account, with better work-life balance and predictable schedules and shifts—key components in the equation to enhance job satisfaction and decrease turnover (Tripathi & Rosak-Szyrocka, 2024). In a more internal aspect, DHL uses AI to map employee skills and find reskilling paths with the help of programs like Digital Champions and Certified in Logistics so that employees are also, in their turn, part of the growth of technology. This "human + machine" perspective mirrors DHL's philosophy that sustainability and human potential are two sides of the same coin (van Delft, 2024; Rosak-Szyrocka et al., 2025; Tripathi & Rosak-Szyrocka, 2024).
Marriott International	**AI-Powered Workforce Planning for Sustainable Hospitality**	Marriott uses AI to augment workforce planning and help achieve Serve360 sustainability goals. Energy use, food waste, and water consumption are tracked in real time using AI-based systems, a part of the company's 2025 environmental commitments to reduce carbon emissions by 30%, food waste by 50%, and water usage by 15% (Marriott International, Serve360). AI also contributes to Marriott's responsible sourcing strategy in tracking supply chain compliance and making intelligent purchasing decisions (Ramirez, 2024).. The company is aiming to have 50% of fresh produce purchased locally and more than 95% of priority purchases meet responsible sourcing (Marriott International, Serve360).

		Marriott also incorporates AI in its learning platforms to provide specific employee training. The latter indicated that it trained 70% of corporate employees in human rights and responsible hiring, in line with the company's objective to educate 100% of the staff from its hotels in human rights, responsible hiring, and anti-trafficking practices by 2025 (Marriott International, Serve360). Through this data-driven, values-oriented approach, Marriott illustrates that sustainability and workforce empowerment are mutually reinforcing priorities in the hospitality industry.
Schneider Electric	**AI for Sustainable Workforce and Energy Management**	Schneider Electric is using AI to drive transformation both in energy and in the shaping of the workforce. Its AI-based Open Talent Market, involving 60% of its employees in two months, released 127,000 hours of internal potential and promoted talent mobility (Bersin & Enderes, 2022). In parallel, the company announced an agentive AI ecosystem—autonomous systems that support decision-making in emissions tracking, climate risk, and resource efficiency (Green, 2025). From 2023, Schneider has also started to work with Generative AI in collaboration with Microsoft Azure OpenAI. Other tools, such as Resource Advisor Copilot and Knowledge Bot, are designed to help customers and teams analyze ESG information, streamline reporting, and improve service quality. A committed GenAI Core Team uncovers fresh use cases across departments. All of our solutions are built based on the principles of frugal AI—most efficient service with minimal energy consumption (Electric, 2025). AI is now at the heart of Schneider's innovation model and is speeding up the rate of both digital transformation and sustainability impact in their operations, with talent and in customer engagement.
Accor Hotels	**AI for Workforce Planning in Sustainable Hospitality**	AI technologies are used for energy management (leading to a reduction of usage by up to 15%) and food waste reduction in partnership with startups such as Orbisk, Winnow, and Fullsoon (sales teams of each hotel saving over 15 tons of food each year) (Bridgenext, 2024). And Accor is also a bridge between technology and human progress. 93% of corporate employees leaned in with mandatory climate, biodiversity, and impact strategy training via the "School for Change" program. On the other hand, the "Reveal Talent" program helps non-graduate employees rise to the managerial roles too, promoting inclusivity and internal mobility (Accor impact report, 2023). AI also allows guests to choose between eco-friendly decisions or personalization of their services. By combining intelligent tools with social and educational support, Accor shows how AI can simultaneously enable operational efficiency and ethical, sustainable business strategy. This combination of human and machine intelligence makes Accor a pioneer in sustainable mesh-based hospitality transformation (Accorgroup, NaN; Cousins, 2023).

(*Continued*)

TABLE 8.5 (*Continued*)

Case study	AI use area	Description
Ford	**AI for Sustainable Workforce Planning in Manufacturing**	The way Ford is working to sustain its workforce is a combination of cutting-edge technology and age-old dedication to the health and happiness of its employees. Expanding on its 2013 "Sustainable Workforce" program, which focused on strategic hiring, safety and health, and immersive training, Ford now leverages AI and data analytics to bring workforce planning to the next level (Automotive Manufacturing Solutions, 2025b; Sarahrudge, 2024). Ford has centralized production and labor data on its "Manufacturing 360" platform and is using the information to predict what types of skills will be needed, optimize staffing levels, and steer reskilling programs. AI assists in modeling workforce scenarios, and virtual factory simulations train employees effectively and safely. The company also supports ergonomic risk prevention and chronic condition healthcare programs through digital precision and a human-centered approach (Automotive Manufacturing Solutions, 2025a). Ford's approach demonstrates that digital transformation is not only about automation—it's about bringing into existence a resilient, adaptable, and high-functioning workforce. Ford's innovative approach in combining AI with societal and environmental purposes creates a template for how manufacturing companies can leverage technology to serve people and the planet while also promoting economic growth (Automotive Manufacturing Solutions, 2025c).
IKEA	**AI for Workforce Planning and Sustainability in Retail**	IKEA's digitalization harmonizes efficiency with profound ethical responsibility. Via tools like Demand Sensing, IKEA employs AI to predict demand by store based on over 200 variables, enabling smart workforce scheduling while minimizing waste and maximizing product availability. Those accurate predictions allow for more tranquil employee shifts, less emissions from unnecessary transportation, and cost savings handed off to customers (IKEA, 2025). Since 2019, ethical AI has been integrated within IKEA's core values, inspired by principles of transparency, fairness, and inclusivity. The company listens to its 165,000 employees; retools them with new skills; and makes human dignity the centerpiece of AI design. A large AI and data literacy program is now teaching thousands of co-workers across the world. By integrating leading technology with people-centric values, IKEA is establishing a new model for responsible AI within the retail sector that promotes efficiency in operations, employee welfare, and meeting long-term environmental targets.

Source: Own study.

8.4 CASE STUDY 4: AI-POWERED WORKFORCE PLANNING IN SUSTAINABLE COMPANIES

The planning and the development of the workforce are fundamentally changing due to artificial intelligence (Rosak-Szyrocka, 2024; Rosak-Szyrocka et al., 2022a; Rosak-Szyrocka & Tiwari, 2023; Tripathi & Rosak-Szyrocka, 2024). With increasingly short technology cycles, uncertain markets, and a growing awareness regarding sustainability, the classical "hire and fire" model is no longer viable. McKinsey (2023) states that as much as 30% of the time spent in the workplace today could be automated by 2030, requiring organizations to use agile, predictive, and AI-enabled workforce planning practices (McKinsey, 2023).

Companies embracing AI-powered planning aren't just predicting skills and talent demand more accurately; they're nurturing resilient, inclusive, and sustainable workforce ecosystems. AI enables the determination of skill gaps, promotion of internal mobility, boosting of well-being, and optimization of resource utilization. And most importantly, it is a solution that connects operational efficiency with social and environmental responsibility (Sakhwalkar, 2025). The following case studies highlight the ways in which AI is shaping the new world of work, from industry giants like Intel to companies like IKEA, and how its adoption has enabled greater organizational flexibility, increased talent mobility, and the emergence of more sustainable modes of working. Table 8.5 presents case studies of AI-powered workforce planning in sustainable companies.

REFERENCES

Accenture. (2024, November 29). *Thrive with responsible AI: Embedding trust can unlock value.* Accenture. www.accenture.com/pl-en/insights/data-ai/rai-from-risk-to-value

ACCOR. (2023). Impact report, accelerating our hospitality sustainable transformation. https://group.accor.com/-/media/Corporate/Commitment/Documents/2024/05/28/ACCOR_IMPACT_REPORT_2023.pdf?rev=4da770f825694e6482de45721cc958ca

Accorgroup. (NaN). *Food waste: AI supporting Accor hotels – Accor – Newsroom.* Retrieved June 09, 2025, from https://press.accor.com/food-waste-ai-supporting-accor-hotels/?lang=eng&utm_source=chatgpt.com.

AI HR Institute. (2025). *IBM HR AI: transforming the future of human resources with artificial intelligence.* Retrieved June 08, 2025, from www.aihr-institute.com/blog/ibm-hr-ai-transforming-the-future-of-human-resources-with-artificial-intelligence.

Alam, F., & Akter, T. (2025). *Leadership evaluation and strategy effectiveness: a case study of Walmart Canada's Store Manager.* SAGE Publications; SAGE Business Cases Originals.

Alokai. (2025, February 20). *Salesforce Commerce Cloud: Insights from 80+ top executives* [Report]. Alokai. https://alokai.com/lpd/salesforce-commerce-cloud-report

Aly, M. (2025). *AI-powered sustainability: how Unilever cut waste by 40% with predictive analytics – Em Vide.* Retrieved June 08, 2025, from https://emvide.com/ai-powered-sustainability-how-unilever-cut-waste-by-40-with-predictive-analytics-2/.

Amazon. (2024). *2023 Sustainability Report.* https://sustainability.aboutamazon.com/2023-sustainability-report.pdf

Anuradha, A., & Sailaxmi, S. S. (2024). Growth hacking business analytical tools for small and medium enterprises. *Journal of Business Analytics, 7*(4), 292–317.

AP News. (2024). *Intel exec on bringing artificial intelligence into the workplace.* Retrieved June 09, 2025, from https://apnews.com/article/ai-workforce-intel-training-initiatives-26772553fe7ed82b535b41a8169ac078.

Automotive Manufacturing Solutions. (2025a). *Blueprint for building the smart factory of the future.* Retrieved June 09, 2025, from www.automotivemanufacturingsolutions.com/smart-factory/blueprint-for-building-the-smart-factory-of-the-future/46508.article.

Automotive Manufacturing Solutions. (2025b). *Blueprint for building the smart factory of the future.* Retrieved June 09, 2025, from www.automotivemanufacturingsolutions.com/smart-factory/blueprint-for-building-the-smart-factory-of-the-future/46508.article.

Automotive Manufacturing Solutions. (2025c). *Blueprint for building the smart factory of the future.* Retrieved June 09, 2025, from www.automotivemanufacturingsolutions.com/smart-factory/blueprint-for-building-the-smart-factory-of-the-future/46508.article.

Bersin, J., & Enderes, K. (2022). *Schneider Electric pioneers the talent marketplace.* The Josh Bersin Company. https://resources.gloat.com/wp-content/uploads/TM-22_10-Schneider-Electric-Pioneers-the-Talent-Marketplace-Case-Study-3.pdf

Bridgenext. (2024). *Revolutionize sustainability in travel and hospitality with AI* – Bridgenext. Retrieved June 09, 2025, from www.bridgenext.com/blog/revolutionize-sustainability-in-travel-and-hospitality-with-ai/.

Casu, M., Triscari, S., Battiato, S., Guarnera, L., & Caponnetto, P. (2024). AI chatbots for mental health: a scoping review of effectiveness, feasibility, and applications. *Applied Sciences, 14*(13), 5889.

Chakraborty, C., Pal, S., Bhattacharya, M., Dash, S., & Lee, S.-S. (2023). Overview of chatbots with special emphasis on artificial intelligence-enabled ChatGPT in medical science. *Frontiers in Artificial Intelligence, 6*, 1237704, from https://www.frontiersin.org/articles/10.3389/frai.2023.1237704/full.

Consumer Goods Technology. (2025). *Nestle using AI to convert CO2 into green products & recycle wastewater | Consumer Goods Technology.* Retrieved June 08, 2025, from https://consumergoods.com/nestle-using-ai-convert-co2-green-products-recycle-wastewater.

Coursera. (2025). *Siemens Improves Employee Retention with Coursera | Coursera.* Retrieved June 08, 2025, from www.coursera.org/enterprise/resources/casestudy/siemens.

Cousins, F. (2023). *Accor adopts food waste AI to halve excess.* Retrieved June 09, 2025, from https://sustainablehotelnews.com/accor-adopts-food-waste-ai-to-half-excess/?utm_source=chatgpt.com.

Daly, N. (2025). *Managerial AI skill stacking: a new professional skillset for the AI-driven workplace.* Available at SSRN: https://ssrn.com/abstract=5277762 or http://dx.doi.org/10.2139/ssrn.5277762

Deloitte Insights. (2025a). *2023 Global Human Capital Trends.* Retrieved June 07, 2025, from https://www2.deloitte.com/us/en/insights/focus/human-capital-trends/2023.html.

Deloitte Insights. (2025b). *Deloitte 2023 Global Human Capital Trends.* Retrieved June 07, 2025, from https://www2.deloitte.com/us/en/insights/focus/human-capital-trends/2023/future-of-workforce-management.html.

DHL. (2025). *Strategy.* Retrieved June 09, 2025, from https://group.dhl.com/en/about-us/the-group/strategy.html?utm_source=chatgpt.com.

Electric, S. (2025). *Schneider Electric announces multi-year initiative in AI-native ecosystem for sustainability and energy management.* Retrieved June 09, 2025, from www.prnewswire.com/news-releases/schneider-electric-announces-multi-year-initiative-in-ai-native-ecosystem-for-sustainability-and-energy-management-302456420.html.

Emerj Artificial Intelligence Research. (2025a). *Artificial intelligence at DHL – two applications at the world's largest logistics company – Emerj Artificial Intelligence Research.* Retrieved June 09, 2025, from https://emerj.com/artificial-intelligence-at-dhl-two-applications/?utm_source=chatgpt.com.

Emerj Artificial Intelligence Research. (2025b). *Artificial intelligence at DHL – two applications at the world's largest logistics company – Emerj Artificial Intelligence Research.* Retrieved June 09, 2025, from https://emerj.com/artificial-intelligence-at-dhl-two-applications/?utm_source=chatgpt.com.

Fairwork. (2024, June). *Fairwork Amazon Report 2024: Transformation of the Warehouse Sector through AI.* Global Partnership on AI. Retrieved from https://fair.work/wp-content/uploads/sites/17/2024/06/Fairwork-Amazon-Report_June24-2.pdf

Forbes. (2022). *Nestlé's IT HR transformation: realizing values on a global scale.* Retrieved June 08, 2025, from www.forbes.com/sites/sap/2021/11/19/nestls-hr-transformation-realizing-values-on-a-global-scale/.

George, G. (2005). Slack resources and the performance of privately held firms. *Academy of Management Journal, 48*(4), 661–676.

Green, A. (2025). *Schneider Electric launches AI-native initiative for sustainability and energy management.* CarbonCredits.com. Retrieved June 09, 2025, from https://carboncredits.com/schneider-electric-launches-agentic-ai-native-sustainability-initiative/.

Hayes, M., & Downie, A. (2025). *AI agents in human resources.* IBM Consulting. www.ibm.com/think/topics/ai-agents-in-human-resources

IBM ASEAN Newsroom. (2025). *IBM and Happily.ai help organizations enhance employee experience with AI.* Retrieved June 08, 2025, from https://asean.newsroom.ibm.com/press-releases?item=122412.

IKEA. (2025). *Using AI for smarter demand forecasting – IKEA Global.* Retrieved June 09, 2025, from www.ikea.com/global/en/stories/design/using-artificial-intelligence-for-smarter-demand-forecasting-210527/.

Intel. (2021, 3 sierpnia). *Intel's AI for Workforce Program brings AI education to community colleges across the U.S.* [Blog post]. Intel. https://community.intel.com/t5/Blogs/Intel/Intel-s-AI-for-Workforce-Program-Brings-AI-Education-to/post/1333301

Isolomons. (2021a). *Facebook diversity update: increasing representation in our workforce and supporting minority-owned businesses.* Retrieved June 07, 2025, from https://about.fb.com/news/2021/07/facebook-diversity-report-2021/.

Isolomons (2021b). *Facebook diversity update: increasing representation in our workforce and supporting minority-owned businesses.* Retrieved June 07, 2025, from https://about.fb.com/news/2021/07/facebook-diversity-report-2021/.

JPMorgan Chase & Co. (n.d.). *JPMorgan Chase | Home.* JPMorgan Chase & Co. Retrieved August 9, 2025, from www.jpmorganchase.com/

Kingson, J. A. (2023). *Google flexes its health care AI muscle.* HealthLeaders Media. Retrieved June 08, 2025, from www.axios.com/2023/03/15/google-ai-chatgpt-healthcare-youtube-chatbot-health?utm_source=chatgpt.com.

Kishorre Annanth, V., Abinash, M., & Rao, L. B. (2021). Intelligent manufacturing in the context of industry 4.0: a case study of Siemens industry. *Journal of Physics: Conference Series, 1969*(1), 12019.

Li, L., & Wang, F.-Y. (2023). Motivation: complexity of service in the digital age. In: *Parallel Services* (pp. 9–19). Springer Briefs in Service Science. Springer. https://doi.org/10.1007/978-3-031-25333-1_2

LinkedIn Corporation. (2021, October 20). *Our 2021 workforce diversity report.* LinkedIn News. Retrieved August 9, 2025, from https://news.linkedin.com/2021/october/2021-workforce-diversity-report

LinkedIn Corporation. (2025). *Global impact.* LinkedIn. Retrieved August 9, 2025, from https://socialimpact.linkedin.com/

Mann, J. (2025). *Meta plans AI-driven hiring overhaul, internal doc reveals.* Retrieved June 07, 2025, from businessinsider: www.businessinsider.com/meta-hiring-ai-recruitment-interviews-candidates-docs-coding-2025-6?IR=T.

Marriott International. (n.d.). *Serve360.* Retrieved June 09, 2025, from https://serve360.marriott.com/

Mathews, A. (2024). *How Nike is using AI to transform product design, customer experience, and operational efficiency.* Retrieved June 08, 2025, from https://aimresearch.co/market-industry/how-nike-is-using-ai-to-transform-product-design-customer-experience-and-operational-efficiency.

McIntyre, L.-R. (2024, October 23). *2024 Global Diversity & Inclusion Report: Our Most Global, Transparent Report Yet.* Microsoft. www.microsoft.com/en-us/diversity/inside-microsoft/annual-report

McKinsey & Company. (2023, August 1). *The state of AI in 2023: Generative AI's breakout year* [McKinsey Global Survey on AI]. McKinsey & Company. www.mckinsey.com/capabilities/quantumblack/our-insights/the-state-of-ai-in-2023-generative-ais-breakout-year

Mental Health Innovations. (2025). *Using AI to help people get the mental health support they need.* Retrieved June 08, 2025, from https://mentalhealthinnovations.org/news-and-information/reports-and-research/transforming-digital-mental-health-support-with-artificial-intelligence/using-ai-to-help-people-get-the-mental-health-support-they-need/.

Microsoft. (2025). *WorkLab: Research and insights on AI at work.* Retrieved August 9, 2025, from www.microsoft.com/en-us/worklab/

Microsoft 2025 annual Work Trend Index. (2025). *Microsoft 2025 annual Work Trend Index.* Retrieved June 08, 2025, from https://news.microsoft.com/annual-work-trend-index-2025/.

Milanesi, C. (2024, 16 kwietnia). *Amazon's AI-driven approach to sustainable packaging and efficient delivery.* Creative Strategies / The Heart of Tech. www.linkedin.com/pulse/amazons-ai-driven-approach-sustainable-packaging-carolina-milanesi-p4ioe/

myHRfuture. (2025). *How IBM uses AI to Transform Their HR Strategies | myHRfuture.* Retrieved June 08, 2025, from www.myhrfuture.com/digital-hr-leaders-podcast/how-ibm-uses-ai-to-transform-their-hr-strategies.

Napathorn, C. (2022). The development of green skills across firms in the institutional context of Thailand. *Asia-Pacific Journal of Business Administration, 14*(4), 539–572, from www.emerald.com/insight/content/doi/10.1108/apjba-10-2020-0370/full/pdf?casa_token=hkhhb-0mcg8aaaaa:e4xhojszphl7koc0tlfsiq9j5uykx0z-3siopqqsky1njpucxe3hdtlt1th7d-90nqiw-5yymog1rgozdawkuuctgzg7z0hrk2x107vadnsw796y.

Nike, Inc. (2023). *FY22 NIKE, Inc. Impact Report.* https://purpose.nike.com/fy22-

Olawade, D. B., Wada, O. Z., Odetayo, A., David-Olawade, A. C., Asaolu, F., & Eberhardt, J. (2024). Enhancing mental health with artificial intelligence: current trends and future prospects. *Journal of Medicine, Surgery, and Public Health, 3,* 100099.

PricewaterhouseCoopers. (2025). *Inclusion and diversity.* Retrieved June 07, 2025, from www.pwc.co.uk/who-we-are/annual-report/annual-report-2023/people/inclusion-and-diversity.html?utm_source=chatgpt.com.

Raji, I. D., & Buolamwini, J. (01272019). Actionable auditing. In V. Conitzer, G. Hadfield, & S. Vallor (Eds.), *Proceedings of the 2019 AAAI/ACM Conference on AI, Ethics, and Society* (pp. 429–435). ACM.

Ramirez, M. (2024, March 31). *Marriott International: AI use cases 2024*. PitchGrade. https://pitchgrade.com/companies/marriott-international-ai-use-cases

Reuters Events & Siemens. (2024). *A new pace of change: industrial AI × sustainability*. Siemens. https://assets.new.siemens.com/siemens/assets/api/uuid:920c58c5-1b3f-4280-84a3-6e58f02f68e5/A-New-Pace-of-Change-Report.pdf

Rosak-Szyrocka, J. (2024). The role of artificial intelligence in digital education. *Zeszyty Naukowe. Organizacja i Zarządzanie / Politechnika Śląska, 2024*(195), 477–499, from https://yadda.icm.edu.pl/baztech/element/bwmeta1.element.baztech-60b404c0-03e1-43cb-a14a-535b6138e365.

Rosak-Szyrocka, J., Apostu, S. A., Ali Turi, J., & Tanveer, A. (2022). University 4.0 sustainable development in the way of Society 5.0. *Sustainability, 14*(23), 16043, from www.mdpi.com/2071-1050/14/23/16043.

Rosak-Szyrocka, J., Gupta, S. K., Shahbaz, M., & Launer, M. (2025). *Enhancing smart universities with emotional intelligence*, Routledge.

Rosak-Szyrocka, J., & Knop, K. (2024). Sustainable development universities-opportunities & challenges on the road to society 5.0 from the key stakeholder perspective. *PLOS ONE, 19*(8), e0308929, from https://journals.plos.org/plosone/article?id=10.1371/journal.pone.0308929.

Rosak-Szyrocka, J., & Tiwari, S. (2023). Structural Equation Modeling (SEM) to test sustainable development in University 4.0 in the ultra-smart society era. *Sustainability, 15*(23), 16167, from www.mdpi.com/2071-1050/15/23/16167.

Rosak-Szyrocka, J., & Wolniak, R. (2025). *Smart universities in Smart Cities*, Routledge.

Rosak-Szyrocka, J., Żywiołek, J., Nayyar, A., & Naved, M. (2023). *The role of sustainability and artificial intelligence in education improvement*, CRC Press.

Sakhwalkar, R. (2025). *Embedding AI-driven workforce planning into business strategy*. LinkedIn. www.linkedin.com/pulse/embedding-ai-driven-workforce-planning-business-rohit-sakhwalkar-7xxdf/

Sarahrudge. (2024). *Inside Ford's strategic push for a digital future*. Retrieved June 09, 2025, from https://scw-mag.com/news/inside-fords-strategic-push-for-a-digital-future/.

Shrivastava, M. (2017). *Learning Salesforce Einstein*, Packt Publishing Ltd.

Staff, I. W. (NaN). *With Intel's help community college students can earn degree in AI | IndustryWeek*. Retrieved June 09, 2025, from www.industryweek.com/talent/article/21175122/with-intels-help-community-college-students-can-earn-degree-in-ai?utm_source=chatgpt.com.

The Coca-Cola Company. (2024). *Sustainability*. Retrieved August 9, 2025, from www.coca-colacompany.com/about-us/sustainability

The Coca-Cola Company. (2025). *Sustainability*. Retrieved August 9, 2025, from https://www.coca-colacompany.com/about-us/sustainability

Tripathi, S., & Rosak-Szyrocka, J. (2024). *Impact of artificial intelligence on society*, CRC Press.

Unilever (2025). *Leading in the next era of corporate sustainability*. Retrieved August 9, 2025, from www.unilever.com/sustainability/

USA, G. H. R. (2025a). *Nestlé says its GenAI tool saves employees 45 minutes a week*. Retrieved June 08, 2025, from www.hrgrapevine.com/us/content/article/2024-07-23-nestl-says-its-genai-tool-saves-employees-45-minutes-a-week.

USA, G. H. R. (2025b). *Nestlé says its GenAI tool saves employees 45 minutes a week.* Retrieved June 08, 2025, from www.hrgrapevine.com/us/content/article/2024-07-23-nestl-says-its-genai-tool-saves-employees-45-minutes-a-week.

van Delft, L. (2024, August 2). *Sustainability in logistics: Your questions answered.* DHL Discover. Retrieved August 9, 2025, from https://www.dhl.com/discover/en-global/logistics-advice/sustainability-and-green-logistics/dhl-expert-interview-sustainability

Walmart Inc. (2025, June 4). *Walmart's Retail Rewired Report 2025: Agentic AI at the heart of retail transformation.* Retrieved August 9, 2025, from https://corporate.walmart.com/news/2025/06/04/walmarts-retail-rewired-report-2025-agentic-ai-at-the-heart-of-retail-transformation

Weisi, H., & Hajizadeh, S. (2025). LinkedIn as a platform: the pragmatic strategies of self-presentation and self-praise. *Social Sciences & Humanities Open, 11*, 101266.

Workplaces, A. (2024). *Inside Facebook's culture: innovation, transparency, and employee well-being.* Retrieved June 07, 2025, from https://amazingworkplaces.co/inside-facebooks-culture-innovation-transparency-and-employee-well-being/.

World Economic Forum. (2025a). *The Future of Jobs Report 2020.* Retrieved June 07, 2025, from www.weforum.org/publications/the-future-of-jobs-report-2020/.

World Economic Forum. (2025b). *Annual Report 2023-2024.* Retrieved June 08, 2025, from www.weforum.org/publications/annual-report-2023-2024/.

Xiong, Y., Chen, H., Zhao, M., & An, B. (2018). HogRider: Champion Agent of Microsoft Malmo Collaborative AI Challenge. *Proceedings of the AAAI Conference on Artificial Intelligence, 32*(1), 4767–4774, from https://ojs.aaai.org/index.php/aaai/article/view/11581.

www.linkedin.com/pulse/diversity-equity-inclusion-dei-workplace-8kmyf/?utm_source=chatgpt.com

V

Strategic Roadmap for Sustainable AI-Driven HRM

CHAPTER 9

Policy and Regulatory Frameworks for AI in HRM

9.1 NAVIGATING GLOBAL AI REGULATIONS IN HRM

AI is today part of HR functions. The shift has gargantuan ethical, legal, and operational implications. Most prominently, the intersection of AI and data privacy, algorithmic fairness, accountability, and transparency poses dazzling complexities for organizations operating in a global environment (Radanliev, 2025; Sozinova, 2025). As governments worldwide begin to create independent regimes of AI regulation, HR professionals will need to take a proactive approach in adapting their systems to preempt future legal demands in an effort to establish risk avoidance along with ethical management. This article reflects on the most significant global AI laws applicable to HRM and their practical applications and provides a systematic guide to the incorporation of legal and ethical aspects into AI-based HR processes.

AI regulation remains patchwork across nation-states but is informed by national agendas and legal traditions. Certain seminal regulations have, however, set precedents that are being adopted more and more in international practice—especially where transparency of decision-making and data privacy are most critical, i.e., in HRM (Cao & Power, 2025; Pantos, 2024).

The General Data Protection Regulation (GDPR) remains the foundation of data protection within the EU and internationally. Article 22 of the GDPR prohibits decisions in automated processing with significant influence on data subjects in a strict manner subject to certain conditions being met—such as explicit consent or contractual performance necessity (European Union, 2016). In HRM, this directly targets algorithmic hiring, promotion, or termination. Employers must make sure that any AI system utilized

DOI: 10.1201/9781003668282-14

in employee decisions guarantees human intervention, explainability of results, and contestability.

The upcoming EU AI Act, pending the final stages of legislative debate at the time of writing in 2024, classifies AI systems in terms of risk. Quite surprisingly, employment-focused AI applications, including CV screening or worker surveillance, are classified as "high-risk" (European Union, 2024). Classifying them places strict obligations on labor-focused AI software, including evaluation conformity procedures, transparency record-keeping, and continuous oversight post-deployment. This means that for multinational companies' Europe-based operations, this entails significant compliance costs and the requirement of rigorous vendor diligence whenever there is an acquisition of AI tools.

The United States, unlike the EU, lacks a federal AI or data protection law. It is instead regulated at state levels (e.g., the California Consumer Privacy Act – CCPA) and through industry-based regulation (Equal, 2023). There has been guidance issued by the Equal Employment Opportunity Commission (EEOC) on employment decision-making use of AI, specifically with respect to Title VII of the Civil Rights Act. The main issue is algorithmic bias—i.e., where AI software will inadvertently perpetuate bias based on race, gender, age, or disability (California, 2020).

The legacy of regulation in China is about state authority, social stability, and algorithm transparency. The "Internet Information Service Algorithmic Recommendation Management Provisions" of 2022 obligates algorithm providers to be fair, non-discriminatory, and transparent. In HR contexts, AI systems should never deceive candidates, offer transparency in recommendation processes, and abide by state-led ethical standards. Enactment is state-driven and usually opaque, but Chinese companies and multinationals operating within China must strictly comply with national guidelines.

In addition to national binding legislation, soft-law instruments such as OECD's AI Principles (2019) and UNESCO's Recommendation on the Ethics of Artificial Intelligence (2021) provide ethical guidelines. These would include human rights, transparency, robustness, and accountability, among others. Not being a legally binding arrangement, they actually influence national policy-making and thereby inform stakeholder expectations. These translate into the pressure for explainable AI, worker involvement, and ethical impact assessments before actual deployment for HRM.

The changing policy environment presents risks as well as opportunities for HR professionals. In applying AI and the consequent legal-ethical misalignment, there may be reputational damage, legal liability, and a possible erosion of trust on the part of employees. Some concerns are as follows:

- Data privacy and consent.
- Algorithmic bias and discrimination.
- Transparency and explainability.
- Accountability and human oversight.

HRM AI would draw most often on enormous quantities of personal data that would include sensitive categories such as health metrics, biometric information, or behavioral data. For GDPR and similar regimes, organizations need to obtain explicit opt-in or base their processing on legitimate interests. Data minimization and purpose limitation principles also constrain the scope of data to be collected. HR managers will, therefore, need to ensure that AI technologies don't "overcollect" and deduce more than strictly necessary.

Algorithmic discrimination is among the more egregious risks of AI in HR. Historical data will inevitably bear the prejudices of society with it, and they will be replicated by machine learning algorithms without realizing it. That would mean racially discriminatory hiring, sexed performance reviews, or age-discriminatory screening. Legal mandates such as the disparate impact doctrine in the US demand that the tools be audited and certified for fairness. HRM needs to include robust fairness audits, varied training data, and recurring retraining of models to avoid discrimination.

For instance, legal obligations, such as in the case of GDPR, which has the right to explanation, demand that people know why and how the algorithm will decide something. That is an organizational and technical challenge, particularly with models that are black boxes, like deep neural networks. HR must focus on explainable AI systems or those equipped with layers of explainability, transforming model behavior into easily understandable explanations (Soprana, 2024; Guha et al., 2024).

Rules are now requiring that AI-based HR decisions are never unaccompanied. Human review processes need to be designed into processes to validate outputs, reverse decisions, and provide recourse. Assignment of accountability to a specific entity—be it the IT vendor, an HR function, or an internal AI ethics board—is most critical for adverse outcomes or regulatory examination.

For legal and ethical compliance requirements to be implemented effectively, HRM needs a formalized governance process well adapted to AI use. Organizations have to start with the general mapping of all relevant AI and data privacy legislation in each country or state in which they have operations. This encompasses statutory law, such as GDPR, CCPA, and soft-law documents, as well as local laws, like NYC Local Law 144. Internal policies will also have to be modified to integrate legal imperatives into procurement, deployment, and oversight structures of AI solutions.

Prior to deployment, AI HR tools should be subjected to a formal risk assessment that considers harms to individuals, including discrimination, invasion of privacy, or emotional distress. Some jurisdictions (e.g., EU and Canada) are starting to require such assessments, namely, Algorithmic Impact Assessments (AIAs), for high-risk uses (Treasury, 2020). Similarly, these must be reviewed over time as systems change.

AI tools must be regularly audited for accuracy, fairness, and harm. This involves statistical bias audits, accuracy benchmarking, and feedback loops from users. Where there are exceptions, remediation mechanisms must be activated with expedience, e.g., suspension of the tool where appropriate. Record-keeping of all audits and interventions facilitates legal defensibility and organizational learning (Litwin & Racabi, 2024; Wang & Zhang, 2025).

Managerial and HR personnel must be trained in the weak areas and danger potentiality of AI. Legal compliance, ethics, and bias recognition must accompany proper governance mechanisms in training (Bartlakowski, 2025; Shetty et al., 2025; Humeres et al., 2025; Vujnovic et al., 2025). Companies would be able to launch multifunctional AI ethics commissions with members from legal, technology, and HR departments so that a constant interfusing of values and practices takes place.

Global regulation of AI will grow with larger numbers of countries adopting risk management practices, transparency expectations, and enforcement (Kajava et al., 2025)). Complacency is no longer a feasible option for HRM. Progressive organizations will internalize explainable AI and inclusive systems, develop ethics-auditing capability, and emphasize human-centered design for algorithmic assets. Therefore, in meeting the requirements of regulations, they also shape work culture based on dignity, equity, and responsibility (Dubey et al., 2025).

Table 9.1 presents a comparative summary of the premier international and national regulation norms that govern the use of artificial intelligence in HRM. The table spotlights relevant legal instruments—from hard-law data protection legislation such as the EU GDPR and Brazil LGPD (Brasil, 2018) to soft-law proposals such as OECD AI Principles and UNESCO's ethical guidelines (United, 2021)—and addresses their relevance to the HR sector. It identifies the most important fields in which such regulation intersects with AI-powered HR practices, such as restrictions on automated decision-making, transparency obligations, anti-discrimination obligations, and consent obligations for data processing. In so doing, the table discusses the growing importance of incorporating legal compliance into AI-based HR systems and cautions that both legal enforceability and the normative force of international soft law need to be considered by HR professionals in developing or procuring AI tools.

Table 9.2 summarizes all the regulatory requirements into simple, step-by-step actions for the organizations and the HR practitioners engaged with AI solutions. For example, the GDPR requires human oversight and express consent to process sensitive employee information—general principles of legality and accountability. The EU AI Act requires internal audit trails and supplier transparency and tries to leverage the supply chain visibility. United States CCPA and EEOC practice comprises fairness testing and traceability of data and data subject opt-out testing by the users. Auditability and Chinese algorithmic transparency are supported by soft-law tools such as UNESCO Ethics and OECD Principles that require ethical government, AI fairness deployment, and development through participation. Testing algorithms and record-keeping of legal processes are the highest priority for Canada and Brazil in their data protection and automated decision-making legislations. In short, the table is a guide to calls to action for global HRM practitioners to reconsider their AI policies, both in terms of compliance with the law and changing ethical standards.

9.2 ETHICAL AI ADOPTION: TRANSPARENCY, BIAS MITIGATION, AND DATA PRIVACY

Sophisticated ethical issues arising from growing AI usage of sensitive employee and candidate data will revolve around questions of explainability in algorithms, preventing

TABLE 9.1 Comparative overview of key international and national regulatory implications

Jurisdiction / Framework	Key regulation / Initiative	Scope relevant to HRM	Implications for AI-powered HR processes
European Union (EU)	General Data Protection Regulation (GDPR, 2016)	Protection of employee and candidate data; limits on automated profiling	Avoids highly automated decisions causing legal or serious effects unless with protections (Art. 22); requires express consent and right to explanation
	AI Act (2024, pending full implementation)	Classification of HR AI tools as "high-risk" systems (e.g., recruitment, testing, surveillance)	Requires conformity testing, transparency records, and constant oversight; penalties can be extreme
United States	Equal Employment Opportunity Commission (EEOC) Guidance (2023)	Non-discrimination in AI recruitment, promotion, and performance of employees	Organizations that deploy AI must ensure compliance with Title VII; processes cannot disproportionately impact protected classes
	California Consumer Privacy Act (CCPA, 2020)	Employee and job applicant data processing rights	Requires notice when collected, right to erasure, and opt-out of sale or profiling; low but increasing HR applicability
China	Provisions on the Management of Algorithmic Recommendations (2022)	Algorithmic decision-making on employment platforms and digital labor	It requires fairness, non-discrimination, and the absence of manipulation, along with a clear explanation of the AI tool's rationale and the explicit articulation of its objectives
OECD (Soft Law)	OECD AI Principles (2019)	Cross-sectoral and cross-border ethical framework for trustworthy AI	Encourages transparency, accountability, resilience, and human rights alignment
UNESCO (Soft Law)	Ethics of Artificial Intelligence	Promotion of ethical, inclusive, and rights-based AI systems	Ensures prioritization of non-discrimination, explainability, social inclusion, and sustainable development
Canada	Directive on Automated Decision-Making (2020)	Federal law-regulated HR processes, especially in public service recruitment	Requires mandatory Algorithmic Impact Assessments (AIAs) where AI systems affect people; necessity of transparency, redress, and human oversight
Brazil	Lei Geral de Proteção de Dados (LGPD, 2020)	Protection of personal data in the context of HR	Requires legal foundation for the processing of personal and sensitive data, especially in recruitment and surveillance

Source: Author's own work.

systems bias, and the protection of the privacy of the data. Consequently, the proper application of AI in HRM has to be premised on fairness, accountability, and trust principles. This article discusses best practices for ethical AI implementation in HRM with emphasis on the three interconnected pillars of transparency, minimizing bias, and data privacy,

TABLE 9.2 Comparative overview of key international and national regulatory-compliance recommendations

Jurisdiction / Framework	Key regulation / Initiative	Compliance recommendations
European Union (EU)	General Data Protection Regulation (GDPR, 2016)	Ensure human-in-the-loop decision-making; obtain explicit opt-in for sensitive information; offer mechanisms for challenging decisions
	AI Act (2024, pending full implementation)	Implement internal audit trails; utilize only vendors that provide CE-compliant AI systems; include risk management processes
United States	Equal Employment Opportunity Commission (EEOC) Guidance (2023)	Conduct algorithmic bias testing; utilize diverse and representative datasets; allow appeal mechanisms for AI-based decisions
	California Consumer Privacy Act (CCPA, 2020)	Offer privacy notices within AI tools; track data sources and usage; allow opt-outs as and when necessary
China	NYC Local Law 144	Have HR tech vendors perform audits annually; caution applicants clearly about AI usage; maintain audit trail for examination
	Provisions on the Management of Algorithmic Recommendations (2022)	Post open accounts of algorithmic rationale; avoid elusive recommendation systems; ensure employee access to monitoring routes
OECD (Soft Law)	OECD AI Principles (2019)	Establish AI ethics oversight boards; document AI-driven choices; prioritize safety and fairness tests in HR algorithms highest
UNESCO (Soft Law)	Ethics of Artificial Intelligence	Embrace ethical influence assessments; integrate participatory design methods in AI work; maintain ethical standards for the acquisition of HR technology
Canada	Directive on Automated Decision-Making (2020)	Apply AIA methodology before system implementation; offer transparent explanations to affected individuals
Brazil	Lei Geral de Proteção de Dados (LGPD, 2020)	Identify legal grounds for each instance of HR data processing; document data flows; grant data subjects rights to access and correction

Source: Author's own work.

each of which is an important pillar for responsible innovation in people management (Rao & Zhao, 2025).

Transparency or clear description is central in ethically adopting AI. In the context of HRM, this implies that both the operational aspects of AI—how it functions and the nature of the data it processes—and the rationale behind its recommendations or decisions are made transparent, thereby enabling clear and accessible understanding. This is especially the case in matters related to recruitment, performance analysis, and promotions since, most times, decisions derived from AI influence professional lives significantly, and a professional's future too (Madanchian & Taherdoost, 2025).

An explainable HRM AI system requires three things: explicability, accessibility, and auditability. Explicability is the ability of an AI model to give human-understandable explanations for its outputs. This is most ordinarily accomplished through integrating explainable AI (XAI) methods, which allow stakeholders and HR practitioners to view the decision rationale, i.e., why a particular candidate was ranked or why a worker was given a particular performance rating (Muralidharan et al., 2024). Accessibility guarantees that the respective stakeholders such as human resource practitioners, job candidates, and employees have ready access to information regarding how the system operates. Auditability allows internal or external auditors to perform an audit of the AI system's integrity, follow the steps involved in data processing, and examine the logs of decisions (Mahade et al., 2025' Wolniak, Stecuła, & Aydın, 2024; Wolniak & Stecuła, 2024).

Best practice is the publication of AI impact assessments, just like the Data Protection Impact Assessments (DPIAs) under the General Data Protection Regulation (GDPR). Such assessments address not only data security considerations but also the ethical concerns, fairness elements, and possible unintended consequences of AI implementation. In addition, interdisciplinary governance boards should be formed in businesses and comprise ethicists, data scientists, HR professionals, and attorneys who will assess AI technologies periodically to ensure that they are compliant with ethical standards (Raja & Manoharan, 2024; Tursunbayeva, 2024).

Bias in AI systems happens in situations where algorithms replicate or even amplify social inequities that exist in training data or in the development decisions of creators. HRM biases can take on many forms, from demographic type-based applicant preference to penalty imposition based on bias against members of minority groups in performance appraisal. In this regard, the moral obligation is to detect, evaluate, and mitigate bias at every stage of AI system development and deployment (Madanchian and Taherdoost, 2025).

One of the fundamental methods to minimize bias is extremely meticulous auditing of AI models' training data. Biased historical data, for instance, historical hiring data that reflects discriminatory practices, can contaminate even highly sophisticated machine learning models. Preprocessing techniques involve rebalancing data, anonymizing the data, or even creating synthetic data to minimize representational disparities (Koo et al., 2025). In-processing techniques involve the integration of fairness constraints into the training process itself, algorithmically, whereas post-processing techniques attempt to modify outcomes after model predictions with a perspective to ensuring fair treatment (Bankins, 2021).

Integration with fairness-testing software, such as IBM's AI Fairness 360 or Google's What-If Tool, to detect overrepresentation by gender, race, age, or other protected classes is also a requirement. This software could be added to the model loop, tracking how the algorithm is doing on every subgroup and alerting against discriminatory trends (Chen, Tallant, & Selig, 2025).

Avoiding bias goes far beyond technical tweaks. Ethical AI requires constant human oversight and interpretive intelligence. HR practitioners have to be vested with the expertise and power to challenge AI-derived results and reverse decisions that contradict ethical considerations or organizational D&I goals. Cross-training the HR function on data literacy and ethical thinking will accomplish this. In addition, mechanisms for redress must be available so that a person affected by an AI-generated decision can lodge an appeal with a request to have a human review the determination, thus still ensuring procedural justice and accountability (Arjanto & Aditama, 2025; Zhang, Hu, & Zhou, 2025).

Finally, because the HRM AI tools rely very much on humongous personal data, all from resumes, psychometric tests, behavioral patterns, and even biometric markers, data privacy is a question of concern. Regulatory requirements like the GDPR in the EU and the CCPA in the US set stringent conditions on the collection, processing, and storing of personal data, especially in the workplace. Ethical AI solutions must not only meet these regulatory requirements but also exceed them to create trust and respect for people's digital sovereignty (Bani Ahmad, 2024).

Such good practices begin with data minimization: gathering only the bare minimum data required for a specific purpose. AI technology must be developed to work optimally with a minimum of personal data and, consequently, expose individuals as little as possible to privacy-harming risks. The second necessary practice is purpose limitation, where the information gathered with the intent of satisfying a purpose, say recruitment, will not be used to satisfy a different purpose, say marketing analysis, unless by explicit consent (Singh & Kumar, 2024).

Consent management must be robust and transparent. Job applicants and employees must be informed of what information is being collected, how the information will be used, and what rights they retain regarding access, correction, and erasure. PETs like differential privacy, federated learning, and homomorphic encryption can be used with a view to enabling AI systems to learn from data without having express access to raw personal information (Rana et al., 2024).

Similarly, robust data governance must be in place. This would involve appropriate data stewardship functions, data security measures, i.e., encryption, access controls, breach notification protocols, and routine privacy audits. Lastly, privacy-by-design must be an ethical HRM practice. For instance, data protection should be integrated into the design of AI systems from the get-go, and not as an afterthought (Hayes, 2024; Ooi & Wilkinson, 2024).

HRM companies that plan to deploy AI ethically are likely to have a comprehensive, interdisciplinary approach that would provide ethical considerations at every stage of the cycle of implementing AI. These include technical countering measures and organizational policy architectures and cross-functional governing architectures and proactive engagement with evolving regulatory standards. Ethical AI in HRM is actually not a matter of compliance but one of social responsibility and institutional integrity—a perpetual commitment to balancing technological progress and human dignity (Hussain, Wang, & Li, 2024; Joseph et al., 2024).

The recap of best practices in ethical AI use in HRM is displayed in Table 9.3, with emphasis on actionable strategies to ensure fairness, responsibility, and data protection. The table is organized under the three broad ethical themes—AI transparency, bias mitigation, and data privacy—with a definition and an instance of in-practice implementation (Abderrahim et al., 2024). Data auditing, fairness-aware algorithms, and human-in-the-loop decision-making processes transcend prevention of algorithmic bias and fair treatment of demographic groups. Data privacy is ensured by data minimization

TABLE 9.3 Best practices for ethical AI adoption in Human Resource Management (HRM)

Best practice	Description	Implementation example
Data auditing	Oversight of datasets for gender, ethnicity, age, and other protected class imbalances on a regular basis.	Conduct quarterly reviews of hiring datasets to identify and address demographic gaps.
Fairness-aware algorithms	Use fairness-constrained algorithms during model training.	Employ fairness metrics like demographic parity or equal opportunity in candidate ranking.
Human-in-the-loop decision-making	Have final decisions checked and approved by HR practitioners.	Grant HR the capability to override algorithmic suggestions that are perceived as biased or unethical.
Diverse development teams	Have diverse and multidisciplinary teams involved in model development to reduce design biases.	Include HR, legal, data science, and DEI representatives on AI project teams.
Continuous monitoring and testing	Use ongoing monitoring of model performance over different demographic groups.	Utilize tools like IBM AI Fairness 360 for subgroup analysis in hiring outcomes.
Data minimization	Collect only data that is necessary and relevant to the HR function being performed.	Do not collect social media data unless it is directly related to job performance.
Consent and transparency mechanisms	Transparency: clearly inform subjects regarding the data being collected and obtain informed consent.	Use digital consent forms outlining data use in AI testing.
Privacy-enhancing technologies (PETs)	Use technologies like differential privacy or federated learning.	Utilize federated learning to train models on employee data locally, as opposed to centrally.
Robust data governance	Establish roles, procedures, and policy to protect sensitive HR data.	Assign a Data Protection Officer (DPO) to oversee AI-related data processing.
Privacy by design	Design privacy defense mechanisms in the system from the initial stages of development.	Design recruitment chatbots with default anonymization of data and shorter retention policies.
Explainable AI (XAI)	Implement models that can provide human-readable explanations for outputs.	Use SHAP or LIME tools to explain why a candidate received a specific score.
AI impact assessments	Explore social and ethical impacts before implementing AI tools.	Include algorithmic risk assessment as part of HR technology procurement.
Stakeholder access to system information	Provide clear information to relevant users (HR staff, candidates) about how the AI functions.	Provide candidate-facing FAQs or dashboards showing AI decision logic.
External auditing	Allow third parties to check and authenticate the legality and equity of AI tools.	Have independent auditors review AI systems used in promotions and appraisals.
Documentation and logging	Maintain complex records of AI decision-making procedures and changes.	Keep all model updates and outputs for five years for traceability and compliance audits.

Source: Author's own work.

policies, privacy-enhancing technologies, and robust governance frameworks that cumulatively protect sensitive employee information and guarantee regulatory compliance. At the same time, the transparency of AI is carried out by explainable AI solutions, accessibility of system rationale to stakeholders, and rigorous documentation, allowing users to understand, evaluate, and trust AI-powered HR processes. Together, these practices constitute a comprehensive ethical framework for organizations using AI technologies in their HR operations responsibly (Shahid, Singh, & Chauhan, 2024; Rahman, 2024).

9.3 THE ROLE OF HR LEADERS AND POLICYMAKERS IN AI GOVERNANCE

As organizations become more reliant on algorithmic software to decide who to hire, promote, and engage, the regulation of AI systems is a burning question. Leading that regulation are two major players: policymakers and HR leaders. Those leaders must work side by side to make sure the use of AI in workplace environments is not just effective but also ethical. Their shared responsibility is to jointly craft a regulatory and operational environment that not only complies with evolving legal requirements but also sustains the pillars of fairness, transparency, accountability, and human dignity (Mahade et al., 2025; Nayak, Budhwar, & Malik, 2025).

Human resource leaders hold a unique position at the intersection of human capital and technology. As custodians of organizational culture, ethics, and employee welfare, they have a significant role to play in the ethical implementation of AI systems in HR operations. They start by carefully balancing the prospective advantages and risks of AI adoption. AI offers efficiency and objectivity but is also risky in terms of possible bias, non-explainability, and impersonalization. HR leaders are thus integrally involved in AI strategy formulation, insisting on systems that enhance, not undermine, human judgment (Dutta & Mishra, 2025).

The most important task for HR professionals is mapping AI systems onto organizational ethical norms and values. This entails participation in AI procurement and development activities such that vendors provide transparent documentation of algorithmic rationale, training data provenance, and fairness audits. By incorporating ethics into technology audits and supplier agreements, HR leaders can factor in accountability at the start of the AI implementation process (Mori et al., 2025; Xiao, Yan, & Bamber, 2025).

HR leaders must be advocates for diversity and inclusion through an examination of AI applications for the potential to produce discriminatory outputs. For example, historical bias in training sets can lead to algorithms that unjustly penalize job applicants from minority groups. In this context, there is a requirement for HR practitioners to engage in ongoing bias auditing and model retraining processes, and demographic balance measures must be included in AI systems' key performance indicators (Malik et al., 2025; Narzary et al., 2025; Skubis, Wolniak, & Grebski, 2024; Stecuła, Wolniak, & Grebski, 2023).

As organizations are ever more accountable for regulatory oversight, HR leaders must also acquaint themselves with regulations pertaining to AI workforce utilization. The European Union's 2024 Artificial Intelligence Act, for instance, classifies many

HR-related applications of AI—i.e., those utilized in hiring, performance management, and surveillance—as "high-risk" systems. The designation comes with requirements pertaining to risk management, record-keeping, transparency, and post-deployment monitoring. In the US, state privacy laws (e.g., CCPA in California) and the Equal Employment Opportunity Commission (EEOC) mandate employers utilizing AI technologies to ensure that they do not have disparate impact on protected groups (Prikshat et al., 2025).

Managing these regulatory frameworks entails a different kind of HR leadership—a legally conscious, technology-friendly, and morally alert one. HR operations have to develop governance structures that would be compliant with these legislations. These include adopting practices such as (Park et al., 2025; Janghbahadur et al., 2025; Ahmić & Cosić, 2025):

- Algorithmic transparency, through disclosure of the impact of AI tools on decisions concerning people to workers.
- Explainability requirements, thus enabling individuals to challenge or contest decisions made by or based on algorithms.
- Human-in-the-loop decisioning, with ultimate decisions subject to human override and checking.

HR executives must form AI ethics boards or cross-functional governance bodies that are made up of not only legal and technical specialists but also representatives of employee groups. These bodies can serve as discussion fora for AI usage scenarios, risk assessments, and development of above-compliance organizational rules that assume best practices in ethics (Revillod, 2025).

While HR professionals operate internally within the organization, policymakers have a contribution to make toward shaping the external environment through legislation, regulation, and public consultation. The complexity and rapid evolution of AI demand agile and forward-thinking policy-making. Governments and regulatory agencies must create legal frameworks that not only protect individual rights but also foster responsible innovation (Madanchian & Taderdoostr, 2025). The decision-makers need to have a clear concept of what is perceived as discriminatory or adverse use of AI in workplaces. The policy framework needs to be specific enough to establish enforceable commitments, but also versatile enough to be adapted to various organizational environments. The EU AI Act, in this regard, is successful at having multi-level categories of risk and imposing mandatory requirements on high-risk systems (Maghsoudi et al., 2025; Gong, Fan, & Bartram, 2025).

The second area where policymakers have a role to perform is standardization. Through working in liaison with international bodies, governments can help facilitate the development of technical standards for algorithmic fairness, robustness, and accountability. They help standardize practice across jurisdictions, which is especially critical for multinational organizations that operate under different legal regimes. The policymakers should also give the regulating authorities the mandate and resources to audit the AI systems, investigate complaints, and impose sanctions for noncompliance (John & Paramila, 2025; Kim, Battaglia, & Kim, 2025). They should also finance public education campaigns and digital literacy workshops that educate employers and employees on AI rights and risks. Policymakers can also be moral innovation facilitators by providing finances, incentives, and regulatory sandboxes to test responsible uses of AI in HR. This can allow experimentation without crossing ethical boundaries (Milhem et al., 2025).

As they are complementary in nature, both policymakers and HR leaders are required to have substantive communication with one another. This cooperation can take the shape of public-private partnerships, multi-stakeholder dialogues, and types of co-regulation that combine legislative demands and industry self-regulation. The collaborative governance vision depends on mutual accountability, continuous learning, and adaptive flexibility in the face of emerging issues. HR professional bodies and associations can serve as intermediaries in the process by translating regulation imperatives into actionable suggestions and contributing training modules on ethical AI application (Antony & Vinayagam, 2025). At the same time, such associations can also serve as feedback mechanisms, alerting policymakers to real issues and unintended effects of AI regulation (Khan et al., 2025; Soni et al., 2025).

A very promising strategy is the co-development by employers, regulators, civil society, and technology providers of AI governance arrangements. These can include sectoral codes of conduct, certification schemes, and public reporting obligations that offer additional transparency and stakeholder confidence. Co-governance allows for contextualization. The application of AI in a high-tech multinational corporation can have different ethical implications than its application in a small home-country services business. Sectoral and organizational realities are made relevant and effective by bespoke governance (Karbekova et al., 2025; Revillod, 2025).

As the pace of change is technology-driven, AI workplace regulation can no longer be left to IT or compliance departments alone. It demands collective leadership, with HR practitioners and policymakers working together as co-designers of a technologically sophisticated but ethically sustainable future (Kyriakidou, 2025).

HR leaders must embrace their new roles as custodians of data, guardians of ethics, and change agents. They must build internal capabilities to evaluate, adopt, and manage AI applications through the lens of fairness, inclusivity, and workforce empowerment. Policymakers, in turn, must craft thoughtful, forward-looking legislation providing legal certainty and room for ethical innovation (Soleimani et al., 2025). Lastly, sound AI governance in HRM is not a technical or legal issue—it is an issue of values. It is an issue of preserving human agency in the age of automation, of ensuring that technology works for the people and not the other way around, and of protecting the dignity of labor in the age of algorithms. It is only through collective, synergistic effort on the part of HR leaders and policymakers that this vision is achievable (Choudhari et al., 2025).

Table 9.4 below depicts the complementary roles of HR leaders and policymakers in artificial intelligence governance in workforce management, needing to work hand in hand to ensure ethical, transparent, and legally sound AI adoption. HR practitioners offer

TABLE 9.4 The role of HR leaders and policymakers in AI governance

Dimension	Role of HR leaders	Role of policymakers	Collaborative actions
Policy development	Call for responsible AI practices in internal HR policies	Formulate legal and ethical AI frameworks for the workplace	Co-create industry codes of conduct and governance models
Fairness and bias mitigation	Examine HR algorithms for discrimination; promote fairness-aware models	Mandate anti-discrimination safeguards in AI systems	Enable shared measures and benchmarks for demographic fairness
Transparency and explainability	Ensure that employees understand how AI-driven decisions are made and that they can appeal them	Impose transparency and explainability expectations for high-risk AI systems	Develop shared standards for explainability of algorithms and justification of decisions
Compliance and legal alignment	Periodically monitor organizational compliance with AI-specified labor laws	Enforce compliance with privacy, labor, and anti-discrimination laws	Provide HR-friendly legal counsel and compliance toolkits
Human oversight	Implement human-in-the-loop procedures in AI-driven HR decisions	Regulate limits on fully automated decision-making in the workplace	Implement human oversight for high-impact decisions (e.g., hiring, dismissal, promotion)
Workforce advocacy	Ensure employee rights, gain informed consent, and uphold data dignity	Guarantee fundamental rights and safeguards in AI-controlled work environments	Enforce shared mechanisms for employee grievances and redress
AI literacy and training	Educate HR teams to understand and deal responsibly with AI technologies	Fund public training initiatives on AI rights and workforce implications	Co-develop training modules in ethical AI for HR and compliance officers
Technology procurement	Examine vendors and AI solutions for inclusive and ethical design	Set procurement standards and certification requirements for HR tech	Integrate procurement with established certifications (e.g., bias-tested, GDPR-compliant)
Monitoring and accountability	Conduct regular performance audits and post-deployment monitoring of AI systems	Form auditing agencies and issue penalties for abuse	Establish joint auditing standards and accountability scorecards
Innovation and governance dialogues	Share HR-specific challenges and innovations with regulators	Involve industry stakeholders in the development of policy	Participate in multi-stakeholder forums and AI governance coalitions

Source: Author's own work.

internal implementation, including bias auditing, employee support, human judgment, and ethical procurement of AI technologies, and policymakers offer the guarantee of creating legal frameworks, compliance, and national and global standards. They both engage in shared activities like co-designing training modules, creating mutual accountability systems, and engaging in multi-stakeholder forums to achieve a balance between technological innovation and human values and regulatory safeguarding.

REFERENCES

Abderrahim, F., Mkik, M., Ghernouk, C., Aziz, H., & Hebaz, A. (2024). Revolutionizing healthcare: the impact of artificial intelligence in connected medicine – unleashing the power of real-time diagnostics, personalized treatment and ethical AI adoption. In *Lecture Notes in Networks and Systems* (Vol. 1108, pp. 17–30).

Ahmić, A., & Ćosić, M. (2025). Digital human resource management influence on the organizational resilience. *Organization Management Journal.* https://doi.org/10.1108/OMJ-09-2024-2299. www.emerald.com/omj/article-pdf/22/2/111/9726831/omj-09-2024-2299.pdf

Antony, S., & Vinayagam, K. (2025). The role of AI in shaping HRM skills and strategies in private banks: a study on manager-employee dynamics in Chennai City. In *2025 International Conference on Automation and Computation (AUTOCOM 2025)* (pp. 353–358). IEEE.

Arjanto, P., & Aditama, M. H. R. (2025). AI in nursing education: from ethical challenges to institutional strategies for effective adoption. *Teaching and Learning in Nursing, 20*(3), 300–301.

Bani Ahmad, A. Y. A. (2024). Ethical implications of artificial intelligence in accounting: a framework for responsible AI adoption in multinational corporations in Jordan. *International Journal of Data and Network Science, 8*(1), 401–414.

Bankins, S. (2021). The ethical use of artificial intelligence in human resource management: a decision-making framework. *Ethics and Information Technology, 23*(4), 841–854.

Bartlakowski, K. (2025). The EU's new AI regulation and its significance on universities, local authorities and libraries | Le nouveau règlement de l'UE sur l'IA et son implication pour les universités, les communes et les bibliothèques. *Information-Wissenschaft und Praxis, 76*(2–3), 113–120.

Brasil. (2018). *Lei nº 13.709, de 14 de agosto de 2018: Lei Geral de Proteção de Dados Pessoais (LGPD).* Presidência da República. www.planalto.gov.br/ccivil_03/_ato2015-2018/2018/lei/l13709.htm (Access data 10.05.2025).

California Civil Code § 1798.100 et seq. (2020). *California Consumer Privacy Act of 2018*, as amended by the California Privacy Rights Act of 2020. Retrieved from https://oag.ca.gov/privacy/ccpa, (Access data 10.05.2025).

Cao, X., & Power, L. (2025). Controlled carefully: How consumer care legitimizes China's AI regulations. *Information, Communication & Society*, 1–17. Routledge. https://doi.org/10.1080/1369118X.2025.2474565

Chen, K., Tallant, A. C., & Selig, I. (2025). Exploring generative AI literacy in higher education: student adoption, interaction, evaluation and ethical perceptions. *Information and Learning Science, 126*(1–2), 132–148.

Choudhari, Y., Shrestha, P., Singh, G., & Bindra, S. (2025). The impact of artificial intelligence (AI) on talent acquisition in human resource management. *Australasian Accounting, Business and Finance Journal, 19*(1), 153–172.

Dubey, A., Yang, Z., Anžel, A., & Hattab, G. (2025). Protocol for implementing the nested model for AI design and validation in compliance with AI regulations. *STAR Protocols, 6*(2), 103771.

Dutta, D., & Mishra, S. K. (2025). Artificial intelligence-based virtual assistant and employee engagement: an empirical investigation. *Personnel Review, 54*(3), 913–934.

www.eeoc.gov/eeoc-guidance

European Union. (2016). *Regulation (EU) 2016/679 of the European Parliament and of the Council of 27 April 2016 on the protection of natural persons with regard to the processing of personal data and on the free movement of such data (General Data Protection Regulation). Official Journal of the European Union, L119*, 1–88. Retrieved from https://eur-lex.europa.eu/legal-content/EN/TXT/?uri=CELEX%3A32016R0679 (Access data 10.05.2025).

European Union. (2024). *Regulation (EU) 2024/1689 of the European Parliament and of the Council of 13 June 2024 laying down harmonised rules on artificial intelligence and amending certain Union legislative acts (Artificial Intelligence Act). Official Journal of the European Union, L 2024/1689*, 1–168. Retrieved from https://eur-lex.europa.eu/eli/reg/2024/1689/oj, (Access data 10.05.2025).

Gong, Q., Fan, D., & Bartram, T. (2025). Integrating artificial intelligence and human resource management: a review and future research agenda. *International Journal of Human Resource Management, 36*(1), 103–141.

Guha, N., Lawrence, C. M., Gailmard, L. A., Liang, P., & Ho, D. E. (2024). AI regulation has its own alignment problem: the technical and institutional feasibility of disclosure, registration, licensing, and auditing. *George Washington Law Review, 92*(6), 1473–1557.

Hayes, C. (2024). Building democratisation and agency: the adoption of ethical AI practice in pedagogy. In *Enhancing higher education and research with OpenAI models* (pp. 60–78). IGI Global.

Humeres, M., Cotoras, D., Moretti, R., Correa, T., & López, C. (2025). Cooling down AI regulation controversies: three closure processes in the Chilean legislative arena. *Big Data and Society, 12*(1).

Hussain, T., Wang, D., & Li, B. (2024). The influence of the COVID-19 pandemic on the adoption and impact of AI ChatGPT: challenges, applications, and ethical considerations. *Acta Psychologica, 246*, 104264.

Jangbahadur, U., Ahlawat, S., Rozera, P., & Gupta, N. (2025). The effect of AI-enabled HRM dimensions on employee engagement and sustainable organisational performance: fusion skills as a moderator. *Evidence-Based HRM, 13*(1), 85–107.

John, J. E., & Pramila, S. (2025). Leveraging AI in HR analytics to foster green human resource management. In *Studies in Systems, Decision and Control* (Vol. 555, pp. 1067–1074).

Joseph, N. P., Nassa, V. K., Krishna, M. H., Revathi, V., & Sahai, A. (2024). Critical analysis of the ethical consequences of AI adoption in human resource management. In *Proceedings of International Conference on Communication, Computer Sciences and Engineering (IC3SE 2024)* (pp. 1502–1507). IEEE.

Kajava, K., Gonzalez Torres, A. P., Rannisto, A., & Sakai, S. (2025). Justifying AI regulation: examining multi-stakeholder responses to the AI Act. *Telematics and Informatics, 99*, 102278.

Karbekova, A. B., Tashbolotova, S. A., Mamatova, A. B., & Uraimhalilova, A. (2025). Intelligent support for personnel decision-making and socially responsible HRM using big data and AI. In *Studies in Big Data* (Vol. 168, pp. 3–11).

Khan, M., Kumari, A., Sengar, V., Shaikh, Z. H., & Rani, N. (2025). Leveraging generative AI and well-being oriented HRM to address social isolation and quiet quitting in the workplace. In *Studies in Big Data* (Vol. 171, pp. 581–593).

Kim, J., Battaglia, S., & Kim, H. H. (2025). Collaborative intelligence achieved from AI-enabled recruitment: a case study of POSCO in South Korea. *Asia Pacific Business Review, 31*(1), 180–199.

Koo, I., Zaman, U., Ha, H., & Nawaz, S. (2025). Assessing the interplay of trust dynamics, personalization, ethical AI practices, and tourist behavior in the adoption of AI-driven smart tourism technologies. *Journal of Open Innovation: Technology, Market, and Complexity, 11*(1), 100455.

Kyriakidou, O. (2025). Algorithms and global diversity management. In *Research handbook on global diversity management* (pp. 148–163). Edward Elgar Publishing.

Litwin, A. S., & Racabi, G. (2024). Varieties of AI regulations: the United States perspective. *ILR Review, 77*(5), 799–812.

Madanchian, M., & Taherdoost, H. (2025). Barriers and enablers of AI adoption in human resource management: a critical analysis of organizational and technological factors. *Information (Switzerland), 16*(1), 51.

Maghsoudi, M., Kamrani Shahri, M., Agha Mohammad Ali Kermani, M., & Khanizad, R. (2025). Mapping the landscape of AI-driven human resource management: a social network analysis of research collaboration. *IEEE Access, 13*, 3090–3114.

Mahade, A., Elmahi, A., Alomari, K. M., & Abdalla, A. A. (2025). Leveraging AI-driven insights to enhance sustainable human resource management performance: moderated mediation model: evidence from UAE higher education. *Discover Sustainability, 6*(1), 267.

Malik, A., Lirio, P., Budhwar, P., Nguyen, M., & Fauzi, M. A. (2025). Guest editorial: artificial intelligence (AI) in the world of work: bibliometric insights and mapping opportunities and challenges. *Personnel Review, 54*(3), 781–799.

Milhem, M., Ateeq, A., Al Astal, A., & Almeer, S. (2025). Digital transformation in HRM: navigating the future of human resource management. In *Studies in Systems, Decision and Control* (Vol. 566, pp. 23–33).

Mori, M., Sassetti, S., Cavaliere, V., & Bonti, M. (2025). A systematic literature review on artificial intelligence in recruiting and selection: a matter of ethics. *Personnel Review, 54*(3), 854–878.

Muralidharan, V., Ravi, B., Pachar, S., Chakraborty, N., & Sahaya Lenin, D. (2024). Ethical considerations in applying machine learning to HR practices: balancing efficiency with fairness. In *Proceedings of International Conference on Contemporary Computing and Informatics (IC3I 2024)* (pp. 1392–1398). IEEE.

Narzary, S., Makhecha, U. P., Budhwar, P., Malik, A., & Kumar, S. (2025). A temporal evolution of human resource management and technology research: a retrospective bibliometric analysis. *Personnel Review, 54*(3), 800–823.

Nayak, S., Budhwar, P., & Malik, A. (2025). Unveiling the hidden costs of AI in hospitality industry: the adverse effect of algorithmic human resources management (AHRM) on stress, wellbeing, and commitment. *International Journal of Hospitality Management, 129*, 104206.

Ooi, P. B., & Wilkinson, G. (2024). Enhancing ethical codes with artificial intelligence governance – a growing necessity for the adoption of generative AI in counselling. *British Journal of Guidance & Counselling, 53*(1), 66–80. https://doi.org/10.1080/03069885.2024.2373180.

Organisation for Economic Co-operation and Development. (2019). *Recommendation of the Council on Artificial Intelligence.* Retrieved from https://legalinstruments.oecd.org/en/instruments/OECD-LEGAL-0449, (Access data 10.05.2025).

Pantos, S. (2024). Supervisory approaches to AI regulation in insurance: The case of the UK prudential framework. In *Organizations and technology for sustainability* (pp. 80–112). Springer International Publishing.

Park, S., Chai, D. S., Park, J. J., & Oh, J. (2025). Exploring opportunities for artificial intelligence in organization development. *Human Resource Development Review, 24*(1), 3–36.

Prikshat, V., Kumar, S., Patel, P., & Varma, A. (2025). Impact of organisational facilitators and perceived HR effectiveness on acceptance of AI-augmented HRM: an integrated TAM and TPB perspective. *Personnel Review, 54*(3), 879–912.

Radanliev, P. (2025). Frontier AI regulation: what form should it take? *Frontiers in Political Science, 7*, 1561776.

Rahman, M. M. (2024). Unraveling fear, cultivating awareness: a research proposal for alleviating AI concerns and guiding ethical adoption. In *Proceedings of the 2024 11th IEEE International Conference on Behavioural and Social Computing (BESC 2024)*. IEEE.

Raja, L., & Manoharan, G. (2024). The ethics of machine learning in human resources: navigating fairness and efficiency. In *Proceedings of International Conference on Contemporary Computing and Informatics (IC3I 2024)* (pp. 1637–1642). IEEE.

Rana, N. P., Pillai, R., Sivathanu, B., & Malik, N. (2024). Assessing the nexus of generative AI adoption, ethical considerations and organizational performance. *Technovation, 135*, 103064.

Rao, S., & Zhao, T. (2025). Ethical AI in HR: A case study of tech hiring. *Journal of Computer Information Systems*, 1–18. https://doi.org/10.1080/08874417.2024.2446954

Revillod, G. (2025). Exploring the acceptability of artificial intelligence in human resources management: insights from Swiss organizations. *Systems Research and Behavioral Science*. https://doi.org/10.1002/sres.3140. https://onlinelibrary.wiley.com/doi/abs/10.1002/sres.3140

Shahid, N., Singh, M., & Chauhan, S. (2024). Ethical imperatives and frameworks for responsible AI adoption in digital entrepreneurship. In *Utilizing AI and smart technology to improve sustainability in entrepreneurship* (pp. 228–250). IGI Global.

Shetty, D. K., Vijaya Arjunan, R., Cenitta, D., Bhat, P., & Pullela, P. K. (2025). Analyzing AI regulation through literature and current trends. *Journal of Open Innovation: Technology, Market, and Complexity, 11*(1), 100508.

Singh, G., & Kumar, J. (2024). Navigating the future through adoption of AI in healthcare: legal and ethical perspectives. In *AI healthcare applications and security, ethical, and legal considerations* (pp. 240–260).

Skubis, I., Wolniak, R., & Grebski, W. W. (2024). AI and human-centric approach in smart cities management: case studies from Silesian and Lesser Poland Voivodships. *Sustainability, 16*(18), Article 8279, 1–26.

Soleimani, M., Intezari, A., Arrowsmith, J., Pauleen, D. J., & Taskin, N. (2025). Reducing AI bias in recruitment and selection: an integrative grounded approach. *International Journal of Human Resource Management*. (ahead-of-print) 1–36. https://doi.org/10.1080/09585192.2025.2480617

Soni, A., Shaikh, Z. H., Alhejair, A., Gulati, N., & Saseendran, H. (2025). AI in expanded HR ecosystems: mapping research trajectories and future prospective. In *Studies in Big Data* (Vol. 171, pp. 473–483).

Soprana, M. (2024). Compatibility of emerging AI regulation with GATS and TBT: the EU Artificial Intelligence Act. *Journal of International Economic Law, 27*(4), 706–722.

Sozinova, A. A. (2025). AI regulation of the labour market in a smart city to close the gap between the markets of higher education and work. In *Education in the Asia-Pacific Region* (Vol. 73, pp. 109–116).

Stecuła, K., Wolniak, R., & Grebski, W. (2023). AI-driven urban energy solutions—from individuals to society: a review. *Energies, 16*(24), 7988, 1–34.

Treasury Board of Canada Secretariat. (2020). *Directive on Automated Decision-Making.* Government of Canada. www.tbs-sct.gc.ca/pol/doc-eng.aspx?id=32592 (Access data 10.05.2025).

Tursunbayeva, A. (2024). Augmenting human resource management with artificial intelligence: towards an inclusive, sustainable, and responsible future. In *Contributions to management science* (Part F3983, pp. 1–148).

United Nations Educational, Scientific and Cultural Organization. (2021). *Recommendation on the Ethics of Artificial Intelligence.* UNESCO. https://unesdoc.unesco.org/ark:/48223/pf0000380455, (Access data 10.05.2025).

Vujnovic, M., Kruckeberg, D., Swiatek, L., & Galloway, C. (2025). AI regulation and ethical considerations surrounding the use of artificial intelligence in PR: the need for transparency and accountability. In *Public relations and the rise of AI* (pp. 77–93). Routledge.

Wang, S., & Zhang, H. (2025). Generative artificial intelligence and internationalization green innovation: roles of supply chain innovations and AI regulation for SMEs. *Technology in Society, 82*, 102898.

Wolniak, R., Stecuła, K., & Aydın, B. (2024). Digital transformation of grocery in-store shopping – scanners, artificial intelligence, augmented reality and beyond: a review. *Foods, 13*(18), Article 2948, 1–34.

Wolniak, R., & Stecuła, K. (2024). Artificial intelligence in Smart Cities—applications, barriers and future directions: a review. *Smart Cities*, 7, 1346–1389.

Xiao, Q., Yan, J., & Bamber, G. J. (2025). How does AI-enabled HR analytics influence employee resilience: job crafting as a mediator and HRM system strength as a moderator. *Personnel Review, 54*(3), 824–843.

Zhang, X., Hu, J., & Zhou, Y. (2025). The role of perceived utility and ethical concerns in the adoption of AI-based data analysis tools: a multi-group structural equation model analysis among academic researchers. *Education and Information Technologies*, 120880. Routledge. https://doi.org/10.1007/s10639-025-13535-3

CHAPTER 10

Preparing for the Future of AI-Driven HRM

10.1 WORKFORCE UPSKILLING AND RESKILLING IN AI-ENABLED HRM

While AI technologies are reshaping the very nature of work, Human Resource Management (HRM) has a dual mandate: leveraging the potential of AI to drive organizational performance and preparing the workforce for the digital economy. Reskilling and upskilling the workforce become strategic imperatives, not operational processes, in this context (Xiao, Yan, & Bamber, 2025; Jangbahadur et al., 2025). The objective is not only to future-proof work but to establish flexible and agile workforces with the ability to match the irrepressible pace of technological advancement. Strategic planning for upskilling and reskilling in AI-based HRM with regard to digital readiness, capacity-building, and long-term sustainability in the talent value chain is the focus of this chapter (Biswas, Giri, & Chatterjee, 2024).

The Fourth Industrial Revolution, which is fueled by AI, machine learning, automation, and big data analytics, is revolutionizing the need for human skills at a very rapid rate. According to the World Economic Forum, over 44% of the existing skills in the workforce will have evolved by the year 2027, which will necessitate humongous investment in learning and development. AI is substituting for humans in work that is not necessary but also opening new opportunities toward the resolution of complicated problems, innovation, and digital competence. Traditional HR models based on fixed job descriptions and straight-line careers are thus untenable (Zhou, Wang, & Chen, 2023; Xiao, Yan, & Bamber, 2023).

DOI: 10.1201/9781003668282-15

HR leaders must institute a dynamic model of building capability that looks to obsolescence in capability and accelerates the learning of new capabilities. This requires a future-focused talent development and learning strategy and frequent surveillance of new technologies and their influence on the work role. The strategic role of HRM nowadays is to identify future skills needs, design competency-based career paths, and utilize AI-powered tools to customize and scale up learning interventions (Band et al., 2024; Muralidharan et al., 2024). It also entails addressing structural disparities in internet access, thereby fostering inclusion in the future of work. Upskilling, in this context, refers to enhancing the capabilities of existing staff to meet evolving job requirements. Upskilling within AI-facilitated organizations increasingly entails learning digital skills, AI literacy, and analytical thought patterns. The focus broadens from IT skills to encompass cognitive flexibility, flexibility, and cross-functional teamwork (Goyal, Nagar, & Sharma, 2024).

One such effective approach is the utilization of AI-driven learning platforms such as LXPs, which enhance content delivery in a more personalized manner depending on user engagement, learning behavior, and performance indicators. Such platforms can also detect skill gaps through predictive analysis and suggest customized learning modules accordingly. For instance, IBM and SAP have managed to create productive AI-facilitated internal talent marketplaces that connect staff profiles to future growth positions, mentorship, and stretch assignments (Band et al., 2024).

Micro-credentialing and modular streams of learning have also been useful tools. With standalone, stackable modules of learning, companies make it possible for employees to master knowledge at their own pace as they map content to changing strategic priorities. Badges and digital certificates also provide transparency regarding emergent skills, making it convenient to move people around internally and to plan for succession. Foremost of all, however, HR practices must generate a culture of lifelong learning with psychological safety and management roots so that workers may learn without threat of penalty or failure (Patil et al., 2024; Mahade et al., 2025).

Upskilling is intended to improve current work, while reskilling is the transition to entirely new work or sectors, typically as a consequence of redundancy or automation. Reskilling initiatives must thus be comprehensive, strategic, and appropriately aligned with organizational workforce planning. They must include stringent examination of employment displacement patterns and complementary skill pathways that can facilitate horizontal or vertical transfer (Nayak, Budhwar, & Malik, 2025). Insight-driven reskilling begins with skills mapping—an action that contrasts existing workforce capacity with new requirements. That skill-mapping exercise is facilitated by AI-powered software that contrasts job architecture and competency models to spot transferable skills. For example, a customer service representative who has been made redundant by a chatbot can possess communication and empathy skills that can be repurposed for user experience design or employee advocacy roles (Dutta & Mishra, 2025; Mori et al., 2025).

Effective reskilling programs are co-designed with the input of line managers, L&D professionals, and external training providers so that they can be scaled and applicable. Public-private partnerships are also reshaping reskilling at the ecosystem level. Initiatives such as Microsoft's Global Skills Initiative and the Pact for Skills of the European

Commission are excellent models of collaborative initiatives, with corporate investment and government policy mutually reinforcing one another to propel grand-scale workforce reconfiguration (Narzary et al., 2025; Antony & Vinayagan, 2025). Effective reskilling initiatives involve career counseling and psychosocial counseling, considering the intellectual and emotional energy required to switch jobs. Adult learners go through dislocation of identity, self-doubt, and economic insecurity; HRM must therefore offer guided direction, mentoring, and involvement in the community so as to sustain interest and morale (Xiao, Yan, & Bamber, 2025; Malik et al., 2025).

Digital readiness is not only the equipment required to deliver digital training but also the intellectual and cultural competence of the workers to embrace AI integration. Organizations must ensure equal access to digital resources, platforms, and connectivity—particularly in hybrid or remote workplaces where digital divide challenges might be more intensive. From an HRM perspective, digital readiness begins with a digital skills audit across function areas. This audit is the foundation of digital competencies such as data interpretation, virtual collaboration, cybersecurity awareness, and productivity tool mastery. Specific intervention is then created to keep constantly developing these capabilities, experiential training, in-use feedback, and working implementations in real life taking priority (Prikshat et al., 2025; Park et al., 2025).

An electronically enabled workforce is also one that remains responsive to the ethical dimensions of AI, including data confidentiality, algorithmic bias, and transparency. Some of the trainings should, therefore, incorporate governance and ethics aspects in the context of digitization. For example, the application of AI by HR practitioners in recruitment should be mindful of the risk of biased decision-making and should involve training on bias-reduction methods, model explainability, and adherence to new AI regulation (i.e., the EU AI Act). Employees' development of a growth mindset is critical for digital readiness. HRM must create a firm rationale for utilizing AI as a complement, rather than a substitute, for human effort. Interventions in change management must be accompanied by open communication, participative discussion, and listening to overwhelm aggression and skepticism (Jangbahadur et al., 2025).

Long-term sustainable HRM consists of creating strong, inclusive, and dynamically evolving talent systems. Rather than turning to short-term, reactive one-off upskilling or reskilling programs, organizations must inscribe sustainable learning cultures into business strategy. That means constructing lifelong learning as an organizational culture pillar (Revillod, 2025; Ahmić & Cosić, 2025). One of the ways that it can be constructed with learning organizations—one that has inculcated knowledge creation, transfer, and application via function and hierarchies—is needed. These organizations bring in AI for applying experiential learning and making it democratized using knowledge management systems (Kim, Battaglia, & Kim, 2025). They also bring learning KPIs into team dynamics, leadership development, and performance appraisals (Madanchian & Taherdoost, 2025).

The second is talent mobility. HRM must facilitate smooth career flows whereby employees can scan cross-functional possibilities based on adjacency of skills, and not remain in a stringent role hierarchy. Talent intelligence platforms with artificial intelligence capabilities can place employees into new roles based on their hidden potential and learning history, thereby facilitating internal mobility and turnover (John and Pramila, 2025). Long-term sustainability requires embedding DEI (Diversity, Equity, Inclusion) in upskilling and reskilling. AI applications must be experimented on with respect to objectivity, learning content must be made culturally relevant, and training must be extended to all demographic segments. And it is only through this and by this, once the proper actions are taken by HRM, that the AI revolution will compound existing disparities instead of being an engine for social progress (Maghsoudi et al., 2025).

Upbringing and upscaling are the nucleus of change. Through expenditure on expert learning, digital literacy, reskilling streams, and ethical education, organizations can craft robust, well-secured working forces. HRM, previously a back-office department, today leads the charge on strategic reinvention—tasked not only with managing human capital but with developing it for the age of AI. Organizations most likely to thrive in this emerging world order are those that embrace learning as a strategic asset, inclusion as a design force, and human potential as an unlimited asset (Gong, Fan, & Bartram, 2025; Milhem et al., 2025).

Tables 10.1–10.4 summarize the most important strategic pillars for workforce readiness in an AI-enabled Human Resource Management (HRM) setup. Table 10.1 summarizes workforce upskilling initiatives, such as building digital and cognitive competencies through AI-driven learning platforms customized to the company, a continuous learning culture, and internal talent mobility platforms. Table 10.2 focuses on reskilling strategy in the sense of emphasizing the need for systematic career transition to new occupations, cross-ecosystem collaboration with the external world, and utilization of support systems to ease the workers through role redefinition. Table 10.3 focuses on digital readiness, referencing the demand for equal access to infrastructure, digital literacy as a company agenda, and ethical AI governance training implantation. Table 10.4 centers on organizational learning systems, future leadership development, and diversity-, equity-, and inclusion-driven upskilling paths to long-term sustainable HR. Together, these tables present a detailed and hands-on guide to workforce competitiveness in an AI economy.

TABLE 10.1 Strategies for workforce upskilling

Focus area	Strategic description
Digital and cognitive capability building	Organizations are investing in personalized, AI-driven learning platforms that adapt to a user's learning pace, style, and performance. These systems allow employees to develop the essential digital literacy, analytical reasoning, and cognitive flexibility necessary to thrive in AI-enhanced workplaces.
Continuous learning culture	The long-term upskilling strategy requires learning to be embedded in the organizational culture. Companies are rewriting performance measures to include learning objectives, and they are establishing psychological safety to foster experimentation and ongoing learning of new capabilities.
Talent internal mobility	Firms are designing internal talent marketplaces powered by AI, which facilitate the redeployment of employees into new roles based on their evolving skillsets. This allows workforce planning agility and fosters continuous development.

Source: Author's own work.

TABLE 10.2 Strategies for workforce reskilling

Focus area	Strategic description
Transition to emerging roles	Reskilling targets enable employees to shift into fresh career families aligned with the developing requirements of the digital economy. Through transferable skills mapping and matching with strategic needs, corporations provide systematic prospects for career transition.
Ecosystem collaboration	Successful long-term reskilling is frequently reliant on collaboration with schools, government agencies, and non-profits. These partnerships expand access to funding, minimize training expense, and synchronize curricula to reflect the realities of the labor market.
Support for learning transitions	Reskilling is typically linked with stress related to role and identity. Organizations are therefore providing one-on-one mentoring, coaching, and counseling to enable employees to meet these challenges boldly and hopefully.

Source: Author's own work.

TABLE 10.3 Strategies for digital readiness

Focus area	Strategic description
Infrastructure and access	Facilitating equal access to digital resources is at the heart of digital readiness. Firms are equipping employees with necessary hardware, software, and secure connectivity, especially in rural and hybrid work settings.
Digital mindset and literacy	Companies are implementing enterprise-wide digital literacy initiatives aimed at encouraging workers' comfort with data utilities, virtual meeting places, and digital models of problem-solving, thus establishing confidence and self-efficacy.
AI ethics and governance	To deploy AI ethically in HR functions, businesses are training employees—HR, legal, and compliance teams in particular—on matters such as algorithmic fairness, data protection, and explainability, in alignment with future global regulations such as the EU AI Act.

Source: Author's own work.

TABLE 10.4 Strategies for HR sustainability

Focus area	Strategic description
Organizational learning systems	Long-term HR sustainability is being maintained through the creation of learning organizations that are capable of capturing, managing, and sharing institutional memory. AI-driven platforms are being used to formalize tacit knowledge and enhance organizational memory.
Future-ready leadership	Companies are investing in leadership development that integrates digital literacy with soft skills such as empathy, inclusion, and flexible thinking. Leaders are being trained to exemplify continuous learning and lead teams through ongoing change.
Diversity, equity, and inclusion (DEI) in learning	DEI principles are being embedded in learning design to ensure that upskilling and reskilling programs remain inclusive, accessible, and culture-responsive. AI-driven applications are audited to prevent bias in learning suggestions and talent grading.

Source: Author's own work.

10.2 AI LITERACY AND DIGITAL READINESS FOR HR PROFESSIONALS

AI literacy as a part of HR activity is well beyond technical skills. It is being able to critique algorithmic recommendations, question the results of machine learning algorithms, and work positively with data scientists and coders (Chandel & Lim, 2025). Since HR decisions often touch people's careers, paychecks, and opportunity for career progression, errors, bias, or unforeseen consequences in AI deployment can have dire ethical and legal implications. HR practitioners thus need to be familiar with some key AI concepts such as training data, predictive modeling, supervised and unsupervised learning, algorithmic bias, and model transparency (Li et al., 2025).

Bias in AI is particularly worrying. AI model training will typically employ historical data that has social bias and produce outputs that are discriminatory against people on the basis of gender, race, age, or other protected attributes (Ghani et al., 2025; Promma et al., 2025). HR professionals are often unaware that they can inadvertently facilitate discriminatory hiring software or deceptive performance assessments. There should be a chance to identify sources of bias—data labeling, feature selection, model hyperparameter adjustment, or data acquisition. In addition, HR must also have the ability to demand fairness audits, explainability reports, and validation tests from AI vendors (Bećrović, Polz, & Tinkel, 2025; Zhang et al., 2025).

Equally important is the skill of interpreting algorithmic output. AI applications don't give deterministic solutions; they give probabilistic estimates. HR managers must recognize the probabilistic nature of AI analysis and not depend too heavily on model projections. For instance, a tool that suggests there's a 70% possibility of a candidate doing great in a position does not mean it will do so with absolute certainty and does not even account for contextual and growth factors. HR professionals should be literate in order to make use of such tools as a supplement—and not a substitute—to human decision-making (Kim, Battaglia, & Kim, 2025; Lew et al., 2025; Yang et al., 2025).

Table 10.5 displays dimensions of AI literacy anticipated from HR professionals today in order to work in more algorithm-ruled and digitalized workplaces.

All the aspects, ranging from possessing a basic knowledge of AI concepts to operating in systems of law and ethics, equip HR professionals with the skills to critically reflect on AI technologies. Through acquiring skills of algorithmic interpretation, detection of bias, explainability, and data governance, HR professionals can not only enhance decision-making, but also enable transparency, fairness, and accountability. Embracing continuous learning and inter-functional communication represents a doubling down on the adaptive role of HR as a strategic business partner and an ethical guardian in applying AI for managing human capital.

In addition to individual literacy, digital readiness addresses organizational culture and infrastructure for AI change. Companies attempt to make use of AI solutions without granting their HR competencies the potential to maximize its usage rightfully and ethically. Digital readiness consists of robust data governance processes, ongoing learning cycles, cross-functional collaboration models, and ethics-driven innovation culture. A learning culture for HR professionals is one of the essential elements of readiness.

TABLE 10.5 Dimensions of AI literacy for HR professionals

AI literacy dimension	Description	Relevance to HR professionals	Example applications
Basic AI concepts	To value the basic building blocks of artificial intelligence, such as machine learning, algorithms, training data, and model output.	Empowers HR to engage meaningfully with technical teams and evaluate AI tools used for hiring or performance management.	Learning AI fundamentals courses; learning HR technology platforms like Workday AI.
Algorithmic bias awareness	To understand that AI systems may perpetuate social, gender, or racial biases learned from past, unbalanced datasets.	Critical to ensuring fairness and avoiding discrimination in hiring, promotion, and evaluation practices.	Detecting biased hiring models; being part of fairness audits.
Interpretation of AI outputs	Read, understand, and question capabilities of AI-recommended insights while valuing the probabilistic, non-deterministic nature thereof.	Enables HR to make well-balanced decisions without undue reliance on machine output.	Auditing AI-generated performance ratings coupled with human ratings.
Transparency and explainability	To discover how and why AI systems arrived at particular conclusions and to demand comprehensible explanations.	Critical to building trust with employees and compliance with transparency legislation.	Using explainability techniques (e.g., SHAP, LIME) to interpret candidate scoring models.
Ethical implications	Awareness of ethical considerations like consent, surveillance, autonomy, and human implications of automation.	Ensures HR compliance with organizational values and employee rights through alignment of AI use.	Developing in-house AI ethics guidelines for HR applications.
Human-in-the-loop understanding	Knowledge of human oversight necessary in decision-making use of AI.	Prevents over-automation and ensures accountability in high-risk HR decisions.	Conducting final interviews through HR in spite of AI-based screening.
Data literacy	Awareness of the data lifecycle, from data collection and cleansing to analysis and storage, and data privacy policies.	Empowers HR to practice responsible data usage and comply with legal requirements like GDPR.	Taking care of consent and safe handling of candidate data in AI systems.
Legal and regulatory literacy	Knowledge of international and local laws controlling AI and automated decision-making in HR contexts.	Averts legal non-compliance and promotes ethical AI usage in workforce management.	Mapping HR algorithms to the EU AI Act or EEOC guidelines.
Communication with technical teams	Ability to explain HR goals and ethical concerns to developers and data scientists.	Ensures that AI tools are co-developed with technical competence and HR significance.	Attending AI tool development meetings with data engineers.
Continuous learning mindset	Commitment to keeping AI knowledge current and abreast of new technology and ethical controversy.	Empowers HR to evolve with future AI trends and maintain competence in AI governance.	Attending AI literacy workshops and HR tech conferences.

Source: Author's own work.

Long-term learning must be one of the core HR competencies, and the professionals must have constant upskilling and reskilling. These can be data analytics training, ethical AI courses, or experiential workshops with AI tools such as natural language processing for candidate screening or predictive modeling of turnover (Alfadhli et al., 2025; Aftab et al., 2025; Katsamba, 2025).

As much of an element of readiness is critical departmental collaboration. HR departments must closely work with IT, legal, and data science departments in a bid to co-design and run AI tools. Interdepartmental collaboration helps ensure that HR-specific ethical values such as fairness, transparency, and psychological safety are built into algorithmic systems right from the beginning. Digital preparedness also means technical infrastructure: secure data lakes, workflow automation, and AI performance monitoring software for real-time tracking of population segments (Almurtadha, 2024; Weritz, Wache, & Hönigsberg, 2024; Jonek-Kowalska & Wolniak, 2023). At the strategic level, digital preparedness enables HR functions to transition from reactive administration to proactive, evidence-driven planning. Workforce analytics powered by AI can identify skills gaps, forecast labor shortages, and even model the impact of leadership succession. But for those insights to be executed, HR practitioners would require digital technologies in addition to interpretation skills to place them in a responsible application (Shonubi, 2024; Frick et al., 2021; Rosak-Szyrocka & Wolniak, 2025; Jonek-Kowalska & Wolniak, 2025).

Table 10.6 is a list of digital readiness dimensions that are needed by HR professionals to deal with the subtleties of AI-enabled and data-driven organizational culture. From the development of a digital mindset through continuous upskilling, to encouraging ethical leadership, to cross-functional collaboration, all the dimensions hold the sophisticated capabilities needed to operate and gain value from digital change in human capital management. These considerations combined allow HR departments to be strategic agents of transformation, rather than negotiating the capabilities of technology, but also ethical, responsible, and people-centric adjustment, in the age of AI.

Although HR practitioners take part in the development of AI and data protection law, they must act amidst developing legal frameworks. Laws like the European Union (EU GDPR) General Data Protection Regulation, the forthcoming AI Act, and other state-state algorithmic transparency laws place stakeholders who leverage AI in HRM contexts under unprecedented pressures. Some of these pressures are consent demands, explanations of automated decision-making, and non-discrimination assurance in outcome (Rocha et al., 2025; Huang et al., 2025).

AI literacy is pertinent to regulation too. HR practitioners need to be able to identify where AI-based recruitment or performance management software is "high-risk" from a regulatory viewpoint. They need to be able to implement "human-in-the-loop" controls, where machine decision-making is piloted and overridden by human beings (Singh et al., 2025; Amoako et al., 2024). This is a stronger moral imperative than a regulatory firewall for guaranteeing justice, accountability, and respect in human capital management. AI ethical regulation is a matter of in-house rule-making and not compliance-making

TABLE 10.6 Dimensions of digital readiness for HR professionals

Digital readiness dimension	Description	Relevance to HR professionals	Example applications
Digital mindset and culture	Openness to innovation, flexibility, and forward-looking approach in the adoption of new technologies.	Invites HR to act as change agents and digital transformation champions in organizational environments.	Fostering AI-supported workflows in performance management and onboarding.
Continuous learning and upskilling	Institutionalized mechanisms for learning that enable ongoing digital competency development.	Empowers HR teams to remain nimble and skilled in new tools and technologies.	Offering internal AI literacy training and certifications.
Technological infrastructure	Availability and integration of digital tools, platforms, and cloud systems.	Enables efficient and scalable deployment of AI-driven HR functions.	Enabling platforms like SAP SuccessFactors, Oracle HCM, or AI chatbots.
Change management capability	Organizational ability to manage digital changes, including resistance, communication, and alignment.	Prepares HR to facilitate culture change and help employees adapt to new systems.	Organizing communication plans for AI deployment.
Data governance and security	Data privacy mechanisms, consent management, ethical usage, and compliance systems with laws.	Ensures HR use of AI tools aligns with GDPR, CCPA, and other data protection laws.	Creating secure digital files for employee and recruitment analysis.
Cross-functional collaboration	HR, IT, legal, and analytics functions' alignment of interaction.	Facilitates HR to shape AI solutions and strategies both in organizational goals and compliance requirements.	Participating in cross-functional AI development task forces.
Digital talent management	Utilizing digital technologies to enable recruitment, development, and retention of digitally savvy employees.	Helps HR to strategically align talent plans with digital capability needs.	Deploying AI-powered candidate screening and internal mobility platforms.
AI-driven decision support	Use of data analytics and AI reports to inform strategic HR decision-making.	Arms HR with predictive workforce trend, attrition, and engagement data.	Using dashboards and predictive analytics for turnover forecasting.
Agility and responsiveness	Ability to act quickly in response to technological shifts, disruptions, or emerging HR challenges.	Ensures resiliency in talent plans and management of employee experience.	Rapidly developing remote work policies using digital HR tools.
Ethical digital leadership	Ensuring ethical conduct in the adoption and management of digital and AI systems.	Saves employee trust and reputation of the organization.	Adopting internal AI governance codes and transparency channels.

Source: Author's own work.

and enforcement (Bagheri & van Wetering, 2024; Paz et al., 2023). Most of the world's largest companies already possess AI ethics boards or cross-functional task forces that are approving and vetting AI systems before roll-out. They are HR professionals who are supposed to be champions of such models and recommend inclusive design, minimization, and regular audits. They know the workforce thoroughly, and therefore, they can foresee and predict how to prevent the evil of automation (Natanel & Bracha, 2024).

From algorithmic advising to informed attempts at ethical governance, HR professionals are being asked to balance human values and technical competency. They are not being asked to become data specialists but to be learners, savvy buyers, and stewards of AI technologies. They will be asked to obtain those competencies, not just to implement AI effectively to deliver HR practice, but to promote equity, transparency, and human dignity in the face of algorithmic decision-making.

10.3 FUTURE-PROOFING HRM: BUILDING RESILIENT AND SUSTAINABLE AI STRATEGIES

HRM resilience means that the company can absorb and weather, and recover from, internal or external shocks and maintain the ability to continue operating and developing. Within AI work spaces, this will be contingent upon adaptive algorithmic systems, inclusive data stewardship, adaptive learning environments, and firm human control mechanisms. Sustainability will also take into account environment and society concerns. It involves ethically designing, deploying, and operating AI applications in such a way as to provide long-term value to stakeholders, employees, and society. Sustainable AI in HRM should incorporate concepts of transparency, equity, and accountability in such a way that automated decisions will be based on non-discrimination and non-prejudice. The combination of toughness and sustainability has a robust support structure for long-term growth. Resilience systems can manage volatility and provide continuity of operation, whereas sustainable systems can provide ethical integrity and public trust. Both combined are in a position to future-proof HRM against the uncertainty of technological, economic, and regulation fluctuations (Antony & Vinayagam, 2025; Mollah et al., 2024).

Human values-first governance starts off with good AI governance. It refers to the establishment of AI ethics boards, multiple stakeholders' involvement in algorithm development, and developing explainability and contestability frameworks. For instance, transparency systems for the HR units such that the employees can observe how the AI system is reviewing their performance or eligibility for promotions must be in place. Human-in-the-loop (HITL) frameworks must identify decision-critical areas in a particular way to deliver accountability and curtail over-trusting automatic risk (Choudhuri et al., 2024).

All successful AI-HRM ventures have to involve investment in future digital upskilling initiatives. General algorithmic ability, critical data thinking, and digital co-working are the kind of skills that have to be accessible to all at all organizational levels. Likewise, learning architectures have to be created that will bridge the digital divide and facilitate upskilling for everyone across age, context, and profession. Accenture and IBM, among others, launched in-house talent marketplaces and micro-credentialing platforms to

TABLE 10.7 Competencies for managing and regulating AI-based workforce strategies

Competency area	Specific skills	Application in HRM context
AI literacy and fundamentals	Knowledge of AI principles, 3 of machine learning, and reasoning through algorithms	Enables HR practitioners to comprehend how AI systems operate in talent acquisition, assessment, and performance prediction.
Data governance and privacy	Knowledge of data ethics, GDPR, CCPA, consent management, and anonymization	Makes HR systems compliant with data protection law and ethically handles employee data.
Bias detection and fairness-auditing	Capability for detecting, analyzing, and minimizing bias in algorithms and datasets	Enables fair recruitment and promotion practices and prevents discrimination by performing regular algorithm audits.
Algorithmic transparency	Explainability skills in clarifying AI decision-making and creating explainability	Builds employee trust and enables HR to explain AI-generated outcomes when facing internal or legal scrutiny.
Human-in-the-loop decision-making	Designing flows that include human monitoring in AI systems	Ensures that key decisions (e.g., hiring, firing) remain in human hands, reducing automation risk.
Ethical AI implementation	Deployment of frameworks of responsible AI, e.g., OECD or UNESCO guidelines	Aligns AI adoption with overall ethical and societal values, enhancing HR's role in sustainable innovation.
Change management and digital adoption	Managing organizational transition, AI employee onboarding, and training employees	Facilitates easy adoption of AI tools in HR departments and minimizes resistance from employees.
AI-driven workforce planning	Use of predictive analytics to forecast skills, succession planning, and workforce optimization	Allows HR leaders to anticipate future talent needs and balance human capital strategies with AI-generated insights.
Interdisciplinary collaboration	Working alongside data scientists, legal experts, and IT professionals	Guarantees integrated design and governance of AI systems by closing technical and operational knowledge gaps.
Continuous learning and innovation	Staying up-to-date with the most recent AI trends, tools, and HR tech solutions	Maintains HR's strategic edge and nimbleness amidst a rapidly evolving digital landscape.

Source: Author's own work.

support agile career mobility in AI-intense roles. Creating an AI-fueled HR infrastructure requires a modular and interoperable system architecture (Ramu et al., 2024; Kadirov et al., 2024; Skubis, Wolniak, & Grebski, 2024). They consist of cloud-based platforms, API integrations, and secure data warehouses to enable real-time analytics and dynamic decision-making. Data resilience, or the preservation of data security, availability, and integrity from coercion, is what AI sustainability is all about. Safeguarding from redundancy, encryption, and decentralized storage of data needs to be integrated into HR systems to ensure safeguarding from cyber attacks and data loss (Budhwar et al., 2023). Organizations require data minimization practices and comply with upcoming data protection legislation such as the EU AI Act and CCPA in California.

Table 10.7 presents the competencies of HR professionals capable of leading and managing AI-based workforce initiatives. It requires a multidisciplinary competency that encompasses technical knowledge regarding artificial intelligence, data governance, ethical management, and change management. These competencies not only enable HR leaders to read and interpret AI systems but also influence their appropriate usage in recruiting, performance management, and workforce planning. By enabling individuals to bring IT into alignment with law, the capabilities also enable the application of human judgment and ongoing learning to create strong, open, and ethics-based AI-HRM systems.

Bias in AI-based HR decision-making can lead to reputation and legal disasters. Active bias reduction must hence be incorporated at every stage of the AI lifecycle—ranging from data collection for training and model choice to deployment and impact monitoring. A few tools such as IBM AI Fairness 360 and Microsoft Fairlearn have very good model fairness-auditing mechanisms across demographic subgroups. These green AI applications also require planning for fairness audits as a standard practice within predetermined cycles and the incorporation of redressal mechanisms for those harmed by algorithmic consequences (Arslan et al., 2022).

To future-proof HRM in reality, organizations will have to carry out scenario-planning exercises replicating shocks generated by AI in the future. They also entail stress-testing AI deployments against market meltdown, pandemics, workers' strikes, or tensions in geopolitics. Stress-testing AI systems for their robustness in such instances reveals hidden weaknesses and allows the organization to develop contingency plans. Simulations, for instance, can prove the impact of an auto payroll or a recruitment pipeline AI system breakdown on organizational as well as legal damage in instances of such breakdown (Ozturk et al., 2022). Such discoveries are a concrete contribution of this study.

Unilever has also pioneered AI-based recruitment via gamified mental ability tests, video interview tests, and machine learning (Wolniak & Stecuła, 2024; Stecuła, Wolniak, & Grebski, 2023). But the firm marries technological automating with man phases of evaluation and maintains data usage policy compliance transparency accessible to job applicants, as required by GDPR laws. This marriage of man and machine software guarantees efficiency gain while not sacrificing on transparency and accessibility. SAP has also embraced a Responsible AI Charter which provides tangible benchmarks of ethical standards for creating and applying algorithms. SAP provides international ethics of AI training modules, bias removal, and digital accountability for HR professionals too. The program drives sustainable, long-term workforce transformation and builds internal capability to implement AI systems responsibly.

As AI HR goes global in the world, there is a need to create global ethical standards to bring in fairness, transparency, and accountability. The guidelines need to set up definite requirements of explainable AI, human discretion, right to appeal against automated decision-making, and protection of employees' personal information. Global organizations such as the OECD, ILO, and European Commission need to work in tandem to develop international AI guidelines for the uses of AI in HRM that foster cross-border coherence and prevent regulatory fragmentation (Coetzee & Deas, 2021).

National governments and trade unions need to call for all entities that use AI in HRM to include robust transparency and audit measures. These entail mandatory disclosures of how AI systems affect decisions around recruitment, promotion, performance appraisals, and termination. Bias tests, fairness tests, and effects testing for all applications with high-risk exposures need to be conducted on a regular basis to uncover and avoid discriminatory impacts. Governments need to license unbiased third-party auditors to perform such tests, e.g., financial audits, to facilitate trust and accountability (Arslan et al., 2022).

In order to facilitate equitable access to AI workplaces, there ought to be publicly funded programs in AI literacy, digital reskilling, and worker adjustment. These programs need to reach both HR professionals, who will be running and maintaining AI systems, and workers, whose jobs and career development depend on these technologies. Tax credits, public-private partnerships, and grants can be used to incentivize companies to invest in lifelong learning and reskilling initiatives, especially in sectors or regions at risk of automation displacement (Rachma et al., 2024; Wolniak, Stecuła, & Aydın, 2024a; 2024b).

Policy rules must classify AI-related HR goods by risk level, like the EU AI Act's "high-risk" categorization system. AI technologies applied to recruitment, surveillance of employees, pay, and termination must be assessed as high-risk based on the likelihood that they have to impact human rights and livelihoods considerably. That would trigger certain regulatory needs like pre-deployment conformity tests, human intervention requirement, and continuous post-deployment surveillance to ensure that AI deployment is not merely legal but also morally correct (Devi et al., 2025; Lekshmi et al., 2024).

Regulation of AI in HRM cannot be entrusted to technology providers or attorneys exclusively. Institutional representative systems between governments, workers, employers, labor unions, human rights commissions, AI ethicists, and civil society must be created. These platforms can facilitate discussion of emergent AI innovation, sound alarms regarding regulatory gaps, and co-design policies balancing innovation with protecting workers. Through enabling policy-making in an integrated fashion, the models mentioned above ensure that HRM's artificial intelligence systems are based on varied perceptions and democratic assumptions instead of sectarian business or computer thinking (Khushk et al., 2025; Choudhuri et al., 2024).

Table 10.8 is a long list of ten strategic propositions of policies for responsible, ethical, and futuring introduction of artificial intelligence into human resource management (HRM). All the proposals individually address a particular policy space—algorithmic transparency and international ethics, all the way to data sovereignty, workforce upskilling, and risk management. Overall, the proposals constitute an organic agenda on how to align the application of AI in HR with human rights, regulation requirements, and technology. Having been primed to adopt multi-stakeholder governance, responsive regulation, and long-term social and environmental responsibility, the table presents a model for institutional and policy design to policymakers and institutions that wish to provide for AI in HR processes not just in the service of operational effectiveness but for democratic accountability and distributive workforce formation as well.

Future-proofing HRM in the age of AI is not an exercise in technology or organizational innovation but an organizational renaissance authored by moral imagination, strategic agility, and co-innovation. Organizations can ensure that digitalization works for

TABLE 10.8 Policy recommendations for future AI usage in Human Resource Management

Focus area	Policy recommendation	Expanded description
Ethical standards	**Establish global ethical standards for AI in HRM**	Work with international organizations to develop standard guidelines for fairness, human intervention, consent, and explainability of AI-powered HR processes.
Transparency and accountability	**Mandate algorithmic transparency and auditing mechanisms**	Enforce regulatory requirements on organizations to offer explanations of AI-powered decisions, release paperwork, and conduct fairness and bias audits on a routine schedule.
Workforce readiness	**Fund AI literacy and upskilling initiatives**	Establish national programs to raise the digital literacy and AI literacy of HR professionals and employees through grants, public-private partnerships, and certification programs.
Risk classification	**Develop AI risk classification frameworks**	Install legal regimes that classify AI HR tools by risk level, with higher controls on higher-stakes uses such as automated hiring or workplace surveillance.
Inclusive governance	**Institutionalize multi-stakeholder governance councils**	Create governance institutions with industry, labor, regulator, ethicist, and civil society representation for democratic accountability and transparency.
Worker protection	**Ensure human oversight and appeal rights**	Make human review of all AI-generated employment decisions (e.g., hiring, promotion, firing) mandatory and allow workers to appeal or contest them.
Regulatory harmonization	**Align AI-HRM regulations across jurisdictions**	Promote regulatory convergence at regional (e.g., EU, ASEAN) and international (e.g., G20) levels to minimize compliance complexity for multinationals and protect labor rights across borders.
Data privacy and security	**Enhance data governance and employee data sovereignty**	Implement stringent data requirements on collection, storage, and processing in HRM contexts, e.g., anonymization, encryption, and consent-based access to personal data.
Sustainability and long-term impact	**Require environmental and social impact assessments of AI**	Make reporting mandatory for enterprises to assess the environmental footprint and societal implications of AI use in HRM and encourage responsible and green AI.
Monitoring and adaptive regulation	**Establish dynamic regulatory sandboxes for HR AI**	Provide test spaces where organizations may pilot AI-HRM applications subject to regulatory oversight so that policy adjustments will be responsive as technology develops.

Source: Author's own work.

and not against human thriving by co-designing AI technology and HRM practice with resilience and sustainability. The path forward is to develop AI solutions that are not only intelligent but also wise—value-aligned, function-explainable, and disruption-resistant. This is the way HRM operates as an integral pillar in shaping workplaces that are agile, fair, and ready to address a future that is uncertain.

REFERENCES

Aftab, J., Stan, M., Srivastava, M., Wei, F., & Abid, N. (2025). The impact of digital leadership on performance: examining the roles of big data analytical capabilities, green innovation, and

AI change readiness in Italian SMEs. *Business Strategy and the Environment*. https://doi.org/10.1002/bse.4322. https://onlinelibrary.wiley.com/doi/abs/10.1002/bse.4322

Ahmić, A., & Ćosić, M. (2025). Digital human resource management influence on the organizational resilience. *Organization Management Journal, 22*(2), 111–125.

Alfadhli, M., Onat, N. C., Kucukvar, M., & Al-Maadeed, S. (2025). Analyzing AI readiness through digital transformation and data management: a case study of Qatar's government sector. *Applied Mathematics and Information Sciences, 19*(3), 497–507.

Almurtadha, Y. (2024). AI prediction model to investigate the GovTech Maturity Index (GTMI) indicators for assessing governments' readiness for digital transformation. *Journal of Applied Data Sciences, 5*(4), 1838–1849.

Amoako, G. K., Kumi, E., Appiah, T., & Ofori, K. S. (2024). The effects of digital transformation, technological readiness, leadership support, and psychological contract on turnover intentions among healthcare professionals in Ghana: a mediated, moderated study. *SN Business and Economics, 4*(12), 167.

Antony, S., & Vinayagam, K. (2025). The role of AI in shaping HRM skills and strategies in private banks: a study on manager-employee dynamics in Chennai City. In *Proceedings of the 2025 International Conference on Automation and Computation (AUTOCOM 2025)* (pp. 353–358). IEEE.

Arslan, A., Cooper, C., Khan, Z., Golgeci, I., & Ali, I. (2022). Artificial intelligence and human workers interaction at team level: a conceptual assessment of the challenges and potential HRM strategies. *International Journal of Manpower, 43*(1), 75–88.

Bagheri, S., & van de Wetering, R. (2024). RPA ready? Unlocking organizational RPA readiness. In *Lecture Notes in Computer Science (*Vol. 14907, pp. 14–28*)*.

Band, G., Bapat, S., Sonkul, D., Nandurkar, P., & Ahmad, M. I. (2024). Assessing the efficacy of utilizing artificial intelligence for human resources management in the Indian IT industry. *Nanotechnology Perceptions, 20*(S5), 499–506.

Bećirović, S., Polz, E., & Tinkel, I. (2025). Exploring students' AI literacy and its effects on their AI output quality, self-efficacy, and academic performance. *Smart Learning Environments, 12*(1), 29.

Biswas, S., Giri, A., & Chatterjee, S. (2024). How can AI-enabled HRM (artificial intelligence-enabled Human Resource Management) help to change the future of multi-speciality hospitals?: An empirical investigation in India. In *Perspectives in finance and digital transformations in business* (pp. 248–257). IGI Global.

Budhwar, P., Chowdhury, S., Wood, G., Tung, R. L., & Varma, A. (2023). Human resource management in the age of generative artificial intelligence: perspectives and research directions on ChatGPT. *Human Resource Management Journal, 33*(3), 606–659.

Chandel, P., & Lim, F. V. (2025). Generative AI and literacy development in the language classroom: a systematic review of literature. *Ubiquitous Learning, 18*(2), 31–49.

Choudhuri, S., Veeranalla, S., Gamini, P., Priya, U., & Katta, S. K. (2024). AI-powered HR marketing revolutionizing employee recruitment and retention strategies. In *Intelligent Computing and Emerging Communication Technologies (ICEC 2024)*. Springer.

Coetzee, M., & Deas, A. (2021). *Redefining the psychological contract in the digital era: issues for research and practice* (pp. 1–335). Springer.

Devi, K., Singh, J., Garg, N., Shaik, N., & Elangovan, M. (2025). Measuring AI's impact on HR strategies and operational effectiveness in the era of Industry 4.0. In *Communications in Computer and Information Science* (Vol. 2125, pp. 97–107).

Dutta, D., & Mishra, S. K. (2025). Artificial intelligence-based virtual assistant and employee engagement: an empirical investigation. *Personnel Review, 54*(3), 913–934.

Frick, N. R. J., Mirbabaie, M., Stieglitz, S., & Salomon, J. (2021). Maneuvering through the stormy seas of digital transformation: the impact of empowering leadership on the AI readiness of enterprises. *Journal of Decision Systems, 30*(2–3), 235–258.

Ghani, M. M., Mustafa, W. A., Bakhtiar, D. L. S., & Khairudin, M. (2025). A comprehensive study: AI literacy as a component of media literacy. *Journal of Advanced Research in Applied Sciences and Engineering Technology, 53*(2), 112–121.

Gong, Q., Fan, D., & Bartram, T. (2025). Integrating artificial intelligence and human resource management: a review and future research agenda. *International Journal of Human Resource Management, 36*(1), 103–141.

Goyal, M., Nagar, P., & Sharma, A. (2024). Exploring theoretical artificial intelligence applications: HR's emerging frontiers. In *Lecture Notes in Networks and Systems* (Vol. 1007, pp. 199–209).

Huang, J., Raja Yusof, R. N., Abd Rahman, A., & Ab Rahman, R. (2025). Determinants of digital technology adoption and its impact on firm performance in manufacturing firms. *Journal of Manufacturing Technology Management.* www.emerald.com/jmtm/article-abstract/doi/10.1108/JMTM-08-2024-0475/1256321/Determinants-of-digital-technology-adoption-and?redirectedFrom=fulltext

Jangbahadur, U., Ahlawat, S., Rozera, P., & Gupta, N. (2025). The effect of AI-enabled HRM dimensions on employee engagement and sustainable organisational performance: fusion skills as a moderator. *Evidence-Based HRM, 13*(1), 85–107.

John, J. E., & Pramila, S. (2025). Leveraging AI in HR analytics to foster green human resource management. In *Studies in Systems, Decision and Control* (Vol. 555, pp. 1067–1074).

Jonek-Kowalska, I., & Wolniak, R. (2023). Towards sustainability and a better quality of life?, Routledge.

Jonek-Kowalska, I., & Wolniak, R. (2025). Exclusion in Smart Cities assessment and strategy for strengthening resilience, Routledge.

Kadirov, A., Shakirova, Y., Ismoilova, G., & Makhmudova, N. (2024). AI in human resource management: Reimagining talent acquisition, development, and retention. In *Proceedings of the 2024 International Conference on Knowledge Engineering and Communication Systems (ICKECS 2024).* IEEE.

Katsamba, D. (2025). Digital readiness and big data analytics: moderating roles in achieving social sustainability through AI-CRM and competitive advantage. *Journal of Management Practices, Humanities and Social Sciences, 9*(1), 1–18.

Khushk, A., Zhiying, L., Yi, X., & Aman, N. (2025). AI-driven HR transformation in Chinese automotive industry: strategies and implications. *Business Process Management Journal.* https://doi.org/10.1108/BPMJ-11-2023-0915. www.emerald.com/bpmj/article-abstract/doi/10.1108/BPMJ-11-2023-0915/1254557/AI-driven-HR-transformation-in-Chinese-automotive?redirectedFrom=fulltext

Kim, J., Battaglia, S., & Kim, H. H. (2025). Collaborative intelligence achieved from AI-enabled recruitment: a case study of POSCO in South Korea. *Asia Pacific Business Review, 31*(1), 180–199.

Lekshmi, R. S., Mary, V. S., Arasuraja, G., Kaliappan, S., & Selvameena, R. (2024). AI-driven HR optimization strategies in finance and marketing: methodological framework and applications. In *Proceedings of the 2024 International Conference on Innovative Computing, Intelligent Communication and Smart Electrical Systems (ICSES 2024)*. IEEE.

Li, R., Ouyang, J., Lin, J., & Ouyang, S. (2025). Mediating effect of AI attitudes and AI literacy on the relationship between career self-efficacy and job-seeking anxiety. *BMC Psychology, 13*(1), 454.

Liew, T. M., Foo, J. Y. H., Yang, H., Koh, G. C.-H., & Thumboo, J. (2025). PENSIEVE-AI: a brief cognitive test to detect cognitive impairment across diverse literacy. *Nature Communications, 16*(1), 2847.

Madanchian, M., & Taherdoost, H. (2025). Barriers and enablers of AI adoption in human resource management: a critical analysis of organizational and technological factors. *Information (Switzerland), 16*(1), 51.

Maghsoudi, M., Kamrani Shahri, M., Agha Mohammad Ali Kermani, M., & Khanizad, R. (2025). Mapping the landscape of AI-driven human resource management: a social network analysis of research collaboration. *IEEE Access, 13*, 3090–3114.

Mahade, A., Elmahi, A., Alomari, K. M., & Abdalla, A. A. (2025). Leveraging AI-driven insights to enhance sustainable human resource management performance: moderated mediation model: evidence from UAE higher education. *Discover Sustainability, 6*(1), 267.

Malik, A., Lirio, P., Budhwar, P., Nguyen, M., & Fauzi, M. A. (2025). Guest editorial: artificial intelligence (AI) in the world of work: bibliometric insights and mapping opportunities and challenges. *Personnel Review, 54*(3), 781–799.

Milhem, M., Ateeq, A., Al Astal, A., & Almeer, S. (2025). Digital transformation in HRM: navigating the future of human resource management. In *Studies in Systems, Decision and Control* (Vol. 566, pp. 23–33).

Mollah, M. A., Rana, M., Amin, M. B., Rahaman, M. A., & Fenyves, V. (2024). Examining the role of AI-augmented HRM for sustainable performance: key determinants for digital culture and organizational strategy. *Sustainability (Switzerland), 16*(24), 10843.

Mori, M., Sassetti, S., Cavaliere, V., & Bonti, M. (2025). A systematic literature review on artificial intelligence in recruiting and selection: a matter of ethics. *Personnel Review, 54*(3), 854–878.

Muralidharan, V., Ravi, B., Pachar, S., Chakraborty, N., & Sahaya Lenin, D. (2024). Ethical considerations in applying machine learning to HR practices: balancing efficiency with fairness. In *Proceedings of International Conference on Contemporary Computing and Informatics (IC3I 2024)* (pp. 1392–1398). IEEE.

Narzary, S., Makhecha, U. P., Budhwar, P., Malik, A., & Kumar, S. (2025). A temporal evolution of human resource management and technology research: a retrospective bibliometric analysis. *Personnel Review, 54*(3), 800–823.

Natanael, M., & Bracha, M. (2024). Chasing career readiness: raising engineers for critical and ethical information gathering and analysis to solve complex problems. In *SEFI 2024–52nd Annual Conference of the European Society for Engineering, Proceedings: Educating Responsible Engineers* (pp. 2619–2624). European Society for Engineering Education.

Nayak, S., Budhwar, P., & Malik, A. (2025). Unveiling the hidden costs of AI in hospitality industry: the adverse effect of algorithmic human resources management (AHRM) on stress, wellbeing, and commitment. *International Journal of Hospitality Management, 129*, 104206.

Ozturk, A., Bayraktar, N., Bayraktar, M., Bozok, T., & Ceylan, M. R. (2022). Evaluation of amino acid profile in serum of patients with COVID-19 for providing a new treatment strategy. *Journal of Medical Biochemistry, 41*(4), 526–533.

Park, S., Chai, D. S., Park, J. J., & Oh, J. (2025). Exploring opportunities for artificial intelligence in organization development. *Human Resource Development Review, 24*(1), 3–36.

Patil, S., Upadhye, P., Khandekar, S. R., Ghewari, A., & Bhattacharya, U. (2024). Artificial intelligence and data science approaches to analyzing human resource management in hybrid and remote work models. In *Proceedings of the 2024 International Conference on Innovative Computing, Intelligent Communication and Smart Electrical Systems (ICSES 2024).* IEEE.

Paz, J. P., de Moraes, J. B., de Freitas Rocha Loures, E., & Deschamps, F. (2023). Agility-readiness assessment of teams for digital transformation: a multicriteria decision approach. In *Proceedings of the American Society for Engineering Management 2023 International Annual Conference and 44th Annual Meeting* (pp. 902–912). American Society for Engineering Management (ASEM).

Prikshat, V., Kumar, S., Patel, P., & Varma, A. (2025). Impact of organisational facilitators and perceived HR effectiveness on acceptance of AI-augmented HRM: an integrated TAM and TPB perspective. *Personnel Review, 54*(3), 879–912.

Promma, W., Imjai, N., Usman, B., & Aujirapongpan, S. (2025). The influence of AI literacy on complex problem-solving skills through systematic thinking skills and intuition thinking skills: an empirical study in Thai Gen Z accounting students. *Computers and Education: Artificial Intelligence, 8*, 100382.

Rachma, Y., Sutarman, A., Andayani, D., Haryani, H., & Johnson, S. A. (2024). Analysis of HR career development strategies in the era of artificial intelligence. In *Proceedings of the 2024 3rd International Conference on Creative Communication and Innovative Technology (ICCIT 2024).* IEEE.

Ramu, M., Ilakkiya, T., Venkatesh, P., Krishnamoorthi, M., & Senthilnathan, C. R. (2024). Understanding the scope of artificial intelligence in HR technology e-recruitment: a theoretical perspective. In *Proceedings of the 4th International Conference on Power, Energy, Control and Transmission Systems (ICPECTS 2024).* IEEE.

Revillod, G. (2025). Exploring the acceptability of artificial intelligence in human resources management: insights from Swiss organizations. *Systems Research and Behavioral Science.* https://doi.org/10.1002/sres.3140. https://onlinelibrary.wiley.com/doi/abs/10.1002/sres.3140

Rocha, C. F., Quandt, C., Deschamps, F., & Cruzara, G. (2025). Digital transformation readiness in large manufacturing firms: a building block model proposition. *Journal of Manufacturing Technology Management, 36*(1), 45–68.

Rosak-Szyrocka J., & Wolniak, R. (2025). *Smart universities in Smart Cities shaping the future of education and urban innovation*, Routledge.

Shonubi, O. A. (2024). Advancing organisational technology readiness and convergence of emerging digital technologies (AI, IoT, I4.0) for innovation adoption. *International Journal of Technology and Globalisation, 9*(1), 50–91.

Singh, R., Joshi, A., Singh, A., Raghuveer, K., & Kumar, V. (2025). Synergising HR practices and social performance for adoption of digital circular economy: a case of developing country perspective. *Strategy and Leadership, 53*(4), 434–456.

Skubis, I., Wolniak, R., & Grebski, W. W. (2024). AI and human-centric approach in smart cities management: acse studies from Silesian and Lesser Poland Voivodships. *Sustainability, 16*(18), Article 8279, 1–26.

Stecuła, K., Wolniak, R., & Grebski, W. (2023). AI-driven urban energy solutions—from individuals to society: a review. *Energies, 16*(24), 7988, 1–34.

Weritz, P., Wache, H., & Hönigsberg, S. (2024). How digital readiness relates to the intention to use generative AI in workplace service systems. In *30th Americas Conference on Information Systems (AMCIS 2024)*. Association for Information Systems.

Wolniak, R., Stecuła, K., & Aydın, B. (2024a). Digital transformation of grocery in-store shopping - scanners, artificial intelligence, augmented reality and beyond: a review. *Foods, 13*(18), Article 2948, 1–34.

Wolniak, R., Gajdzik, B., Grebski, M., Danel, R., Grebski, W.W. (2024b). Business models used in Smart Cities—theoretical approach with examples of smart cities. *Smart Cities, 7*, 1626–1669.

Wolniak, R., & Stecuła, K. (2024). Artificial intelligence in Smart Cities—applications, barriers and future directions: a review. *Smart Cities, 7*, 1346–1389.

Xiao, Q., Yan, J., & Bamber, G. J. (2025). How does AI-enabled HR analytics influence employee resilience: job crafting as a mediator and HRM system strength as a moderator. *Personnel Review, 54*(3), 824–843.

Yang, Y., Zhang, Y., Sun, D., He, W., & Wei, Y. (2025). Navigating the landscape of AI literacy education: insights from a decade of research (2014–2024). *Humanities and Social Sciences Communications, 12*(1), 374.

Zhang, D., Wijaya, T. T., Wang, Y., Li, X., & Damayanti, N. W. (2025). Exploring the relationship between AI literacy, AI trust, AI dependency, and 21st century skills in preservice mathematics teachers. *Scientific Reports, 15*(1), 14281.

Zhou, Y., Wang, L., & Chen, W. (2023). The dark side of AI-enabled HRM on employees based on AI algorithmic features. *Journal of Organizational Change Management, 36*(7), 1222–1241.

Index

For Product Safety Concerns and Information please contact our EU representative GPSR@taylorandfrancis.com Taylor & Francis Verlag GmbH, Kaufingerstraße 24, 80331 München, Germany